ROUTLEDGE LIBRARY EDITIONS: GERMAN LITERATURE

Volume 12

THE GERMAN POETS OF THE FIRST WORLD WAR

THE GERMAN POETS OF THE FIRST WORLD WAR

PATRICK BRIDGWATER

LONDON AND NEW YORK

First published in 1985 by Croom Helm Ltd

This edition first published in 2020
by Routledge
2 Park Square, Milton Park, Abingdon, Oxon OX14 4RN

and by Routledge
52 Vanderbilt Avenue, New York, NY 10017

Routledge is an imprint of the Taylor & Francis Group, an informa business

© 1985 Patrick Bridgwater

All rights reserved. No part of this book may be reprinted or reproduced or utilised in any form or by any electronic, mechanical, or other means, now known or hereafter invented, including photocopying and recording, or in any information storage or retrieval system, without permission in writing from the publishers.

Trademark notice: Product or corporate names may be trademarks or registered trademarks, and are used only for identification and explanation without intent to infringe.

British Library Cataloguing in Publication Data
A catalogue record for this book is available from the British Library

ISBN: 978-0-367-41588-4 (Set)
ISBN: 978-1-00-301460-7 (Set) (ebk)
ISBN: 978-0-367-43602-5 (Volume 12) (hbk)
ISBN: 978-0-367-43609-4 (Volume 12) (pbk)
ISBN: 978-1-00-300456-1 (Volume 12) (ebk)

Publisher's Note
The publisher has gone to great lengths to ensure the quality of this reprint but points out that some imperfections in the original copies may be apparent.

Disclaimer
The publisher has made every effort to trace copyright holders and would welcome correspondence from those they have been unable to trace.

The German Poets of the First World War

Patrick Bridgwater

CROOM HELM
London & Sydney

© 1985 Patrick Bridgwater
Croom Helm Ltd, Provident House, Burrell Row,
Beckenham, Kent BR3 1AT
Croom Helm Australia Pty Ltd, First Floor,
139 King Street, Sydney, NSW 2001, Australia

British Library Cataloguing in Publication Data
Bridgwater, W.P.
    The German poets of the first world war.
    1. German poetry — 20th century — History
    and criticism
    I. Title
    831'.912'09   PT551
ISBN 0-7099-3237-5

Printed and bound in Great Britain
by Billing & Sons Limited, Worcester.

CONTENTS

Foreword		vii
Acknowledgements		viii
1.	The Aesthetics of War	1
2.	Georg Trakl	19
3.	August Stramm	38
4.	Lichtenstein, Ball and Klemm	62
5.	Anton Schnack	96
6.	Lersch, Bröger and Engelke	120
7.	Epilogue	154
Translations of German Quotations		165
Bibliography		204
Index of Poems		207

DEN OPFERN

FOREWORD

This is a study of what seem to me to be the most interesting poems by the best German poets of the First World War. My concern is therefore almost entirely with the work of front-line poets writing in the line of death between 1914 and 1918. War poetry is like any other poetry in that most of it is bad. Hundreds of poets and thousands of poems had to be mustered before this book could even be contemplated; let it never be forgotten that in August 1914 some 50,000 poems were written *daily* in Germany. The best war poem, as I shall try to show, is that in which poetry and morality are fused together. Neither poetry nor morality is enough by itself. In making my selection of poets and poems I was inevitably guided by moral as well as aesthetic criteria. But having made the selection I have concentrated on the poetry as such since, while the undergraduate readers to whom the book is addressed will need no help with the morality, they will not spurn help with the poetry, which frequently has to be very closely read before its real significance is revealed. Practically all the poems discussed are quoted in full, in the original German, and it is on this that the often very close readings are based. In order to make the study as accessible as possible to the general reader, translations of the German quotations are also included.

Earlier versions of parts of the book appeared in the following: *European Studies Review*, vol. I, no. 2, 1971, 147–86 ('German Poetry and the First World War'); *Londoner Trakl-Symposium*, ed. W.E. Yuill and W. Methlagl, Salzburg: Otto Müller Verlag, 1981 ('George Trakl and the Poetry of the First World War'); *New German Studies*, VIII, 1980, 29–53 ('The War-Poetry of August Stramm'). Prior to that several chapters had in effect been given as papers to the Durham German Department Staff Seminar, to the London Trakl-Symposium organised by the Austrian Institute, and to the universities of East Anglia, Hull and Manchester. Of the many friends and colleagues who have read some or all of the MS and helped me to avoid some of the mines with which the field is scattered, I wish to thank particularly Dr J.W. Smeed, Dr D.J. Constantine and Professor W.E. Yates. My debt to Kathleen Sewell who typed the MS so carefully, is no less great.

ACKNOWLEDGEMENTS

For permission to quote copyright material the author is most grateful to the following publishers and other copyright holders: Eugen Diederichs Verlag for the poems 'Bekenntnis', 'Nachtmarsch' and 'Sang der Granaten' from Karl Bröger, *Kamerad, als wir marschiert*, copyright (c) 1916 by Eugen Diederichs Verlag; Eugen Diederichs Verlag for the poems 'Das rote Wirtshaus' and 'Die Gärten des Todes' from Karl Bröger, *Soldaten der Erde*, copyright (c) 1918 by Eugen Diederichs Verlag; the Gerrit-Engelke-Stiftung for brief extracts from Gerrit Engelke's letters from the front; Verlagsgruppe Langen Müller Herbig for eleven poems by Wilhelm Klemm; Alfred Kröner Verlag for passages from Wilhelm Klemm's letters from the front; Kösel-Verlag for the poems 'Der neue Krieg' and 'Der sterbende Soldat' from Karl Kraus, *Gesammelte Werke in 14 Bänden und 3 Supplementbänden*, hrsg. v. Heinrich Fischer, Kösel-Verlag, München; Eugen Diederichs Verlag for the poems 'Brüder', 'Im Artilleriefeuer II', 'Massengräber' and 'Wenn es Abend wird' from Heinrich Lersch, *Gedichte* (*Ausgewählte Werke*, Erster Band), copyright (c) 1965 by Eugen Diederichs Verlag, Köln; Eugen Diederichs Verlag for extracts from Heinrich Lersch's letters from the front published in Heinrich Lersch, *Erzählungen und Briefe* (*Ausgewählte Werke*, Zweiter Band), copyright (c) 1966 by Eugen Diederichs Verlag, Köln; Erich Schmidt Verlag GmbH for brief extracts from August Stramm's letters from the front published in *August Stramm. Kritische Essays und unveröffentlichtes Quellenmaterial aus dem Nachlass des Dichters*, herausgegeben von J.D. Adler und J.J. White, copyright (c) 1979 by Erich Schmidt Verlag GmbH. Although it was not easy to do so, the author hopes and believes that he has succeeded in tracing all the relevant copyright holders. Mainly as a direct result of the war, much of the work in question is no longer in copyright. Bibliographical details of the work of *all* the poets concerned will be found in the Bibliography.

1 THE AESTHETICS OF WAR

Whereas between the Thirty Years War and the First World War most war poetry was poetry idealising and glorifying war, from winter 1914 onwards most war poetry worth the title has been anti-war poetry written by poets in the line of death. This break with the heroic tradition was caused by the barbarous technology of the 'Great War for Civilisation', which brought about a change in the general attitude towards war and with it a change in the nature of war poetry. So long as war remained essentially a matter of hand-to-hand combat, man versus man, it could be seen in a chivalrous and heroic light and was in fact still seen in such a light in the initial period of euphoria in 1914. But once it had finally become a matter of mechanised (and compulsory) murder, man versus machine, war could no longer be seen in a positive light, could no longer be defined in the basically chivalrous vocabulary and concepts of traditional war poetry, for survival had become a matter of luck rather than of virtue.

The downright impossibility of reconciling modern methods of warfare with traditional concepts of heroism forms the subject of a vitriolic satire by Karl Kraus, entitled 'Der neue Krieg', which could not be published until the end of the war:

> Am schwersten in diesem Krieg wird mir:
> Gasmaske zu einen und Panier.
> Wie ist das? Die vor dem Feind nicht weichen,
> den Tod ihm mit chemischen Mitteln reichen,
> die chlorreich bei der Waffe geblieben,
> ob auch die Sonne über uns scheint –
> sie wurden nicht aus der Armee getrieben
> für rühmliche Feigheit vor dem Feind?

The word 'chlorreich' is coined to pun on *Glor-* ('glory') and *Chlor-* ('chlorine') because the latter is one sure way of attaining the former.

The typical front-line poet of the First World War portrays the suffering and tragedy around him as an implicit or – if he is a satirist – explicit protest against the war in which he is involved. He is committed not to the imperatives of heroic action, but to exposing the futility of heroic action and the tragedy of war. As early as 1914–15 we see the old heroic tradition of war poetry starting to give way to what, in retrospect, can be seen to be a new tradition.

War poetry, and especially modern war poetry, raises some of the fundamental problems of poetry in peculiarly acute forms. Above all it raises the question of the relationship between poetry and morality and obliges us to think through our aesthetic criteria to the point where they merge into moral ones.

The inadequacy of conventional criteria was unwittingly shown by W.B. Yeats, who excluded all British poems of the Great War from his *Oxford Book of Modern Verse* (1936) on the grounds that 'passive suffering is not a theme for poetry'. The relevant part of his introduction reads as follows:

> I have a distaste for certain poems written in the midst of the great war ... The writers of these poems were invariably officers of exceptional courage and capacity ... but felt bound, in the words of the best known, to plead the suffering of their men. In poems that had for a time considerable fame, written in the first person, they made that suffering their own. I have rejected these poems for the same reason that made Arnold withdraw his *Empedocles on Etna* from circulation; passive suffering is not a theme for poetry. In all the great tragedies, tragedy is a joy to the man who dies; in Greece the tragic chorus danced. When man has withdrawn into the quicksilver at the back of the mirror no great event becomes luminous in his mind; it is no longer possible to write *The Persians, Agincourt, Chevy Chase*: some blunderer has driven his car on to the wrong side of the road - that is all.
>
> If war is necessary, or necessary in our time and place, it is best to forget its suffering ...

This must be one of the silliest remarks about poetry by a great poet. Yeats's dictum arises from an exclusive concern with aesthetic qualities and criteria and therefore from a failure of the imagination: a failure (occasioned, no doubt, by his own non-involvement) to understand the nature of modern war and therefore of modern war poetry. He seems to have wanted some heroic gesture, seems to reject modern war poetry because it was in every sense anti-heroic and therefore could not be absorbed into his own hero-myth. It could be said that Yeats has simply got his aesthetic categories wrong and that it is downright absurd to reject modern war poetry out of hand because it happens to be elegiac, for in reality the elegy, in the modern sense of poetry on a subject for which Roman poets would have used elegiacs, notably mourning for the dead, is the natural poetic mode of the war; Owen refers to his 'elegies' and Schnack defined his work as elegiac. This is not to say, of course, that all modern war poems are elegiac, for fear of death could, exceptionally, lead to an intensification of experience and of being which seemed to call for lyrical celebration:

>Sick with delight
>At life's discovered transitoriness,
>Our youth became all-flesh and waived the mind.[1]

In reality it might be truer to say that the omnipresence of seducer death sometimes blew the mind, for it is impossible to celebrate any feeling of being 'sick with delight', impossible to celebrate the excitement and camaraderie of war, that is, without finding oneself, silently, in a pro-war posture. The most forgettable front-line war poems were written by those who 'waived the mind'.

Expression of a similar irrelevant and therefore irresponsible aestheticism can be found also in poems by two of Yeats's German contemporaries: Rilke and George. To substantiate this point, let us consider Rilke's 'Fünf Gesänge, August 1914' (1914) and George's *Der Krieg* (1917).

Rilke's cycle of hymns[2] was written in the first days of the war amid the intense patriotism unleashed by the Declaration and subsequent mobilisation. That Rilke starts by echoing the nationalistic and militaristic sentiments of the day is hardly surprising. While avoiding the jingoism of so many lesser poets, in the first hymn Rilke welcomes war in a way which points straight to Heym's magnificent 'Der Krieg' (discussed in the next chapter):

I

>ZUM erstenmal seh ich dich aufstehn,
>hörengesagter, fernster, unglaublicher Kriegs-Gott.
>Wie so dicht zwischen die friedliche Frucht
>furchtbares Handeln gesät war, plötzlich erwachsenes.
>Gestern war es noch klein, bedurfte der Nahrung, mannshoch
>steht es schon da: morgen
>überwächst es den Mann. Denn der glühende Gott
>reisst mit Einem das Wachstum
>aus dem wurzelnden Volk, und die Ernte beginnt ...

Endlich ein Gott. Da wir den friedlichen oft
nicht mehr ergriffen, ergreift uns plötzlich der Schlacht-Gott,
schleudert den Brand: und über dem Herzen voll Heimat
schreit, den er donnernd bewohnt, sein rötlicher Himmel.

In other words, Rilke's starting-point is not actuality, but art in the form of Heym's 'Der Krieg'. The prophetic grandeur of Heym's poem has become a poetic pose. Rilke's 'war-god' is a far more ambiguous and less terrifying figure than Heym's demon; he is a mythical god and as such at most a source of awe rather than terror. Rilke's 'war-god' is a 'sacred' figure deriving from the heroic world, while the whole point of Heym's demon is his profanity. Rilke's god comes ultimately from Olympos; Heym's demon comes straight from that Hell where youth and laughter go. And there is a further point, for Rilke's first and second hymns are also reminiscent of Hölderlin in terms of diction, syntax and attitude. The rhetorical first and second hymns are based on Hölderlin's view of the poet as the prophetic voice of his people and on his cyclic view of history, which enables Rilke to view the war as necessary. The borrowed prophetic mien is remarkable and basically spurious. It means that Rilke has fallen into the same trap as other, lesser poets in going back to the patriotic tradition of Romantic poetry. His choice of the grotesquely inappropriate hymn form was a clear indication of what was to come.

Three days later, in the third hymn, the poet's attitude has changed, although the god of war is still seen as a primitive demonic force, and as such is still described in language reminiscent of Heym's 'Der Krieg':

SEIT drei Tagen, was ists? Sing ich wirklich das Schrecknis,
wirklich den Gott, den ich als einen der frühern
nur noch erinnernden Götter ferne bewundernd geglaubt?
Wie ein vulkanischer Berg lag er im Weiten. Manchmal
flammend. Manchmal im Rauch. Traurig und göttlich.
Nur eine nahe vielleicht, ihm anliegende Ortschaft
bebte. Wir aber hoben die heile
Leier anderen zu: welchen kommenden Göttern?
Und nun aufstand er: steht: höher
als stehende Türme, höher
als die geatmete Luft unseres sonstigen Tags.
Steht. Übersteht. Und wir? Glühen in Eines zusammen,
in ein neues Geschöpf, das er tödlich belebt.
So auch *bin* ich nicht mehr; aus dem gemeinsamen Herzen

schlägt das meine den Schlag, und der gemeinsame Mund
bricht den meinigen auf.

Now, however, Rilke begins to have doubts about the way in which he welcomed the advent of this legendary war-god. He begins to realise that he has allowed himself to be carried away by his amoral, aesthetic enthusiasm for this radical phenomenon, an enthusiasm shared by his fellow-countrymen. This very reminder that he is speaking for so many others brings the realisation that war, however 'great' in a purely aesthetic sense, is a blind and destructive power. So far so good. If the hymns had ended here, it would have been better. Rilke after all has realised the true nature of war long before most of his contemporaries. The trouble is that the hymns continue and, in so doing, become increasingly irrelevant. Rilke now sees it as his task to praise not the feeling of being 'in gloriously experienced danger, holy to all', but rather the pain and grief which underlie this feeling and which are the real product of war. In the final hymn this 'endless lament' leads to a mystique of *Schmerz*, so that war is virtually idealised for the depth of the grief that it causes:

AUF, und schreckt den schrecklichen Gott! Bestürzt ihn.
Kampf-Lust hat ihn vor Zeiten verwöhnt. Nun dränge der Schmerz
  euch,
dränge ein neuer, verwunderter Kampf-Schmerz
euch seinem Zorne zuvor.
Wenn schon ein Blut euch bezwingt, ein hoch von den Vätern
kommendes Blut: so sei das Gemüt doch
immer noch euer. Ahmt nicht
Früherem nach, Einstigem. Prüfet,
ob ihr nicht Schmerz seid. Handelnder Schmerz. Der Schmerz hat
auch seine Jubel. O, und dann wirft sich die Fahne
über euch auf, im Wind, der vom Feind kommt!
Welche? Des Schmerzes. Die Fahne des Schmerzes. Das schwere
schlagende Schmerztuch.

After hovering between enthusiasm and doubt, Rilke ends by appropriating war into his private mythology, where it does not belong, in the guise of Grief. The lines just quoted clearly anticipate the Landscape of Grief of the tenth Duino Elegy. In the course of the cycle Rilke's language indeed becomes more and more clearly the rhetorical, emotionally charged and yet abstract language of the *Duino Elegies*.

The real events of August 1914 are absorbed into Rilke's esoteric view of life; war is turned into so much poetry. The real insight of the third hymn deserves all praise, but the cycle as a whole begins and ends with an aestheticism which is not only amoral, but arguably immoral. These hymns are certainly the work of the most considerable German poet of the time and they contain some of the best poetry written during the war; but it could be argued that they are too poetic, too literary and rhetorical to rank highly as war poetry. The decisive criticism was made in August 1914 by the worker-poet Gerrit Engelke, who said that there is too much 'Hölderlin' here.[3]

Rilke's reactions may be sensitive, but he is in some ways too far from his subject. The great war poetry of 1914-18 was written by the front-line poets for whom the 'horrible beastliness of war' (Wilfred Owen) was a matter not of sensitivity, but of grim personal experience and terror. If Wilfred Owen was right to stress that he was 'not concerned with Poetry', then Rilke by contrast appears to be too much concerned with 'Poetry'. While Owen's poetry is deeply personal, Rilke's hymns are personal only in the sense of being esoteric. Otherwise they are impersonal in their lack of deep and genuine emotion, a masterful mistake. It would have been better if Rilke had refused, like Oskar Loerke, to leave his real, inner world; after all, the war, for him, was essentially a threat to his work on the *Duino Elegies*.

Stefan George's *Der Krieg* (1917)[4] shows an objectivity altogether different in kind from that of any other war poetry except Rilke's hymns.[5] Singularly little emotion is present in George's poem, which appears to have been written solely because he felt that an utterance was expected of him. His impassive, prophetic stance conveys nothing so much as a monumental indifference to the war. George had, of course, looked forward to a holy war which would renew the spiritually moribund society of his time; but the particular war that came must have struck him as vulgar and brutal. In *Der Krieg* the opening quotation from Dante's *Divina Commedia* and the biblical allusion in the first line ('getier der wälder' comes from Psalm 50, verse 10: 'Every beast of the forest is *mine*') serve to underline the impassive dignity of George's prophet-persona, the hermit on the mountain. Asked whether he has nothing to say of the cataclysm, he replies:

Was euch erschüttert ist mir lang vertraut .
Lang hab ich roten schweiss der angst geschwizt
Als man mit feuer spielte . . meine tränen
Vorweg geweint . . heut find ich keine mehr.

Das meiste war geschehn und keiner sah..
Das trübste wird erst sein und keiner sieht.
Ihr lasst euch pressen von der äussern wucht..
Dies sind die flammenzeichen.. nicht der kunde.
Am streit wie ihr ihn fühlt nehm ich nicht teil.

This is the crux: George takes no part in the struggle as experienced by others. Except where the death of his own friends is concerned – and his best 'war poems' are unquestionably those written in their memory – the war leaves him completely cold. His attitude is altogether too exalted: 'Nie wird dem Seher dank... Was ist IHM mord von hunderttausenden Vorm mord am Leben selbst?' Though the poet's proper concern is precisely the 'mord am Leben selbst', George shows a brutal indifference to the actual deaths that constitute this slaughter, for either the 'Mord am Leben' is composed of the 'Mord von Hunderttausenden' or the phrase is sententious and callous cant. Of the old prophet – himself – he says: 'SEIN amt ist lob und fem gebet und sühne... IHN packt ein tiefres grausen', but this – however true – again underlines his almost total lack of commitment to real suffering and therefore to real life. His objectivity is at times little short of inhuman. He realises, of course, the nature of modern war:

Zu jubeln ziemt nicht: kein triumf wird sein .
Nur viele untergänge ohne würde ..
Des schöpfers hand entwischt rast eigenmächtig
Unform von blei und blech . gestäng und rohr.
Der selbst lacht grimm wenn falsche heldenreden
Von vormals klingen der als brei und klumpen
Den bruder sinken sah . der in der schandbar
Zerwühlten erde hauste wie geziefer ..
Der alte Gott der schlachten ist nicht mehr.
Erkrankte welten fiebern sich zu ende
In dem getob. Heilig sind nur die säfte
Noch makelfrei versprizt – ein ganzer strom.

It is precisely his realisation that modern war is bestial rather than heroic that explains his distaste for it. No one felt more strongly than he did that the times were diseased; his contempt for his time is matched only by Ezra Pound in 'Hugh Selwyn Mauberley'. George is right, and his prophetic stance is momentarily justified, when he writes the lines that we have just read, for it was precisely many deaths without dignity that this war produced. And he was right, too, in saying that a nation is dead when its gods are dead:

> In beiden lagern kein Gedanke – wittrung
> Um was es geht . . . Hier: sorge nur zu krämern
> Wo schon ein andrer krämert . . ganz zu werden
> Was man am andren schmäht und sich zu leugnen
> Ein volk ist tot wenn seine götter tot sind
> Drüben: ein pochen auf ehmaligen vorrang
> Von pracht und sitte . . während feile nutzsucht
> Bequem veratmen will . . im schloss der hellsten
> Einsicht kein schwacher blink . . . dass die Verpönten
> Was fallreif war zerstören . dass vielleicht
> Ein >Hass und Abscheu menschlichen geschlechtes<
> Zum weitren male die erlösung bringt.
>
> Doch endet nicht mit fluch der sang. Manch ohr
> Verstand schon meinen preis auf stoff und stamm .
> Auf kern und keim . . schon seh ich manche hände
> Entgegen mir gestreckt . sag ich: o Land
> Zu schön als dass dich fremder tritt verheere:
> Wo flöte aus dem weidicht tönt . aus hainen
> Windharfen rauschen . wo der Traum noch webt
> Untilgbar durch die jeweils trünnigen erben . . .
> Wo die allblühende Mutter der verwildert
> Zerfallnen weissen Art zuerst enthüllte
> Ihr echtes antlitz . . Land dem viel verheissung
> Noch innewohnt – das drum nicht untergeht!

In this last section – the penultimate section of the poem – George expresses his love of Germany in a noble and moving way. But after this flash of real and deep feeling, and of brilliant poetry, the oracular pose returns in the final section, where the mythical allusions are unnecessary adjuncts to his pose, unlike the very necessary ritual and mythical allusions in David Jones's *In Parenthesis*.

The conclusion is therefore inescapable that, for all its linguistic brilliance and moments of real insight, George's *Der Krieg* as a whole is uninspired, unconvincing, unnecessary.

Why was it, it will be asked, that Rilke and George, two of the most outstanding poets ever to have written in German, produced such uneven and relatively weak poetic responses to the war? No doubt one reason is that these were responses that they felt were expected of them, rather than deeply felt ones; their concerns were therefore, in the most literal sense, otherworldly. George, writing later in the war, overgeneralises precisely because he sees himself as a prophet with a public duty to perform, not bothering to conceal his distaste for the war. Rilke's concerns were more obviously otherworldly, but George, too, although striking a public stance, was concerned with a private ideal (*his* Germany, not the real one). Both poets' poetic modes were designed to express other, private worlds. In other words, the major reason for their relative failure must be the one that so often lies behind unconvincing poetry: the fact that the poet is not sufficiently deeply or directly involved in what he is writing about. When George, for his part, *was* directly involved, as he was in the *Drei Gesänge* of 1921, he produced far more convincing poetry.

Common to Yeats and George is a fastidiousness that finds modern war not morally but aesthetically unacceptable. Yeats simply cannot see beyond the pre-war literary convention which said that war poetry should be heroic; he cannot see that for those caught up in the intense suffering which it occasions, and which only intensifies as it comes to appear more and more pointless, war is simply not heroic:

> What are the great sceptred dooms
> To us, caught
> In the wild wave?
> We break ourselves on them,
> My brother, our hearts and years.[6]

What Sir Maurice Bowra said about poets, in the early days of the war, not seeing 'the reality of war beyond the mirage of misleading associations',[7] applies very much to Yeats, who, writing his introduction twenty years after the war, should have known better.

Yeats helped to spread the idea that a general feature of the poetry of the Great War was a lack of objectivity and restraint, formal control and historical perspective. This criticism is based on the view that the average front-line poet found his experiences too overwhelming to be viewed objectively, too overpowering to be set within a formal poetic pattern or against an historical perspective. But *is* most war poetry in fact 'subjective', as opposed to intensely personal in origin? It may be very difficult for the war poet to be wholly objective, but Yeats himself writes of officer-poets pleading the suffering of their men; is that 'subjectivity'? I think not. On the contrary, any war poet worth his salt expresses not only his own agony, but that of countless fellow-combatants, so that he speaks for a wider audience than the average poet and indeed ultimately for mankind as such. This does not mean, however, that most poets find it possible to be fully objective about the war in which they are involved, for this is not the case, and a poet like Rosenberg is an exception to almost every rule. Rosenberg's achievement has been admirably described by I.M. Parsons:

> In some extraordinary way, he managed to detach himself emotionally from the terrible things that were going on all round him, to expose himself to them and to record them minutely but objectively, and then to transmute them into poetry of the highest imaginative quality, set in a much broader context than his own personal plight.[8]

This is, however, only to emphasise the exceptional nature of the case. Most poets found it impossible to be wholly objective about their experiences and, in the hands of a lesser poet than Rosenberg, complete objectivity would not have rung true. To see historical perspective as desirable or relevant, or even possible, is wrong. Where was the historical perspective to come from? The whole point of the First World War, particularly from 1916 onwards, is that it is historically unparalleled. Besides, the best poetry of the war is simply not concerned with what Yeats described as 'passive suffering', however much this was a fact of life. Now Yeats's view has been elaborated thus by John H. Johnston:

> A tragic event which is understood only in terms of personal misadventure ceases to be tragic. Tragedy implies a relationship between man and the mysteries of the moral universe. Since the modern war-poet can discern no significant relationships among the phenomena that confront him, he cannot positively relate his experiences to the moral whole of which they are necessarily a part. Of pity, grief, and fear there is much in World War I poetry, but these emotions rarely attain the nobility proper to genuinely tragic emotion[9]

To deny the modern war poet's despair the dignity of being 'genuinely tragic', because one is identifying 'tragic' with 'heroic', shows yet again the inadequacy of purely aesthetic criteria in our context, and Johnston's argument is moreover open to the objection that remarkably little 1914–18 war poetry is concerned merely with 'personal misadventure'. Even if it were, personal misadventure in a world of blind fatality would be tragic enough. Johnston had previously argued that the war was seen, by the English poets, as 'an absolutely unique event' which seemed to have 'no real significance'.While this may be consistent with his view, derived from Yeats, that the tragedy of the war is somehow not really tragic, it remains specious. As a matter of fact a number of German poets – admittedly a small number – had the keenest sense of the moral significance of the war, which they saw as a recapitulation of the Fall of Man, as the Passion of Man, and as an event likely to lead to the permanent brutishness of man.

If it had been made in 1914 there would have been much truth in the statement attributed to Kafka by Janouch, that

> Der Krieg wurde eigentlich noch nie richtig dargestellt. Gewöhnlich werden nur Teilerscheinungen oder Ergebnisse... gezeigt. Das Schreckliche des Krieges ist aber die Auflösung aller bestehenden Sicherheiten und Konventionen. Das animalische Physische überwuchert und erstickt alles Geistige. Es ist wie eine Krebskrankheit. Der Mensch lebt nicht mehr Jahre, Monate, Tage, Stunden, sondern nur noch Augenblicke. Und selbst die lebt er nicht mehr. Er wird sich ihrer nur noch bewusst. Er existiert bloss.[10]

By 1921, however, while remaining profoundly true of war, this was no longer true in relation to war literature, for it is precisely the mere animal level of existence to which man was reduced that is the subject of much 1914-18 war poetry. There is overwhelmingly clear evidence that the war deadened the senses and therefore dehumanised all those who took part in it for any length of time. There was more than jocularity in the term *Frontschwein*. In such circumstances the ideal is not so much to be able to live, as not to have to kill. The point was well made by Edlef Koeppen in 'Loretto':

> Einen Tag lang in Stille untergehen!
> Einen Tag lang den Kopf in Blumen kühlen
> und die Hände fallen lassen
> und träumen: diesen schwarzsamtnen singenden Traum:
> Einen Tag lang nicht töten.

By and large the best poets on either side were concerned not with their own plight, or with the plight of individual combatants; they were concerned with

> whatever mourns in man
> Before the last sea and the hapless stars;
> Whatever mourns when many leave these shores;
> Whatever shares
> The eternal reciprocity of tears.[11]

By far the most far-sighted and fundamental comment on the poetry of this war was made not by a poet who had grown up with the heroic tradition and had indeed developed a personal, Nietzsche-inspired hero-myth (Yeats, George, Rilke), but by one who grew up into the reality of the Great War and knew it to pose unique poetic problems: Wilfred Owen. The most important document of the entire war, from our present point of view, is the Preface to Owen's collected poems:

> This book is not about heroes. English poetry
> is not yet fit to speak of them.
> Nor is it about deeds, or lands, nor
> anything about glory, honour, might, majesty,
> dominion, or power, except War.
> Above all I am not concerned with Poetry.
> My subject is War, and the pity of War.
> The poetry is in the pity.
> Yet these elegies are to this generation in
> no sense consolatory. They may be to the next.
> All a poet can do today is warn. That is why
> the true poets must be truthful.

Concisely and honestly this says it all. Starting from a rejection of the heroic and the subsequent lack of any formal convention within which the modern war poet can grow, Owen goes straight to the point when he implies that the poetry is in the morality, in the attitude, and not merely in the words. He is not, of course, subscribing to what was to become the fallacy that the poetry matters *less than* the underlying morality.

In the ordinary way it is perfectly possible for something to please us morally and displease us aesthetically, and vice versa; Schiller made the point in his essay 'Über das Pathetische':

> Der nämliche Gegenstand kann uns in der moralischen Schätzung missfallen und in der ästhetischen sehr anziehend für uns sein. Aber wenn er uns auch in beiden Instanzen der Beurteilung Genüge

leistete, so thut er diese Wirkung bei beiden auf eine ganz verschiedene Weise. Er wird dadurch, dass er ästhetisch brauchbar ist, nicht moralisch befriedigend, und dadurch, dass er moralisch befriedigt, nicht ästhetisch brauchbar.

From this it follows that good morality does not of itself make good poetry. This goes for war poetry too, although in this case bad morality seems even worse. Many war poets of many different levels of competence show two things equally clearly: that the most brilliant poetry will not pass muster unless the moral attitude is right, and that the most admirable attitude is no substitute for poetry. The conclusion is inescapable that expression and attitude are equally important in the case of war poetry, and the critic cannot hide behind the idea that form is moral; moral, in this case, means the sentiments. In the case of war poetry, more unambiguously and perhaps more so than with other forms of poetry, the morality has to be 'right' before the question of 'poetry' or poetic quality can arise. It could, of course, be argued that the opposite is the case, that the poetry has to be right before the question of morality can arise; for most people, however, morality has to do with ethical rather than with aesthetic forms. The whole question of the relationship between art and morality is a complex one. We always tend to approve aesthetically (or at least to temper our aesthetic criticism) when we approve of the morality of a poem. We often have to make an effort to be aesthetically fair to an 'immoral' poem. And besides we are aware that moral judgements may be as subjective as aesthetic ones. That said, what do we in fact mean by 'good' and 'bad' sentiments in this context? We mean, in the first place, those of which we approve and those of which we disapprove, not doubting the soundness of our own reactions. With the wisdom of hindsight we can also see that there is a more objective criterion: 'good' sentiments are implicitly anti-war sentiments, for it is one of the most soundly based facts in history that the Great War for Civilisation was a barbarous atrocity.

Now sentiments of which we approve are not only no bar to the enjoyment of the poetry in question; they are, in the case of war poetry, an intrinsic part of the more than usually moral pleasure which we derive from it. Bad sentiments, which lead us to argue with the poetry, tend to invalidate it, as they tend to invalidate any poetry, which of its nature deals with universal, and therefore universally acceptable, truths. The very idea of aesthetic pleasure is crucial here, for it is an undeniable fact that poetry gives, and is intended to give, pleasure. It is no less a fact that we are morally disinclined to allow ourselves to take pleasure in the poetry of war. But what is the nature of the 'pleasure' in question? May it not be, above all, the satisfaction of our *moral* requirement: believing war to be an atrocity, we are pleased to see it condemned as such by brave and brilliant men. The pleasure which we take in rhyme, metre, form may be only conducive to that, may, in other words, be less important in war poetry than it normally is in poetry. Keats's 'we hate poetry that has a palpable design on us' is generally accepted; but in the poetry of war we seem, more or less explicitly, to *require* that design, in the sense that we seem to require it to be conducive to pity and indignation. Perhaps we need these to condone, or atone for, the pleasure which we take in the poet's words. Pure aesthetic pleasure, we feel, would be unacceptable. It would also be impossible, for by definition the term carries with it the idea of pleasurable learning. We are pleased, then, to learn the truth about modern war from someone caught up in it, someone who is content to write poetry and who has no palpable design on us beyond telling the truth.

Unfortunately many modern critics fail to distinguish between poetry and propaganda; the moral or even political 'correctness' of the writer's attitude has tended to become the only yardstick by which his work is judged, both in the case of the literature of the First World War and in the whole politicised remainder of the twentieth century. It remains important to recognise that work which embodies sincerely held (and generally accepted) beliefs may be sub-literary in nature and non-literary in aim.

The technical difficulties of dealing with this particular war were immense, so much so that it has even been argued that lyric poetry as such was not a wholly adequate medium in which to express the front-line writer's awareness of war:

> In different ways these three poets [Sorley, Blunden, Owen] were aware that war has no real significance unless it is viewed in terms that are larger and more universally valid than those of patriotism, humanitarianism, or simple personal involvement. The lyric only partially sufficed for the expression of this awareness...which seemed to demand...a fuller and more objective expression in narrative or dramatic form.[12]

This view might seem to be supported by the fact that the most impressive and complete expressions of the 1914-18 war are David Jones's epic *In Parenthesis*, Karl Kraus's 'epic' tragedy of mankind,

Die letzten Tage der Menschheit, and Ludwig Renn's novel *Krieg*, while some of the best war poetry as such, that of Owen and Schnack for instance, has obvious epic qualities. Theoretically modern war might be supposed to be too overpowering, its tragic potentialities too vast to be encompassed and expressed within a given lyrical form. This is, however, a purely theoretical point, for in reality it is precisely lyric and elegiac poetry that is arguably *best* suited to express the vast tragic potentialities of modern war, which is none other than what Alun Lewis, writing during the Second World War, called 'the single poetic theme of Life and Death'. This is the very stuff of poetry. Of course the question is again academic in that the physical conditions in which the poets of 1914-18 wrote dictated the use of the short lyric or elegiac mode. It is a fact that the most *memorable* expressions of the war were produced by the poets on both sides and that few are more memorable than the ultra-short lyrics of August Stramm.

The poets may have been triumphantly successful, but we have still to describe the actual technical difficulties which they faced. Above all there was the basic formal problem involved in dealing with *any* chaotic experience, whether historically unparalleled or not: they had to decide whether to express chaotic experience through an appropriate dislocation of form, or by means of a deliberately 'inappropriate' harmony in form. We shall return presently to the question of whether it is possible to neutralise chaos by superimposing form on it, or whether this involves a falsification of experience. In the meantime there is another, more urgent point: whether the existing poetic tradition is fitted to deal with this wholly new experience.

Here it is necessary to distinguish between different national poetic traditions, or, rather, between poetic traditions in unequal stages of development. English (and French) was at this time rather better equipped than German. One of the great strengths of English poetry had always been its particularity, and this was something which clearly stood it in very good stead when it came to expressing the war in all its hideous details. In Germany it was different, for there the dominant tendency in poetry at the time of the First World War was towards idealisation, abstraction, remoteness from reality. Although German poets and critics do not seem to have recognised the fact, this tendency proved to be a major barrier to the production of adequate war poetry. The abstractions in which the Idealist tradition had ended were simply irrelevancies which led poets further away from the very realities with which they were supposed to be coming to terms. Poetry, like truth, is concrete. Or should be. The trouble is that the majority of German war poets ignored the particularity of much later nineteenth-century poetry and took refuge in the windy rhetoric of the patriotic verse of the Romantic era. Rilke's failure was repeated, on a more trivial level, by countless other poets.

More specifically, the strength of Lichtenstein's Heine-inspired work shows that most German poets ignored what was likely to be most helpful and relevant in their poetic tradition when it came to dealing with something as rudely tangible and as ambivalent as modern war. Johnston has rightly said that 'During the second winter of the war, when the true nature of the struggle was becoming apparent, poets began to react to the horrors around them with a directness almost unprecedented in verse.'[13] This is true, and applies to a poet like Wilhelm Klemm, but by and large this directness was much slower coming to German poets than to British. It may be that non-poetic factors are relevant here, but essentially it is a matter of the poetic tradition. There are literally millions of poems which show how easily German poets at this time raise war into the mythical, how they incline to bombast (even while denouncing war's verbiage-mongers), how they poeticise. Much of the work in question is unbelievably bad. And to make matters worse, the work of the most considerable poet of the time, Rilke, is itself a striking and in some ways shocking example of the unacceptability of aestheticism. In the context of modern war poetry, with its peculiar moral stringencies, his poeticisation of war (the German phrase 'den Krieg zum schönen Bild machen' puts it most clearly) is not just an aesthetic, but is also a moral failure. On the whole, then, the state of the German language and therefore of German poetry in 1914 was parlous, simply not suited to the detailed poetic expression of reality and therefore of the realities of war, whereas English 'Georgian' poetry, for all its supposed shortcomings, *was* suited to it. The view that the Georgians' 'tremulous stability' was achieved at the cost of loss of contact with contemporary reality is, I think, mistaken; it depends upon a misreading of the pulse of pre-war society. The world of normality and peace of which the British war poets dreamt was precisely that described in slow and loving detail by the Georgians. It may be true that 'the characteristic qualities of Georgian poetry – its blandness, its decorum, its homogeneity, its simplicity of attitude, its preoccupation with rural themes (rather than with "nature" as the romantics understood the term) – all reflect the decline of a once powerful imaginative vision'.[14] But what matters in the present context is the fact that it was precisely those same characteristic qualities that were to prove a sheet anchor to the Georgian war poets. So far as German poetry is concerned, it was not until after the Second World War that it was stressed, by Gottfried Benn, that the poet needs to be a great realist, closely attuned to all forms of reality; and it was not really until the 1960s that the kind of realistic particularity in question finally returned to German poetry. And when it came, it derived, ultimately, from Heine. Whereas the English tradition of nature poetry was clearly a source of strength to most of the war poets writing in English, for all sorts of different reasons, the German tradition of nature mysticism was a very considerable handicap, even if most of the poets concerned did not realise this; it led all too many poets into disastrous failure.

Despite all the difficulties, among them the heroic convention, which was a complete red herring until it began to be ironised, the better German poets did succeed in coming to terms with the war. Realism was, of course, the key, but what kind of realism? Recent writers on the English poetry of the war are generally agreed that patriotism, idealism and savage realism are alike inadequate as poetic attitudes to modern war and that it is the 'modern attitude' of 'compassionate realism', which originates with Walt Whitman and is seen, for instance, in the best work of Owen and Rosenberg, that comes closest to conveying a true and truly tragic conception of war. The truth of this is confirmed by the German poetry of the war. Mere patriotism, however noble (and frequently it is but an ignoble mask for prejudice), does not and cannot take account of the gruesome realities of modern war; and indeed idealism of whatever kind is similarly inadequate; most outbreak-of-war verse proves that. Simple and savage realism are not enough, simple realism because it lacks the compassion necessary to convey the tragic aspect of war, savage realism because it lacks humanity and is in danger of glorifying that which it purports to attack. Realism must therefore be combined with compassion and with as much of objectivity as possible.

Notes

1. Robert Graves, 'Recalling War'.
2. Rilke, 'Fünf Gesänge, August 1914', first appeared in *Kriegs-Almanach 1915*; reprinted in his *Neue Gedichte*. A sixth hymn was later discovered; it is to be found among the poet's *Späte Gedichte*.
3. Letter to Jakob Kneip of 10 December 1914, in G. Engelke, *Das Gesamtwerk*, 1960, 383.
4. Stefan George, *Der Krieg*, Berlin, 1917.
5. Cf. also the patriotic sonnets of Eugen Roth's remarkable and virtually

unknown second collection, *Der Ruf* (Berlin, 1923), mostly written in the summer of 1918; though showing that Roth, who was not to find his own style for another decade, was at that time over-influenced by Stefan George, they have more permanent value than the work of many of the recognised war poets.

    6. Isaac Rosenberg, 'In War'.
    7. *Poetry and the First World War*, 1961, 11.
    8. In the Introduction to *The Collected Poems of Isaac Rosenberg*, ed. Ian Parsons, 1979, xxvi.
    9. John H. Johnston, *English Poetry of the First World War*, 1964, 19.
    10. Gustav Janouch, *Gespräche mit Kafka*, 1961 edition, 83f.
    11. Wilfred Owen, 'Insensibility'.
    12. Johnston, *English Poetry*, 249.
    13. Ibid., 13.
    14. Ibid., 8.

2   GEORG TRAKL

Georg Trakl was the most considerable Austrian poet to see active service in 1914-18. The war, when it finally came, must have seemed a mere extension of his inner world, for he lived in a haunting and at times terrifying world of Spenglerian visions, a 'proving-ground for world-destruction' (Karl Kraus) if ever there was one. He raged not against the dying of the light, but against its relentlessness, praying in vain to be able to forget his visions. In his poetry the 'infernal chaos of rhythms and images' of his life is transmuted into a series of visionary pictures of the chaos of the degenerate modern world. His poetic world is stigmatised by a loss of essence and substantiality; his deepest and most traumatic experience was that of things falling apart.[1] What he called his 'criminal melancholy' derives from his vision of a world (of which the Habsburg monarchy was the outward sign) that lacks the spiritual strength to ensure its own survival; modern materialism filled him with as much loathing as it did Kafka; he would have approved Kafka's definition of materiality as the evil in the spiritual world. Kafka and Trakl alike sought to affirm their belief in a spiritual order of things; too many critics have seen their work as negative because they, the critics in question, have been unable to see beyond the material order which both writers negate. When Trakl wrote to Erhard Buschbeck in autumn 1911 that he aimed to give to truth what belongs to truth, he could have been speaking for Kafka as well; with both writers the poetic purity of their work stems from an obsession with truth. Trakl's definition of his poetry as an imperfect atonement shows that he shared, too, Kafka's view of the writer as the scapegoat of mankind. When Kafka told Janouch in 1921 that the terrible thing about war was that the animal in man runs riot and stifles everything spiritual, he was expressing a view which Trakl would have shared; indeed, Trakl saw the destruction of man as a spiritual being as characteristic of his time in general. Kafka saw the war as unleashing evil (to Janouch he described war as a flood of evil which had burst open the flood-gates of chaos), while Trakl saw it as a consequence of evil; in effect both saw the war as the bursting of a festering sore not just on the body politic, but on the 'crimson body of man'. Trakl's poetry no less than Kafka's prose-poetry is a form of prayer; but his war poems are prayer-like in a different sense from most front-line poetry in that he prays not that he may himself be spared, but that mankind may not be destroyed.

As poet of war Trakl stands apart from the tub-thumping *Kriegslyrik* of August 1914; the two poems that he wrote at the front are, rather, 'poems from the field of slaughter' in much the same sense as the poems of the anti-war anthology (*1914-16. Eine Anthologie*) published by *Die Aktion*. He has nothing whatsoever in common with the poeticisers of war. What sets him apart is not just the total absence of chauvinism[2] and rhetoric, but the fact that war is a central, pre-existent part of his whole vision, the embodiment of the decline which has been his subject for some years; it is this fact which gives his poems about war an objectivity, perspective and depth that few, if any, other German-language poems of the First World War possess.

There are relatively few German-language poets of the First World War in whose work real depth of understanding is combined with real poetic quality. Georg Trakl is certainly one of them, for, despite the fact that he wrote only five poems that can be accounted war poems in one sense or another ('Menschheit', a prophetic vision of war comparable to Georg Heym's 'Der Krieg'; a related poem, 'Trompeten'; 'Im Osten', a poem of foreboding written shortly before leaving for the Eastern Front; and, most important, 'Klage [II]' and 'Grodek', his only actual front-line poems), his originality and poetic power are such that these few poems make him one of the outstanding German-language poets of the war. It may be partly because he wrote so little that anthologists of war poetry have reacted erratically to Trakl, but it may equally well be because he wrote poems while most other poets were producing prepoetic or subpoetic statements in which the facts are left in the raw instead of being developed into another, autonomous shape. Be this as it may, he presumably owed the inclusion of 'Grodek' in Ernst Volkmann's nationalistic anthology *Deutsche Dichtung im Weltkrieg* (1934) to the Wagnerian motif; but his omission from Rene Schickele's anthology *Menschliche Gedichte im Kriege* (1918) is inexcusable, for no poet of the war was more deeply concerned with the fate of humanity than Georg Trakl.

In a general sense all Trakl's work is relevant to his war poems, for he was obsessed by death and by a vision of disintegration, of which the war is but the summation. It is possible to separate 'Klage II' and 'Grodek' from 'Der Abend' and 'Das Gewitter' (written only weeks earlier, but before the outbreak of war) only in a very literal and arbitrary way; no interpretation of the former poems is complete if it ignores the two latter poems. But neither can any discussion of Trakl's 'war poems' ignore the two further poems whose pre-Spenglerian theme is the decline of the West: 'Abendländisches Lied' and 'Abendland'.

Ultimately all his poems are variations on a single unwritten and unwritable poem; his imagery is not only serial, but agglomerative and indeed circular. Whereas Rilke would, I think, have done better to refuse to leave his inner world, what made Trakl into a superb war poet was the fact that he did not need to leave his inner world in order to write about war. His visionary mode has no parallel, unless it be in the work of Georg Heym.

As Trakl will have known, the most striking single poem about war by a member of his generation is Georg Heym's visionary and prophetic 'Der Krieg':[3]

Aufgestanden ist er, welcher lange schlief,
Aufgestanden unten aus Gewölben tief.
In der Dämmrung steht er, gross und unerkannt,
Und den Mond zerdrückt er in der schwarzen Hand.

In den Abendlärm der Städte fällt es weit,
Frost und Schatten einer fremden Dunkelheit.
Und der Märkte runder Wirbel stockt zu Eis.
Es wird still. Sie sehn sich um. Und keiner weiss.

In den Gassen fasst es ihre Schulter leicht.
Eine Frage. Keine Antwort. Ein Gesicht erbleicht.
In der Ferne zittert ein Geläute dünn,
Und die Bärte zittern um ihr spitzes Kinn.

Auf den Bergen hebt er schon zu tanzen an,
Und er schreit: ihr Krieger alle, auf und an!
Und es schallet, wenn das schwarze Haupt er schwenkt,
Drum von tausend Schädeln laute Kette hängt.

Einem Turm gleich tritt er aus die letzte Glut,
Wo der Tag flieht, sind die Ströme schon voll Blut.
Zahllos sind die Leichen schon im Schilf gestreckt,
Von des Todes starken Vögeln weiss bedeckt.

In die Nacht er jagt das Feuer querfeldein,
Einen roten Hund mit wilder Mäuler Schrein.
Aus dem Dunkel springt der Nächte schwarze Welt,
Von Vulkanen furchtbar ist ihr Rand erhellt.

Und mit tausend hohen Zipfelmützen weit
Sind die finstren Ebnen flackend überstreut,
Und was unten auf den Strassen wimmelnd flieht,
Stösst er in die Feuerwälder, wo die Flamme brausend zieht.

Und die Flammen fressen brennend Wald um Wald,
Gelbe Fledermäuse, zackig in das Laub gekrallt,
Seine Stange haut er wie ein Köhlerknecht
In die Bäume, dass das Feuer brause recht.

Eine grosse Stadt versank in gelbem Rauch,
Warf sich lautlos in des Abgrunds Bauch.
Aber riesig über glühnden Trümmern steht,
Der in wilde Himmel dreimal seine Fackel dreht

Über sturmzerfetzter Wolken Widerschein,
In des toten Dunkels kalten Wüstenein,
Dass er mit dem Brande weit die Nacht verdorr,
Pech und Feuer träufet unten auf Gomorrh.

Georg Heym, one of the major poets of his generation, was obsessed by a foreboding of war and at the same time longed for war as a forceful interruption of the monotony of his young life and of the banality of the age.[4] Such was his longing for an heroic life – the most that man can hope for, according to his favourite philosopher, Schopenhauer – that he even dreamt, in 1911, of taking part in great battles. The disparity between his dreams of glory and his vision, in this poem, of the carnage to which the heroic leads, is striking. The form of the poem carries clear intimations of the heroic mode, but none whatsoever of the expected immortality. The pervasive enthusiasm is without any illusions; the 'heroic' line is wooden, so that the poem is more like a dance of death than anything else. When Heym wrote it in early September 1911, a year before his tragically early death, 'Der Krieg' must have been at least in part a visualisation of that great battle of which he dreamt; when it was read by others, however, it appeared to be something very different. The poem was in fact to prove a potent influence on the poetry written in the early months of the war. This is why it belongs here.

What strikes the reader at once is the monumental impersonality and barbaric grandeur of the poem, which differs from most 1914-18 war poems in being not at all subjective. What Heym gives is an objective picture of war as such, war as an elemental feature of life. There is terror in this objectivity, as there is later in Ludwig Renn's novel *Krieg*, arguably the outstanding novel of the war. In poems actually written during the war such objectivity is found only in poets who are, for one reason or another, far from their subject.[5] Heym's poem aims to shock; it consists of juxtaposed explosive images which burst like shells in the reader's mind, a technique that was to be further developed during the war, in poetry of a very different kind, by August Stramm. Since the poet sees war as an elemental feature of life, 'Der Krieg' ultimately conveys a visionary and prophetic picture of reality itself. Georg Heym, like T.S. Eliot's Tiresias, 'perceived the scene, and foretold the rest'.

The heavy six-beat trochaic line in which Heym's poem is written makes the accent stalk through the poem like the incarnate demon of war through his apocalyptic landscape. The rhythm and imagery of the poem underline the extreme violence of its subject matter. Occasional deviations from the metrical pattern give the impression both of the poet's vision dominating and threatening to violate his formal resources and of violence continually erupting through the surface of life; the old world represented by the trochaic metre is continually burst open by the violence of the subject matter. The use of rhymed couplets throughout, with all the rhymes masculine ones, is highly appropriate, since the rhyme scheme thus reflects and expresses the primitive, elemental quality of Heym's subject. The poem is 'lyrical' above all in its concentration.

The opening of 'Der Krieg' is majestic in its barbaric grandeur. War is immediately personified into an infernal demon who rises from below, from the collective unconscious, from the primitive depths of life, and at the end stands in all his grim majesty over the apocalyptic landscape that is both his own true element and the scene of mankind's Fall and Passion. What, if not War, is the great power which comes unprompted into men's thoughts, of which Heym wrote in his diary in October 1911.[6] The demon War rises before our eyes on the repeated word 'aufgestanden'. One changed syllable – 'auferstanden' – and the word would refer to a god rising from the dead, but 'aufgestanden' is appropriate here, for War is a chthonic god or demon, a great and unknown power, a figure of utter profanity. Just how terrible this power is, is suggested in the last line of the first stanza, where War is shown crushing the moon in his brute black hand; his colour is the colour of evil and death, for war is the product of evil and the product of war, the whole point and purpose of war, is death. The demon War whose name is Death brings with him the chill of life-denying darkness. In his awful presence life in the city of man is paralysed. At first (second stanza) people are nonplussed; but then (third stanza) the uncanny, threatening atmosphere overcomes them and puzzlement gives way to fear. The jerky, abrupt phrases punch home the confused reactions of men jerked out of their trivial routines who suddenly find themselves faced with primeval violence, that is to say, the violence which all the time had been lurking at the bottom of their own minds (*homo homini lupus*). The peal of bells is a *memento mori* which reduces the staid bourgeois to a figure of fun.

The scene now changes; from the city terrified by this sudden eruption of hitherto suppressed violence we see the demon War moving out into the landscape of war, a landscape that becomes increasingly a prophetic picture of what has been called 'the lunar waste of the Somme', until it finally assumes the proportions of myth: the demon War assumes the proportions of something wholly uncontrollable. Again and again personification is used to control the perspective and gain depth. Thus in the sixth stanza night, the abode of demons, is touched into independent existence by Heym's use of the plural 'nights' which implies a black world full of night demons. Similarly fire is animated into 'a red hound with the screaming of wild mouths': the mythical hell-hound itself carrying off the broken animal bodies of the dead to eternal damnation. The volcanoes which light up the edge of the night-demons' world fill the air with the sulphurous stench of damnation, pointing forward to the final Apocalypse.

In the seventh stanza Death is again personified, as a monstrous stoker feeding the flames with the countless dead in their tall pointed caps (the 'Pickelhauben' of the German war dead in 1914-18). The whole world is turned into a ghastly crematorium. In a brilliant nightmare image deriving from Van Gogh the flames are described as 'Gelbe Fledermäuse zackig in das Laub gekrallt'; the purpose of this memorable metaphor is to be nightmarish. And still the strutting, mechanical rhythms go their incessant, senseless way.

All through the poem War is presented as the sign of evil, and at the end we see the original monster city destroyed by War, destroyed, that is, by the awakened evil within itself. Its fall is made to echo the Fall of Babylon the Great. The earth is reduced to a wasteland dominated by the gigantic figure of Death Triumphant, although at this point Christian iconography fails, for Heym's Death is strongly reminiscent of the Hindu destroyer-god Siva Bhairava with his garland of a thousand skulls and similar figures from Tibetan demonology. Within five years this wasteland was to assume concrete form on the Somme and in Galicia.

'Der Krieg' is a magnificent poem about war, even if it is not a 'war poem' as such. When Heym was writing it in 1911, Georg Trakl had just finished serving in the Austrian army medical corps as a one-year conscript; in April 1912 he re-enlisted for a six-month spell which led to his meeting with Ludwig von Ficker. Following the outbreak of war in 1914, he volunteered for active service and left Innsbruck for Austrian-occupied Poland on 24 August 1914. He wore a red carnation on his cap as he climbed into the cattle-wagon that was to take him to Galicia; his only cause for rejoicing was the hope that the chaos of his life might for a time be replaced by some kind of order short of the ordered finality of death. The unit (Field Hospital 7/14), to which he was attached as lieutenant-pharmacist, was stationed at Rudki in Galicia (the Russian poet Aleksandr Blok had, from St Petersburg, seen the Russian troops departing for Galicia), and was subsequently involved in the battle of Grodek/Rawa-Ruska of 6-11 September. During the battle of Grodek, Trakl was responsible for some 90 severely wounded men lying in a barn with no doctor available for two days and with insufficient drugs to alleviate their suffering. One of the men shot himself in Trakl's presence. Unable to bear the sight Trakl walked outside only to see a row of bodies hanging from trees (they were locals suspected of disloyalty, in other words, of the wrong kind of patriotism).[7] An eyewitness has written of Trakl's horror and despair at what he experienced, which Trakl himself described to Ficker as involving the whole of human misery.[8] It is this misery that is the subject of his last two poems. Trakl's mind was turned by his experiences at Grodek; he tried to shoot himself and was taken into Garrison Hospital 15 in Cracow on 7 October for observation; on 10 October he was reported writing 'various poems' (what happened to them?); on 3 November he died as a result of taking an overdose of cocaine, thus enacting the untranslatable words he wrote in 'Helian': 'Zur Vesper verliert sich der Fremdling in schwarzer Novemberzerstörung.'

The poems on which Trakl was reported working in the last weeks of his life will have included 'Klage [II]' (drafted in September), 'Grodek' (the second version dates from 25-27 October), and 'Menschliche Trauer' (the third version of 'Menschliches Elend', sent to Ficker on 27 October).

Two years previously Trakl may have had a premonition of the Hell of Galicia, for in 1912 he wrote a poem, 'Menschheit', which is, except in a technical sense, almost indistinguishable from his wartime poems. By 1912 he had also written the first two versions of 'Menschliches

Elend'; when he wrote the third and final version of this poem under the title 'Menschliche Trauer' in October 1914, he changed only the title, because no other changes were needed; the whole war situation was already implicit in his work. The original title referred to the human condition as such (cf. Andreas Gryphius's poem with the same title); it is the war which is the specific cause of 'Menschliche Trauer'.

The poem 'Menschheit' is a foreboding vision not just of war, but of world war, the last days of mankind. Like Georg Heym's 'Der Krieg', written only months earlier, Trakl's poem consists of a shocking and eventually overwhelming series of images that are at once concrete and abstract:

> Menschheit vor Feuerschlünden aufgestellt,
> Ein Trommelwirbel, dunkler Krieger Stirnen,
> Schritte durch Blutnebel; schwarzes Eisen schellt,
> Verzweiflung, Nacht in traurigen Gehirnen:
> Hier Evas Schatten, Jagd und rotes Geld.
> Gewölk, das Licht durchbricht, das Abendmahl.
> Es wohnt in Brot und Wein ein sanftes Schweigen
> Und jene sind versammelt zwölf an Zahl.
> Nachts schrein im Schlaf sie unter Ölbaumzweigen;
> Sankt Thomas taucht die Hand ins Wundenmal.

War is immediately unleashed, with the rhythm beating a garish tattoo (we hear the drum-roll in the first line before it is named in the second), and within four lines leads to despair:

> Menschheit vor Feuerschlünden aufgestellt,
> Ein Trommelwirbel, dunkler Krieger Stirnen,
> Schritte durch Blutnebel; schwarzes Eisen schellt,
> Verzweiflung, Nacht in traurigen Gehirnen:

Here there is the same kind of mythical grandeur as in Heym's more famous poem. Common to 'Menschheit' and to Trakl's four other poems is not so much a lack of particularity, as an abstract particularity; the images themselves are as concrete as may be, so that - as with Heym - we have to remind ourselves that they are mostly non-specific, that is, not 'real' (a ridiculous word; as if anything was more real for Trakl). 'Menschheit', like 'Der Krieg', is the product of an obsession with evil, the clearest sign of which, for both poets, was the war which they foresaw.[9] Trakl's attitude towards that war had nothing of Heym's ambivalence. The 'Verzweiflung, Nacht in traurigen Gehirnen' of Trakl's poem is caused not by the preceding vision of war, however, but by the following vision of Man dominated by Mammon. In line 4 Trakl originally wrote 'Und Fratzen gaukeln aus zerstampften Hirnen', which is both too bestial and too specific for any pre-war poem (except Heym's 'Der Krieg', in which it would not be out of place).

'Menschheit' is not only densely imagistic, but very tightly end-rhymed (ababa, cdcdc) and has a clear pattern of front-rhymes and inner rhymes. The metrical pattern emphasises the way in which the poem divides into two distinct and counterbalanced halves, as well as the parallels between the halves.

The first half of the poem, beginning with 'Menschheit' and ending with 'rotes Geld', is a picture of modern man possessed by violence, materialism and despair. The preponderant iambic pentameters and those tight, conventional end-rhymes, which look like little more than a mannerism, give the impression of a formalised, stricken civilisation that is likely to give lip-service only to its beliefs. The dominant sounds are sch and ei, which tends to confirm that we are faced with mere *Schein*, Trakl's melancholy, godless world of *Stein*. The significant rhyme is that front-rhyme to which attention is drawn by the break in the metrical pattern, Menschheit vor/Verzweiflung, for the poem is about mankind driven to despair by its own guilt. The central image in this first 'stanza' (as it really is) is that of the Fall. The first half of the poem conveys, with vivid, lurid precision, the poet's vision of impending war and the reason for it (the Fall; materialism; violence). The first half of the poem ends with the shadow of the Fall ('Hier Evas Schatten, Jagd und rote Geld'), man's betrayal of his God ('rotes Geld' points to Judas), and his subsequent pursuit of the false god of materialism at whatever cost (the epithet 'rot' names the colour of 'Blutnebel'). This melancholy vision of evil is opposed and counterbalanced by a vision of possible salvation which forms the core of the second half of the poem.

The second half is not a mirror image of the first, but does closely follow it. The same end-rhyme scheme is there, as is the same pattern of inner rhymes within the second line (Wein ein/Schweigen, cf. Wirbel/Stirnen in line 2) and within the invisible stanza (bricht/taucht, a near-rhyme which balances and near-rhymes with the full inner rhyme of Nacht/Jagd in lines 4 and 5), and the renewed breaks in the metrical pattern that act as a kind of front-rhyme substitute (Es wohnt in/ Nachts schrein im). The poem, in other words, is as tightly organised as, say, Andreas Gryphius's 'Tränen des Vaterlandes, anno 1636', a classical war poem which similarly ended in a lament for lost faith. What I wish to stress, however, is that what might be thought to be the rigid formalism of the poem is in fact an *exact* expression of its subject matter: the state of modern civilisation.

The fact that the main non-structural connection between the two halves of the poem is biblical, brings us back to the matter of interpretation, for the poem can be read in different, and indeed opposite ('negative' and 'positive') ways. I think the second half of the poem, which has as its central image the Last Supper, indicates man's only hope. Trakl is here pointing to the possibility of redemption and an end to the suffering of the first half. The disciples also suffered, but were saved by their faith. As a Christian, Trakl not only believed that men had never sunk so low as in 1914, that the modern world was bereft of all spirituality; he also believed that only a renascence of primitive Christianity could save the world from destruction. The word 'Abendmahl' in the first line of the second half takes us back to the period before the godless 'Nacht' of the first half, and indeed takes us back to the central symbolical event of primitive Christianity: the Last Supper. The opening image – 'Gewölk, das Licht durchbricht' (the syntax is ambiguous, but the meaning is not) – is a painterly visualisation of a famous biblical passage ('And there came a voice out of the cloud, saying: This is my beloved Son, hear him': St. Luke, IX, 35; cf. St Matthew, XVII, 5; 2 Corinthians, IV, 6). This brings us to the first sign of meaning in the poem – the next line contains the first sentence as such – and points forward to that which Doubting Thomas was forced to recognise and which Trakl himself did recognise: the divinity of Christ. Doubting Thomas is above all an object lesson: what the world needs is faith (this was certainly Trakl's view). But it is important to stress that this *is* a matter of interpretation; the poem is fundamentally ambiguous, and rightly so, for the future can never be read with certainty. Now if Trakl's message, whether positive or negative, had been expressed in abstract moral terms, we should have been faced with a religious tract. But given that it is expressed in the most appropriate poetic terms possible, we are faced with a poem about war whose visionary content matches its visionary nature. If Heym was the first German poet to give adequate expression to the modern, tragic conception of war, Trakl was a very close second. Heym's poem shows the Fall of Mankind; Trakl points to a possible way of averting the tragedy of mankind. Having said this, Lindenberger's comment that 'Menschheit' is a poem which 'succeeds in evoking the horrors of modern war more powerfully than any of the German poems which were to come out of the war itself'[10] is exaggerated; the fact of the matter is that, for all its quality, 'Menschheit' is less powerful than, for instance, any of Anton Schnack's poems.

'Menschheit' was written between 26 September and 10 October 1912 and first appeared in *Der Brenner* on 1 November 1912. Closely related to it is another poem written at the same time, 'Trompeten':

Unter verschnittenen Weiden, wo braune Kinder spielen
Und Blätter treiben, tönen Trompeten. Ein Kirchhofsschauer.
Fahnen von Scharlach stürzen durch des Ahorns Trauer,
Reiter entlang an Roggenfeldern, leeren Mühlen.

Oder Hirten singen nachts und Hirsche treten
In den Kreis ihrer Feuer, des Hains uralte Trauer,
Tanzende heben sich von einer schwarzen Mauer;
Fahnen von Scharlach, Lachen, Wahnsinn, Trompeten.

This poem appeared in the November 1912 issue of *Der Ruf. Ein Flugblatt an junge Menschen*, which was devoted to the theme of war. 'Trompeten' is a much weaker poem than 'Menschheit' (by Trakl's standards the first stanza has no memorable images); in terms of structure, however, it is no less interesting. The obvious (abba, cbbc) formal end-rhyme is complemented by a strong but apparently random pattern of internal assonantal rhymes (Wei/trei/Rei/Krei/Feu/Hai; Kind/Kirch; schauer/Schar; lach/nachts/lach/Lach; Fahnen/Ahorns/Fahnen/Wahnsinn); both the internal rhymes and the preponderance of ei, ach, sch and t sounds are 'artful'[11] in that they are unnecessary. The metrical scheme (basically six-beat iambic) is of no particular interest; the strong caesuras are not supported by any systematic pattern of internal rhymes; indeed, they are nullified by the random pattern we have just discerned. One has the impression that the poem is a five-finger exercise. Each stanza has one long (seven-beat) line ending in the word 'Trauer', the insistent identical rhyme which puts the poem in the context of 'Menschliche Trauer', while the last line with its heavy internal rhyme of Fahnen/Wahnsinn makes Trakl's anti-war position clear. 'Trompeten' is indeed interesting partly for the ambiguous last line, 'Fahnen von Scharlach, Lachen, Wahnsinn, Trompeten' ('Lachen' means both 'laughter' and 'pools of blood'), which Trakl described in a letter to Erhard Buschbeck as a criticism of militaristic madness,[12] partly for the fact that Trakl specifically asked that his anti-war poem should not be followed by a sabre-rattling offering by Paul Stefan, and mainly for the fact that it contains some images (Weiden, Scharlach, des

Hains uralte Trauer) which recur in 'Grodek', thus showing how deeply 'Grodek' is rooted in his personal vision. Otherwise 'Trompeten' reminds me of nothing so much as the formalism of Viennese *fin-de-siècle* poetry ('geschniegelte Wiener Kulturlyrik') which Stadler found in Hofmannsthal; in other words, the formalism which in 'Menschheit' was structurally so important, is here an unnecessary mannerism.

It took less than two years for Trakl's presentiment of war in 'Menschheit' and 'Trompeten' to become reality. According to Ludwig von Ficker, it was in August 1914, probably before he left Innsbruck for the Eastern Front on 24 August, that Trakl wrote 'Im Osten'; if this really is so (and I find it hard to believe), then this, too, is a remarkably prophetic poem, for it reads like a front-line poem, differing from 'Klage' and 'Grodek' mainly in what seems to be its more formal, leisurely structure:

Den wilden Orgeln des Wintersturms
Gleicht des Volkes finistrer Zorn,
Die purpurne Woge der Schlacht,
Entlaubter Sterne.

Mit zerbrochnen Brauen, silbernen Armen
Winkt sterbenden Soldaten die Nacht.
Im Schatten der herbstlichen Esche
Seufzen die Geister der Erschlagenen.

Dornige Wildnis umgürtet die Stadt.
Von blutenden Stufen jagt der Mond
Die erschrockenen Frauen.
Wilde Wölfe brachen durchs Tor.

The key line is the first, for it is the 'wilden Orgeln des Wintersturms' that the whole poem echoes; this can be seen by tracing the pattern of the dominant or/er/ur sounds and occasional variants (or er ur/ er or/ ur ur er/ er er, er er ar/ er/ er er/ er er er, or ür/ -/ er/ ur or) which persists throughout the poem and is, together with the more obvious four-line stanza pattern, the main constant feature; this pattern of sounds is equivalent to and complements the serial imagery. Otherwise the poem is far less regular than it looks. If the first half of the poem is noteworthy for a system of near-rhymes (Sturms/Zorn; Sturms/Sterne; Sturms/Armen; Zorn/Sterne), to say nothing of the full-rhyming Schlacht/Nacht, the second half as such is characterised by a strongly dactylic verse pattern which was not present in the first half (there is one dactyl in the first stanza, while there are six dactyls in each of the last two stanzas; in other words, there are three dactyls in the first half of the poem, ten in the second half); for all the ostensible difference between the poems, this dactylic pattern links 'Im Osten' with 'Grodek'. The near-rhymes of the first half of the poem and the dactylic, near-alcaic ('Hölderlinian') pattern of the second half show that the form of the poem is internalised as the poet moves from actual war to an interpretation first of war and then of history; both halves of the poem are held together not so much by the stanzaic structure as by the recurrent organ notes; it is these which 'order the fragments of wrath into a formal pattern', to re-use the words which Idris Parry used in another context.[13] The successive layers of the poem ranging from obvious (stanzas) to not-so-obvious (near-rhymes) to invisible (dactyls) matches the way in which the poet's concern passes from this war to war in general and thence to human history and the destiny of man.

Sir Maurice Bowra wrote of 'Im Osten' that Trakl 'applies to the whole shapeless panorama of battle his gift for images ... Here the individual elements are taken from fact and give a true picture of war';[14] if, as we are told, the poem was written at Innsbruck, the comment is no longer valid. What is more to the point is that the 'shapeless panorama of battle' has imposed on it both a structural pattern and a pattern of images. War is seen in Hölderlinian terms – and it is Hölderlin who is revealed as the German national poet at this time – as the embodiment of 'des Volkes ... Zorn' (cf. Hölderlin's 'das Zürnen der Welt' in 'Patmos'), the epithet 'finster' implying that this anger is damnable. By saying that the nations' wrath, war, is like the wild organ notes of a winter storm, Trakl seems to imply that war is as necessary as winter; such a cyclic view of history, possibly deriving from Hölderlin, is found elsewhere in his work. The third and fourth lines of the first stanza incorporate Trakl's characteristic symbolism: the epithet 'purpurn' in 'Die purpurne Woge der Schlacht' refers not only to violence, but to man's guilt, to the crimson body of man which can be heard breaking in 'Klage'. In the second stanza Night is likened to Christ on the cross, his brow broken by the crown of thorns, his pale arms (silver-looking in the moonlight) outstretched as though to embrace those crucified by War.

'Im Osten' and 'Klage' are linked by the artful frameworks of violence and darkness, within which man is at the mercy, successively, of 'Die purpurne Woge der Schlacht' and 'die eisige Woge der Ewigkeit'. That the stars, signs of the spiritual, are defoliated, suggests that man is bereft of all spirituality. War is accordingly seen as a sign of man's literal beastliness or animality. The second stanza is by comparison straightforward, although there is inevitably more to it than meets the eye: the colour silver, which Trakl probably took from Hölderlin, who used it to denote the crystalline whiteness of snow, does not only refer to the silvery light of the moon, but is one of the colours of death, the otherworldly light of perdition, for already the landscape is spectral with the peaceless spirits of the slain. The last stanza opens with an allusion to the Passion: 'Dornige Wildnis' refers to Golgotha, the place of the skull (cf. Galicia), thus implying that what is to be enacted in 1914 is the passion of mankind; indeed, Trakl makes the city of man wear a crown of thorns ('Dornige Wildnis umgürtet die Stadt'). The poem ends with a reference to the unrestrained animal ('Wilde Wölfe') in man. 'Im Osten' is basically a Christian poem of despair. The cyclic view of life implied and the reference to the Passion are the only notes of hope. There is little sign of salvation, for the animal in man has the upper hand. Man is not only doomed, but damned by his own actions. Although 'Im Osten', like most of Trakl's poetry, is rooted in reality, his images constantly point beyond themselves to a greater reality. The result is that his poem has an objectivity and a depth unusual in front-line poetry. It is true, as Bowra wrote, that Trakl 'looks upon war from the anguished solitude of a prophet';[15] but it is certainly not true that 'he draws no conclusions and makes no forecasts', for the whole of 'Im Osten' is a forecast, and the poet's conclusions, though implicit, could hardly be clearer.

Both his other war poems, 'Klage' and 'Grodek', were the product of his personal despair. 'Klage' is both a highly personal poem and at the same time an oracular, Hölderlinian one; for all his own spiritual agony, Trakl's greatest fear is that the war may mark the end of man as a spiritual being; he sees mankind in danger of sinking into permanent brutishness:

Schlaf und Tod, die düstern Adler
Umrauschen nachtlang dieses Haupt:
Des Menschen goldnes Bildnis
Verschlänge die eisige Woge
Der Ewigkeit. An schaurigen Riffen
Zerschellt der purpurne Leib
Und es klagt die dunkle Stimme
Über dem Meer.
Schwester stürmischer Schwermut

Sieh ein ängstlicher Kahn versinkt
Unter Sternen,
Dem schweigenden Antlitz der Nacht.

Whether the opening image in 'Klage', the dark eagles of sleep and death, was suggested by the twin-headed eagles of the Austro-Hungarian Empire and Imperial Russia, I do not know, but it seems probable that they were, for the poem clearly has a comparatively realistic starting-point. The first two lines express a state of mind, that of collapse and despair. We assume that 'dieses Haupt' refers to the poet himself, and that it is the despair and indeed derangement to which he had been reduced following the battle of Grodek, that underlies the poem. It is possible that 'dieses Haupt' refers to the wounded soldier who shot himself in the head in Trakl's presence; the despair which the poet expresses could be this man's; but it is more likely that this man's suffering is one of the causes of Trakl's own despair. The poet fears that 'Des Menschen goldnes Bildnis', that is, man's spirituality, his spiritual being, may soon be swallowed up by 'die eisige Woge der Ewigkeit'. Heidegger pointed out that the latter is not a Christian concept, and Michael Hamburger added that Trakl's despair was bound to be coloured by current (Nietzschean) modes of unbelief, but we can be more specific and say that 'die eisige Woge der Ewigkeit' is a variant of Nietzsche's 'Eisstrom des Daseins', which occurs in the context of Nietzsche's view that 'Socratic [modern] man has run his course'.[16] Trakl's view of the decline of the West is strongly tinged by Nietzsche. When he wrote this poem Trakl's mind was possessed by the crimson body of man broken on the reefs of war, so that the poem is an elegy for mankind. There has been much critical discussion of the figure of the 'sister' in Trakl's poetry; in the present context I think that 'Schwester stürmischer Schwermut' refers to Trakl's own sister and that at the end of the poem he is calling upon her to witness his own demise.

In 'Grodek', his last poem, Trakl implies that Western civilisation has reached a turning-point:

Am Abend tönen die herbstlichen Wälder
Von tödlichen Waffen, die goldnen Ebenen
Und blauen Seen, darüber die Sonne
Düstrer hinrollt; umfängt die Nacht
Sterbende Krieger, die wilde Klage
Ihrer zerbrochenen Münder.
Doch stille sammelt im Weidengrund

Rotes Gewölk, darin ein zürnender Gott wohnt,
Das vergossne Blut sich, mondne Kühle;
Alle Strassen münden in schwarze Verwesung.
Unter goldnem Gezweig der Nacht und Sternen
Es schwankt der Schwester Schatten durch den schweigenden Hain,
Zu grüssen die Geister der Helden, die blutenden Häupter;
Und leise tönen im Rohr die dunkeln Flöten des Herbstes.
O stolzere Trauer! ihr ehernen Altäre,
Die heisse Flamme des Geistes nährt heute ein gewaltiger Schmerz,
Die ungebornen Enkel.

That 'Grodek' 'stands at a kind of meeting point between Trakl's private poetic world ... and the pressures of outward, public event'[17] is clearly true. On the surface 'Grodek' appears to be perhaps the most impersonal front-line poem ever written; beneath the surface it is desperately, painfully personal. The evening and autumn of the opening line refer neither solely nor mainly to the aftermath of the battle of Grodek; both have a historical, Spenglerian connotation and bring back the recurrent vision of the destruction of Western civilisation. There is a clear contrast between autumn 1914 and a previous age of golden plains and blue lakes (it is no chance that this ideal landscape bears the colours of Christian and indeed Catholic spirituality), on which the sun is now setting. Night – personified in the manner of Georg Heym and Johann Christian Günther – embraces dying warriors, the wild laments of their broken mouths; compare Charles Sorley's famous lines:

When you see millions of the mouthless dead
Across your dreams in pale battalions go,
Say not soft things as other men have said ...

Although Trakl's scene has a bitterly personal connotation, it is presented in a totally objective, non-specific way; he could be writing about any war in history. The red cloud in which a wrathful god resides is a reflection of the bloodlust by which men's minds are hazed, a symbol of violence and indeed of the profane, finite, physical world; whether the god is Heym's demonic war-god (i.e. Mars), or the Christian god reduced to wrath by man's brutish behaviour, or Moloch, the god to whom children (the unborn grandchildren) are sacrificed, is best left open, for any poem by Trakl is the sum total of its probable interpretations. While the 'zürnender Gott' is clearly an allusion to war, it is also important to recall that the same figure occurred in a similar context in 'Das Gewitter' (written two to three months earlier):

Magnetische Kühle
Umschwebt dies stolze Haupt,
Glühende Schwermut
Eines zürnenden Gottes

The 'mondne Kühle' is the moonlit chill of nightfall, but has the same connotation as the 'icy wave of eternity' in the previous poem, or the 'magnetische Kühle' of 'Das Gewitter'; in other words, the chill is the chill of death as retribution or punishment. The key line in the poem, the one certainty among so many ambiguities, is 'Alle Strassen münden in schwarze Verwesung'; 'schwarze Verwesung' refers not only to physical decay, but also to spiritual corruption (the cause of that decay) and indeed historical disintegration; black is more than one of the colours in the spectrum of putrefaction,[18] it is the colour of damnation. The line 'Alle Strassen münden in schwarze Verwesung' may have the connotation which E.L. Marson has described as 'the coming night as a black edge of decay creeping up from the horizon to engulf Grodek';[19] more certainly it has the connotation of individual lives everywhere ending in death and damnation. In line 12 the ubiquitous sister is transformed into a Valkyrie figure receiving the spirits of the slain into Valhalla, an allusion to the fascination which Wagner's *Die Walküre* held for Trakl; the 'schweigenden Hain', which might appear to be an allusion to the 'schöne Menschlichkeit' of Goethe's Iphigenie and therefore of the ideal sister-figure, is most likely a Hölderlinian echo. The figures of the dead heroes first appeared some weeks earlier in a pre-war poem, 'Der Abend', which begins:

Mit toten Heldengestalten
Erfüllst du Mond
Die schweigenden Wälder

What is new is the context, the 'overwrought Wagnerian pathos',[20] which is no doubt itself the result of the poet's overwrought condition. The dark flutes of autumn sound out not merely to salute the passing of the dead, but to lament a greater loss: the unborn grandsons who have been sacrificed on the brazen altars of war; 'ihr ehernen Altäre' is not only a general reference to war, it is a more specific reference to the phrase 'auf dem Alter des Vaterlandes sterben', which was almost invariably used to announce death at the front, and the pride mixed with sorrow with which such announcements were made. Trakl clearly sees an even greater loss lying behind such deaths: the hot flame of the spirit is sustained by something purer and prouder: grief at the death of the innocents and therefore of innocence. The poem ends with this ambiguous image that has been continually misinterpreted; 'unborn' has both its literal meaning and the figurative meaning of innocent. The ending of the poem, which was less concise in the lost first version, implies that Trakl sees the Fall of Man as being re-enacted on the battlefields of 1914; future generations of innocents will not now be born because man has finally lost his innocence and is therefore doomed.

When Ludwig von Ficker visited Trakl in hospital shortly before his death, the poet asked him whether he wanted to hear what he had written at the front; he added that it was damn all ('blutwenig'), and then proceeded to read 'Klage II' and 'Grodek'. I imagine that it will be agreed that whatever else they are, 'Klage' and 'Grodek' are not 'blutwenig'. Of course, when one bears in mind the fact that between the outbreak of war and Trakl's death 2 million war poems were written in the German language, one can only be more than ever grateful for Trakl's poems. One of the most extraordinary things about 'Klage' and 'Grodek' is that they deliberately dispense with the particularity on which front-line poetry normally depends for its effect. Trakl shuns realism (cf. his use of the unrealistic words 'Krieger' and 'Haupter' in 'Grodek') because his visions were more real to him than the actualities of war; these were important to him only as confirming all his worst fears. It is because his conception of reality is an inward or hallucinatory one that Trakl's metaphors do not follow the normal pattern; whereas a normal metaphor starts with something familiar, Trakl's starting point is frequently something unfamiliar, so that his images tend to exist or operate at two removes from what is normally called reality; but since what is real for him are his own visions, his imagery is appropriate to express *his* reality. Besides, his images, like Kafka's, point deeper and deeper into the work itself and away from the material order which they negate. No one took the war more seriously than Trakl, but no one treated it with more contempt either; most importantly of all, no German-language poet of the war viewed war from a deeper, historic-tragic perspective than Trakl, or produced greater poems while at the front. Kafka's verdict, that Trakl had too much imagination, this being why he could not stand war, which results from an appalling lack of imagination,[21] remains true; but the imagination which drove him out of his mind also made him into a superb poet. Albert Ehrenstein's memorial to Georg Trakl, which forms the preface to his *Den ermordeten Brüdern* (1919), rightly ends with the statement that no Austrian poet has ever written more beautiful poetry than Georg Trakl.

Notes

1. 'Es ist ein so namenloses Unglück, wenn einem die Welt entzweibricht': Letter to Ficker, November 1913 in *Dichtungen und Briefe*, I, 1969, 530.
2. On the whole the patriotism of the early Austrian war poetry is more thoughtful than its German equivalent; more Austrian poets are sensible of the disaster and are therefore opposed to the war from the start, whereas in German poetry the patriotism is mostly blind. This did not, however, cause the Austrian war poets to write better poetry. Most of the poets listed in Stella Herzig's *Oesterreichische Kriegslyrik 1914-18* (Diss., Vienna, 1927) are better forgotten.
3. Georg Heym, 'Der Krieg', in his *Umbra vitae*, 1924 (reprinted 1962 in Insel-Verlag).
4. Heym, *Dichtungen und Schriften*, Bd 3, Tagebücher, Munich, 1960, 89, 164.
5. Cf. Rilke's 'Fünf Gesänge', George's *Der Krieg*, Max Dauthendey's *Des grossen Krieges Not*.
6. Heym, *Dichtungen und Schriften*, Bd 3, 1960, 168.
7. Such a sight seems to have been a common one on the Eastern Front, judging by the photographs in *Krieg dem Kriege*, ed. Ernst Friedrich, Berlin, 1925.
8. Cf. L.v. Ficker: 'Tief habe er sich den Anblick eingeprägt: der Menschheit ganzer Jammer, hier habe er einen angefasst. Nie könne er das vergessen, und auch den Rückzug nicht.' (In *Erinnerung an Georg Trakl*, Innsbruck, 1926, 186f.)
9. 'Der Krieg' was written in early September 1911 and published in Heym's posthumous second collection, *Umbra vitae*, in June 1912. There is no evidence that Trakl knew the poem by the time he wrote his own comparable poem, 'Menschheit', in September-October 1912. The war poem number of *Der Ruf*, in which 'Menschheit' appeared in November 1912, did not contain Heym's poem, although it did contain a poem (Csokor's 'Krieg') that was clearly prompted by it.
10. H. Lindenberger, *Georg Trakl*, New York, 1971, 56.
11. Ibid., 55.
12. Trakl, *Dichtungen und Briefe*, I, 1969, 495.
13. Idris Parry, *Animals of Silence*, 1972, 41.
14. C.M. Bowra, *Poetry and the First World War*, 1961, 19.
15. Ibid.
16. *Die Geburt der Tragödie*, sect. 18.
17. Lindenberger, *Georg Trakl*, 129.
18. 'The colour of the dead faces changed from white to yellow-grey, to red, to purple, to green, to black, to slimy' (Robert Graves, *Goodbye to All That*, 1929, Chapter 15).
19. *GLL*, XXVI, 1972-3, 32-7.
20. Lindenberger, *Georg Trakl*, 132.
21. In G. Janouch, *Gespräche mit Kafka*, 1961, 65.

3 AUGUST STRAMM

August Stramm, a near-sighted dreamer with a sense of duty inherited from his soldier-father (decorated for bravery in the Franco-Prussian war), was born at Münster, Westphalia, in 1874. After a middling performance at school (he subsequently took a degree by part-time study), he entered the German post-office administration in 1893; hard work soon won him promotion. He completed his year's compulsory military service in 1896-7 and within a few years received a commission in the reserve. On being released from the army in spring 1897, he was appointed to a coveted post-office appointment on liners on the Bremen-Hamburg-New York run; this led to several stays in the United States and perhaps also to his love of Ralph Waldo Trine's book *In Tune with the Infinite* (1897), a blood-stained copy of the German edition of which was found in his uniform pocket after his death. He married in 1902. His early work (romantic poetry, painting rather ordinary landscapes and still-lifes, a naturalistic play) was basically unoriginal and derivative. It was not until 1911-12 that he found, in quick succession, a real motivation and a style of his own; from then on he was a dedicated and possessed word-maniac. The plays *Sancta Susanna* and *Die Haidebraut*[1] were written in 1912-13. He was driven to near-despair by his lack of success as a writer; his way-out, experimental lyrical plays were continually rejected. In 1913 he was on the point of destroying everything he had written, when his wife (a romantic novelist with, of course, no such publication problems) suggested that he should contact Herwarth Walden, editor of the avant-garde periodical *Der Sturm* which was described by T.E. Hulme in his 'German Chronicle'[2] of June 1914 as 'a 4d fortnightly, in reality a Futurist and Cubist art-paper, but always containing verse of Futurist type, well worth taking in'; Hulme does not mention Stramm's work, but he does write about the kind of poetry which he heard being read at a meeting of Kurt Hiller's 'Cabaret Gnu', in which 'Very short sentences are used, sometimes so terse and elliptical as to produce a blunt and jerky effect ... it is clear that a definite attempt is being made to use the language in a new way, an attempt to cure it of certain vices', a comment which applies, *mutatis mutandis*, both to Stramm's poetry and to Hulme's. Hulme's chronicle is interesting as a contemporary record of the activities of the avant-garde in German poetry in 1914 and as showing his sympathetic reaction to the German variety of imagism; that he read some of Stramm's poetry, which appeared in *Der Sturm* from April 1914 onwards, seems certain. Stramm duly contacted Walden and his meeting with Walden became the turning-point in his literary career. Not only did Walden actually accept his work, publishing seven of Stramm's plays in the *Sturm-Bücher* series in 1914, but his enthusiasm gave Stramm the stimulus he had needed. This new-found recognition resulted in a release of energy which produced the love poems of *Du* (1915), the long poems 'Menschheit' and 'Weltenwehe', and the war poems of *Tropfblut* (1919).

Tropfblut is one of the most remarkable volumes of poetry of the whole war, but the poetry it contains is so unlike any other poetry of the war that some general account of how Stramm writes, and why, is necessary. He was one of the most radically experimental poets of his generation, perhaps the most experimental writer to continue to produce 'poetry' as such. He composed abstract word patterns whose startling syntax, vivid image clusters and provocative neologisms seek to convey actual sensations (e.g. the fear to which all honest front-line poets owned) in all their immediate dynamism and incoherence and ambiguity (how often are feelings absolutely clear-cut?). All his poetry, but especially his war poetry, is as far as may be from the Apolline, classic-romantic world of 'emotion recollected in tranquillity'; his poems know no tranquillity, nor do they seek to falsify emotion by tranquillising it; his poems are Dionysian-dynamic in that they seek to express emotion in all its raw immediacy; the poetry comes, above all, from the immense concentration of meaning.

This is the most basic characteristic of Stramm's work: that he seeks to express feelings as they are being felt, rather than displaying them, stuffed, under a Victorian glass dome. His premise is, clearly, that description as such is not poetry and that retrospective poeticisation is not honest.

A number of factors combined to make him into the kind of poet that he became. Apart from his emotional personality ('sensation' type), they include his reading of Fritz Mauthner's *Beiträge zu einer Kritik der Sprache* (1901) and Hans Vaihinger's *Die Philosophie des Als Ob* (1911). Mauthner powerfully encourages originality of the kind which Stramm was to show, when he argues that the genuinely original poet finds new words to express new sensations.[3]

The idea that it is the poet's job to find new words and new forms to match his sensations is basic to all Stramm's work and peculiarly relevant to his war poetry. But if Mauthner helped Stramm to find his own style, Vaihinger gave him something even more important: a reason for writing. It was in 1911 that Stramm read Hans Vaihinger's *Die Philosophie des Als Ob*, which quickly became his favourite book. Hans Vaihinger (1852-1933) takes as his starting-point F.A. Lange's statement in the *Geschichte des Materialismus* (2nd edition, 1873-5) to the effect that reality as man imagines it - that is, as an absolutely fixed existence independent of and yet known by us - neither exists nor can exist.[4] This idea is so basic to Vaihinger's book that one can only infer that Stramm agreed with it and accepted the corollary - that the only reality is our sensations.[5] When Stramm read such statements in 1911-12, they will have powerfully confirmed his own experience, for the world of his sensations had always been far more real to him than anything else. Once he started writing in earnest in order to express these sensations, this will in turn have further reinforced the overriding significance of the inner reality by which he quickly became obsessed. Such a view of reality justifies and indeed necessitates the kind of poetry that Stramm proceeded to write, so that the way in which he writes is dictated, in large measure, by his motives in writing. In particular Vaihinger provided him with an ideal justification for his war poetry, for the front-line poet has nothing but his own overwhelming sensations.

Vaihinger remarks that communication is only possible when the medium of communication, the word, is able to express a whole sensation-complex. What Stramm seeks to do, by means of his various kinds of neologism, justified as attempts to express an unparalleled experience of reality, is to turn the mere word into a sensation-complex. In his poetry outward, material reality (and therefore description as such) is suppressed for much the same reason that it is suppressed by Kafka and by Trakl: because the poet denies its significance and, ultimately, its reality. The pattern of words that takes the place of reality dissatisfied Stramm as much as it did Kafka, both of them fearing that the pattern in question was ultimately meaningless.[6] It is, of course, no chance that the word 'unbeschreiblich' occurs so often in Stramm's letters from the front to his wife, which record with a speechless shudder his awareness of the terrible.[7] What cannot be described is not outer reality, which is in fact memorably described in his letters to his wife, but inner reality. What the horrifying outward events mean to him, what is going on behind the eyes that register the horror, can only be conveyed poetically, and then only in the particular sort of poetry that Stramm writes. His war poems are images of indescribable impressions[8] in this sense.

As a captain in the Army Reserve, Stramm was called up immediately on the declaration of war, on the first day of mobilisation, and was posted as a company commander to Landwehrregiment 110, with which he saw action on the Western Front, in the Vosges and in Alsace. In mid-January 1915 he was posted, again as company commander, to the newly formed Infantry Regiment 272 at Oise in the Somme region of northern France. By the end of January he had won the Iron Cross (Second Class) there. After being involved in the heavy fighting in northern France in spring 1915, he was posted to the Eastern Front at the end of April and took part in the Galician campaign. His regiment was straightaway thrown into General von Mackensen's attempt to break through the Russian lines at the Gorlice pass; Gorlice fell on 2 May, the first major success of the German counter-offensive. Stramm distinguished himself and was at one point acting battalion commander, in which role he was involved in the attack on the Russian position at Ostrow. It was here that he won the Austrian Kriegsverdienstkreuz and was recommended for the Iron Cross (First Class). By July his regiment had reached the river Bug, following von Mackensen's recapture of Przemysl and Lwów. At the beginning of August 1915 he had his last leave. It was now – despite the fact that he hated the war, and despite his premonitions of death – that he so characteristically refused a chance to be released from the army. His daughter Inge, who adored him, later described how puzzled she was when her father one day in early August asked her ten-year-old brother to promise never to let himself down ('vor sich selbst ein Schweinehund werden'). It later transpired that at the time Stramm had in his pocket a letter which he had only to countersign to be released from further military service at his publisher's request; although his head was full of things that he wanted to write, Stramm was unable to accept the alibi of a higher duty to literature and returned to the Eastern Front. When he got back to his company after a week-long journey, he found it reduced to 25 men; this was the time of the Russian General Brusilov's successful offensive operations. Again Stramm was involved in the front-line of the 'Riesenkampf um Brest-Litowsk'. He fell on 1 September 1915 (just as the Russian offensive was petering out), shot in the head in hand-to-hand fighting in the Rokitno marshes, and is buried at Horodec (modern David Gorodok, in Russia, some 60 kilometres east of Brest-Litowsk). He had been in action some 70 times in all and was the last man in his company to fall. What is quite extraordinary is that he appears to have found in the hell-on-earth of total warfare around Brest-Litowsk in 1915 the sense of harmony which he had sought for so long; a few weeks before his death he wrote to Herwarth Walden:

> Eigenartig, Tod und Leben ist eins... Beide sind eins... Schlacht und Not und Tod und Nachtigall alles ist eins. Eins! Und Kampf und Schlaf und Traum und Handeln alles ist eins! Es gibt keine Trennung! Es geht alles in eins und verschwimmt und erschimmert wie Sonne und Abgrund. Nur mal herrscht das vor, mal das. So kämpfen hungern sterben singen wir. Alle! Soldat und Führer! Nacht und Tag. Leichen und Blüten. Und über mir scheint eine Hand! Ich schwimme durch alles! Bin alles! Ich![9]

Whether he too, like Trakl at Grodek (not all that far from Brest-Litowsk) the previous autumn, was now at the end of his tether, is not clear; what is clear is that he had finally come into harmony with the Infinite, as Ralph Waldo Trine had urged his readers to do in the book (*In Harmonie mit dem Unendlichen*, 1904) which was found in Stramm's pocket after his death.

While Stramm is known to have enjoyed his peacetime role of reserve officer, he was too sensitive to have any illusions about the war, which he hated (for all the unholy fascination it held for him). On 12 January 1915 he wrote to Walden from the Western Front: 'Ich stehe wie ein Krampf, haltlos, fundamentlos, ins Nichts geklammert, verankert und erstarrt in der Grimasse des Willens und Trotzens', and a few months later he wrote to his wife from Galicia that everything was so dreadful, so unspeakably dreadful. Thus while he was always absolutely sure where his duty lay, he did not write a single chauvinistic war poem even at the time when nearly everybody else in Germany – or so it seemed – was doing so. Nor did he write overtly anti-war poems, which his conscience would not have allowed him to do. In retrospect it seems extraordinary that the poem 'Feuertaufe' should have caused a scandal in the German press in 1915,[10] for its only conceivable fault is its utter honesty, its attempt to convey the feeling of coming under fire for the first time and its implicit refusal to pretend that the feeling in question was one of heroic excitement.

Like Trakl, Stramm regarded war as a grotesque intensification of life. His bewildered reaction to front-line warfare is seen in the words

> Wo bin ich hingeraten... Ich lebe in einer tiefen tiefen Raserei. Innerlich! Äusserlich nicht! Nicht! Tapfer nennen sie mich. Und ich bin auch tapfer und muss die Zähne zusammenbeissen, weil mich das Weinen überkrampft. Nicht um mich, nicht um weiss was. Ich weiss nicht um was.[11]

On 6 October 1914 he wrote to Walden from the front, in a letter which is even more important for an understanding of his war poetry:

> Was soll ich sagen. Es ist unendlich viel Tod in mir Tod und Tod. In mir weints und aussen bin ich hart und roh ... Es ist alles so widersprüchig, ich finde nicht durch das Rätsel ... Ich kann überhaupt nicht mehr lesen und denken. Das Wort schon stockt mir vor Grauen ... ich bin in Unglauben. Lebe gestorben, und bin gesund dabei und stark, wie eine starkwandig taube Nuss. Ich möchte morden morden dann bin ich wenigstens eins mit dem ringsum dann habe ich wieder Grund und Boden dann bin ich nicht so furchtbar allein so in der Luft ohne Flügel. Wo ist der Prediger des Mordes der das Evangelium predigt des Mordes des Mussmordes. Morden ist Pflicht ist Himmel ist Gott. Rasen ... Wo sind Worte für das Erleben ... Ich dichte nicht mehr, alles ist Gedicht umher. Elendes feiges heimtückisches Grausen, und die Luft kichert höhnisch dazu und gurgelt donnernd von den Bergen her ... Es ist alles nicht wahr und alles Lüge.[12]

On 22 November 1914 and 15 May 1915 he reiterated that life was weirdly intensified. Faced with a grotesque intensification of experience, it is hardly surprising that he resorted to intensification of language. It is because the experience of which he writes is genuinely new that his desperate neologisms are fully justified; and it is because they again and again succeed that purist criticism is invalid.

In his war poems, mostly first published in *Der Sturm* and then collected posthumously, Stramm seeks to 'communicate the sights, sounds and horror of war more directly than would be possible in a reasoned and punctuated statement'.[13] This intention is both simple and admirable. He seeks to make war, and one man's reaction to war, speak for itself. In order to do so, he 'chooses his words to act as missiles that will explode in the reader's mind, with the impact of a shell':[14] the poem itself as high-explosive shell with delayed action fuse. Let us now see what happens when some of these shells explode in the mind.

One of the most successful of Stramm's raids on the inarticulate is 'Schlachtfeld' (autumn 1914), which opens with a radically condensed and intensified line, 'Schollenmürbe schläfert ein das Eisen' (literally: 'Clod softness lulls iron off to sleep'), in which 'Mürbe' is made to replace the low-key prosaic 'Mürbigkeit':

Schollenmürbe schläfert ein das Eisen
Blute filzen Sickerflecke

44 *August Stramm*

>   Roste krumen
>   Fleische schleimen
>   Saugen brünstet um Zerfallen.
>   Mordesmorde
>   Blinzen
>   Kinderblicke.

This opening line suggests the omnipresent mud of the battlefield in the Vosges, the continual need for vigilance (relaxed only in death) and the continual threat of exhaustion, the threat of metal and the threat of earth, to which man and his ridiculously aggressive works will return. The iron of shells, grenades, mortar bombs, bayonets, etc., which are the instruments of murder, are rendered harmless once they have landed in the mud; then they too slowly oxidise. After the invisible stop after 'Eisen' we have three line-images juxtaposed in typical Expressionist manner, with two different forms of linguistic intensification involved. The use of the plural instead of the singular is both effective and appropriate; 'Blute' and 'Fleische' in particular are more powerful and suggestive than the singular forms would be, for they remind the reader that it is the blood of many men that clots the patches where they oozed to death (concentrated into the new compound 'Sickerflecke'), that it is the flesh of many men that is turning to stinking slime around which 'Saugen brünstet um Zerfallen'. The revolting verb 'brünsten,' which Stramm rightly prefers to the conventional 'brunsten', is most appropriate for conveying the beastliness of war, which is caused by man's greed but satisfies only that of the worm; 'brünsten', like the verbs 'wühlen' and 'zergehren' which Stramm also uses, serves to stress the totally physical nature of war. Those plurals ('Blute', 'Roste', 'Fleische') also involve personification and therefore another kind of *Potenzierung*; they remind us that the blood that clots, the flesh that 'slimes', is not a mere abstraction or even poeticism; it is something more concrete and more personal: this individual's blood congealing, another individual's rifle rusting, a third individual human being's flesh reverting to earth. War is seen, implicitly, as a matter of personalised, compulsory murder; flesh and metal are reduced to the same level of significance by juxtaposition. The present battlefield scene stands for endless such scenes at either edge of Europe. Murder upon murder is still to come, murder that 'blinks' in 'child eyes' because most of the contestants were only children when they arrived at the front, child murderers and child victims, barely 'of killable age' in Wilfred Owen's phrase. In a letter to Walden, dated 6 October 1914,

Stramm wrote explicitly of the murder you have to commit. By this time he had very likely written 'Schlachtfeld', which was published in *Der Sturm* in January 1915. In another letter (to his wife), dated 5 March 1915, Stramm returns to the question of having to murder and puts it squarely where it belongs, in the context of patriotism; the result is a passage in which the two opposing calls of conscience, to humanity and to country, are summarised with rare insight and honesty:

> Mein Vaterland?! Der Begriff ist mir zu eng, würde nicht mich vor mir selbst entschuldigen! Nein! ich morde, damit der Mord ein Ende nimmt. Ich morde und stifte an, damit das Anstiften keine Macht mehr hat, behält. Ich bin tapfer, ein Draufgänger, so hört ich hier schon! Nicht um des Draufgehns willen nicht aus Rohheit und Lust zur Rohheit! Nein! Aus Wut, aus Hass gegen das unbeschreiblich rohe! unbegreiflich menschenunwürdig Rohe! Ich schleudere meine Kräfte, weil ich rase gegen die Verschleuderung aller Kräfte zum Hohen bestimmt. Ich bin nicht tapfer in dem rohen Sinne, wie man mir nachsagt, wie meine Kerls zu mir aufblicken, ich bin feige, unbeschreiblich feige, weil ich *diese* Art der rohen Tapferkeit aus der Welt schaffen will. Und der Begriff meines Vaterlandes spielt da hinein, weil alles, was mir lieb ist, darin ruht, weil aber auch im letzten Grunde mein Vaterland mir die überzeugte Verkörperung alles dessen ist, was ich an hohem und edlem erstrebe und als das einzige Volk, das zur Zeit den Weg verbürgt, gehen kann und gehen *wird*![15]

Michael Hamburger has written of 'Schlachtfeld' that it 'succeeds in compressing the pity, horror and absurdity of the war into as few words as possible, though once more Stramm had to make up a high proportion of those words, or change the grammatical function of existing words, so as to charge them with the energy he wanted';[16] this is true if exaggerated. C.R.B. Perkins goes even further, however, when he argues that in a line like 'Schollenmürbe schläfert ein das Eisen', Stramm 'goes too far for the reader', adding that 'The result of such lexical and syntactic distortion can only be regarded as bizarre and grotesque.'[17] This comment, typical of critical reactions to Stramm's poetry, is essentially a non-comment, a failure to analyse. We have seen that the first line of 'Schlachtfeld', far from being 'bizarre and grotesque', conveys an exact meaning and one which could only be conveyed with that precise force and concentration. It may be that this is 'primitivism ... akin to the simplification of planes and outlines practised by painters and sculptors of his time',[18] but this not only 'does not prevent that poem from conveying a moral judgement of the war'; more pertinently it does not prevent the poet from writing a unique, powerful, and - given some effort on the reader's part - totally intelligible poem.

Since it was only a matter of time, often a very short time, before men in the front-line were wounded, it is hardly surprising that many poems were written on this subject. Stramm's 'Wunde', published in *Der Sturm* in January 1915 and probably written in November 1914 on the Western Front, is interesting for the way in which it differs from comparable poems. The most striking poems on the subject of the wounded are by Wilhelm Klemm. As an army doctor Klemm writes poems whose clinical matter-of-factness is overwhelming; but it is nausea that is induced rather than pity for the actual victims who are almost lost sight of amid the buckets of blood, piles of amputated limbs, etc.

Stramm's 'Wunde' is quite different. It deals not with the vague subject of 'the wounded', but with the characteristically specific subject of one man being wounded. As usual, Stramm tries to convey the basic gesture concerned, in this case what it is like to be seriously wounded. His poem is set not in a field hospital, but on the earth which looks as though it is bleeding beneath the helmeted head:

Die Erde blutet unterm Helmkopf
Sterne fallen
Der Weltraum tastet.
Schauder brausen
Wirbeln
Einsamkeiten.
Nebel
Weinen
Ferne
Deinen Blick.

What the poem conveys is the working of the wounded man's mind; the whole world is affected by his pain. This is why stars fall. Space 'gropes' because the man is himself groping on the edge of consciousness. Through the swirling mists of half-consciousness and loneliness one thought stands out: the thought of his loved one. This is what remains, or, rather, Stramm's poem is what remains when he himself had become a casualty statistic. Seen thus the poem is an imaginative *tour de force*.

This is important, for while most critics and readers have thought of Stramm's poetry from the point of view of technique, what is most remarkable about his war poems is the imagination and empathy which enable him to convey sensations so concisely and yet so definitively. It is this imagination which makes the neologisms, etc., necessary and thus triumphantly justifies the technique.

The poem 'Gefallen', written at about the same time and first published in *Der Sturm* for February 1915, expresses the final 'gesture' made by so many, that of dying. It complements 'Wunde', for what remains when heaven has glazed the wounded man's eye is his loved one's sorrow. The real monument, however, is not so much this sorrow, or even the poem in which it is expressed, as the poem 'Krieggrab'.

The poem 'Sturmangriff', which first appeared in the February 1915 number of *Der Sturm*, is one of the early war poems dating from Stramm's spell of duty on the Western Front and was presumably written in or before November 1914 (a letter dated 6 October 1914 clearly relates to it); when it subsequently appeared in *Tropfblut* the title was changed (no doubt by Walden) to the even more laconic, but less explicitly brutal 'Angriff'. 'Sturmangriff' is, I am sure, Stramm's definitive title; it is not only more accurate ('Sturmangriff' is the military term for an attack on a fixed position), but more brutally aggressive, and also contains within itself the image of the storm, the successive waves of which the poem conveys:

Aus allen Winkeln gellen Fürchte Wollen
Kreisch
Peitscht
Das Leben
Vor
Sich
Her
Den keuchen Tod
Die Himmel fetzen.
Blinde schlächtert wildum das Entsetzen.

Seen on the printed page, the poem looks like a seventeenth-century figure-poem (cf. Herbert's 'Easter Wings'), but there is no 'false wit' (Addison) here, for the long first and last lines denote the waves of the assault, the waves of gunfire, the successive waves of butcherdom, of men killing and being killed, the waves of fear, the waves of nausea. The first line opens the attack as men come from every corner of the forward lines to go over the top. Stramm does not write of men; he writes of 'Fürchte' - the unnamed men's personified fears': 'Aus allen Winkeln gellen Fürchte Wollen'. The subject is 'Fürchte', an invented plural of the word 'Furcht', appropriate and indeed necessary because the normal 'Befürchtungen' would be altogether too normal, too staid, too prosy and official for what is, after all, an intensely personal emotion; a man's fear is as personal as his language, his love, his death. The fears are made to yell because it is to still their fear that men have been taught to yell as they face death, just as it is to overcome their inhibitions (in other words: their humanity) that they have been taught to yell as they kill. The yells come, the fear comes from every corner of the earth (for this is world war), of the battlefield, of the trenches, of the individual heart and mind ('Winkel' also denotes the recesses of the heart). It is a matter of will-power, of guts, to go on - hence the word 'Wollen' isolated between invisible full-stops. This is, surely, the grimace of determination and defiance ('Grimasse des Willens und des Trotzens') of which Stramm wrote in a letter dated 12 January 1915. With yells and screams of hysteria and pain ('kreisch' is a concentration and therefore an intensification of the normal 'kreischend') life lashes along before it 'gasping' death; the living - the NCOs and officers - drive on the next to die like so many blushing virgins facing a shameful consumation ('keuch' is an intensification of 'keuchend', but also has the sound-connotation of 'keusch'); while this is going on the shooting can be heard, for 'kreisch' and 'peitscht' are rifle shots, each one maybe a consummation for someone; elsewhere Stramm uses the word 'zergehren' to refer to man's wish for the shameful embrace of death as a means of escape from an intolerable situation. The penultimate line, 'die Himmel fetzen' (for 'zerfetzen'), refers to shells exploding in the sky, but the wording implies the heavens - Heaven, even - bursting open, leaving men's faith in tatters. The apocalyptic note accurately expresses Stramm's feeling and, evidently, that of many others. Blindly (if 'blinde' is an adverb, short for 'blindings') the horror by which Stramm was totally possessed butchers out wildly ('wildum' replaces the usual 'wild umher', which would be too long and too figurative: Stramm needs 'wild' to retain its real meaning of savage); his wording emphasises the totally arbitrary nature of the process. If 'Blinde' is object, it is blinded men who are butchered, an even more terrible image. The neologism 'schlächtert' (from 'Schlächter', 'butcher') personifies the horror and terror in question, appropriate because it is individuals who are butchering and being butchered (in a letter dating from the same time Stramm used the word 'Mussmord' to denote the murder which you *have to* commit). Stramm gives only two successive waves, but there was no end to it.

Though 'Sturmangriff' is perhaps slightly less dense than some of Stramm's other war poems, it is typical in that it conveys, as no other more conventional poem could, his own personal reaction to an unheard-of experience. The poem reminds us, specifically, of what he wrote on 6 October 1914: 'Das Wort schon stockt mir von Grauen ... ich bin in Unglauben [cf. 'die Himmel fetzen'] ...Wo sind Worte für das Erleben.' His neologistic intensifications of language, here and elsewhere, express his overriding feeling: that 'Das Dasein ist ganz eigenartig potenziert.'

Stramm's war poems are concerned with particulars, with the brute realities, the basic experiences, the facts of life at the front. It is not until he has been in action for several months that he feels able to write about anything as general as 'Krieg'. But even if the laconic title implies a general view of war - the kind of thing lesser poets *started with* - what the poem actually conveys is a general view only in that the experience of war is objective, not ascribed to any particular person. The experience could, however, be ascribed to almost any particular person, for what the poem conveys is, as it were, the 'Grundgestus' of the experience of war as seen from the trenches. Basic to the poem is the idea that there is no such thing as war in the abstract, only one man's war, one man's sensation of and nervous reactions to war. Stramm had long since - or so it must have seemed, now that every second was lasting an eternity - learned from Hans Vaihinger that our sensations are the sole reality; how much truer, how extraordinarily relevant this must have seemed when he was living on his nerves at the Front.

In the poem 'Krieg' one man's, or everyman's, experience of war is compared to the stages of childbirth:

Wehe wühlt
Harren starrt entsetzt
Kreissen schüttert
Bären spannt die Glieder
Die Stunde blutet
Frage hebt das Auge
Die Zeit gebärt
Erschöpfung
Jüngt
Der
Tod.

The poem can be read in at least two ways. On a general level the onset of war is described metaphorically as the birth of death; it is the age itself which gave birth to war which in turn gives birth to death, just as it is mankind which is seen as waiting, aghast, for the outcome. On an individual level the poem describes the birth of one man's fear, one man's death. In either case the image of childbirth is perverted, for what is created is destruction.

The first line refers to the beginning of labour (Wehe), that is, the pain ('Wehe' is also a cry of pain) or fear beginning to gnaw at his vitals. Rudolf Haller has commented that a Baroque poet might have used allegorical personification in the first three lines of the poem; but personification is precisely what Stramm uses. It may be an abstract personification, for 'Wehe', 'Harren' and 'Kreissen' are abstracts; but they are made all too concrete by the verbs which animate them (the 'wühlt' in line 1 is short for 'einwühlt', which is what a burrowing animal does – a suitable way to express animal fear; the verb turns men into so many trench rats (German is more explicit: *Leichenratten*). Man's waiting (for the balloon to go up, in the contemporary idiom) is made to stare in terror; man becomes his own expectancy and apprehension as the tension rises; the basic gesture of the line is that of numbness. Then the real labour pains begin as fear begins to take hold, shaking him (for 'schüttert' also implies 'erschüttert', and even 'verschüttet' – the hideous possibility of being buried alive), and making him shudder; in a letter dated 12 January 1915 he wrote 'Alles schüttert unter mir, um mich, in mir.' Giving-birth ('Bären' is an abbreviated and therefore intensified version of 'Gebären') tenses his limbs as he screws himself right up waiting for the barrage to begin, waiting for the shell that will bury him or blow him to blazes. Then the bleeding begins; the hour bleeds, or, better, begins to bleed to death ('blutet' short for 'verblutet'). He raises his eye apprehensively to see if his neighbour is any less scared. 'Zeit' means the fateful time of day when the artillery barrage begins (its predictability adding to the tension), the time of death, but also the age, for it is the age which has given birth to the monster, war. Time, then, gives birth to exhaustion and death, or time gives birth to exhaustion, death being renewed in the sense of claiming its latest victim, of being revived, vampire-like (or: whelps, for 'jüngt', short for 'verjüngt', is also made to echo 'jungt'). The syntax at the end is ambiguous, but the meaning is not, for the poem ends, both literally and figuratively, with Death. 'Erschöpfung' is, as it were, a perversion or negation of life (*Schöpfung*), this being the effect of war.

Now let us go back to the beginning to note some further features. The alliteration in the first line underlines the inevitability of what is implied, that is, the way in which anyone waiting for the balloon to go up will be prey to apprehension, which soon turns into outright fear ('Kreissen' is an intensification of 'Wehe'). The second line, 'Harren starrt entsetzt', conveys the gesture of waiting, petrified. The fourth line is a sharpening of the second: 'Bären spannt die Glieder' involves an intensification of the second line through vowel gradation. The way in which line 3 echoes line 1, and line 4 echoes line 2, is shown visually too. After line 4 the second half of the poem begins (the process of birth is described as beginning), and almost before we know what is happening the intolerable tension has been released into death (cf. the similar structural gesture in 'Patrouille'). Death is the end and the aim. Death – every single combatant's own death, to use the Rilkean concept that is suddenly more than an order of words – is what war is about.

Stramm's poem very clearly implies that war is not a matter of rhetoric and heroics, although this is not an explicitly anti-war poem and indeed could not be further removed from anti-war satire (another form of 'Wortmacherei', so far as the poor bloody infantry are concerned). The poem, and with it Stramm's position, is absolutely clear; there are no heroics, no lies, no beating about the bush, not an unnecessary syllable. War, for the person actually involved in it, consists of growing fear and ends in death. Thousands of chauvinistic poems are thereby given the lie.

Stramm seeks to convey 'not a picture or a recollection but the actual sensations of the moment itself'.[19] Thus in perhaps the best of all his war poems, 'Patrouille', he simply tries to convey what it feels like to be out on patrol in 1914-15:

Die Steine feinden
Fenster grinst Verrat
Äste würgen
Berge Sträucher blättern raschlig
Gellen
Tod

The first line is immediately effective: the very stones are hostile (in German the neologism 'feinden' is used for 'anfeinden'). So it must seem to the soldier on patrol in no man's land who faces so many real and imagined dangers. The first line points to one of these dangers:

mines. Another obvious danger was from snipers, hence the equally concentrated second line: 'window grins treachery'. What Stramm is saying here is that to the soldier out on patrol it seems as though the very stones he treads are hostile, it seems as though a sniper is lurking behind every window, it seems (third line) as though every branch which brushes against him is someone trying to strangle him. It is all a question of his own nervous reactions. Each of the first three lines could have a full-stop at the end, and the third would normally require it, for after it the second half of the poem begins. The rhythm in the first three lines has been stealthy, suggesting soldiers creeping along with their nerves on edge, waiting for the sudden danger and death by which their minds and bodies are obsessed. The fourth line is longer and quicker – one imagines the men running for cover as they come under fire – and also even more concentrated. Mountainous bushes ('berge' suggests 'bergige') – that is, bushes which seem mountainous or loom overlarge to them in their overwrought condition – shed their leaves and disintegrate with a whistling sound; but 'berge' also suggests 'bergende' and therefore alludes to the shelter which these bushes fail to give and to the danger which they hide. After the frantic fourth line, the poem tails off into the silence of death: two syllables, followed by one, followed – there is no full-stop – by silence ...

This is surely an excellent example of the Expressionist war poem. Highly condensed and highly expressive, it conveys in an absolute minimum of words, and with total precision, the state of mind in question. Because the war which provokes this state of mind is unparalleled, Stramm's neologisms are fully justified.

In September 1915, at the time of his death, the best-known of Stramm's war poems will have been 'Feuertaufe'. First published in *Der Sturm* in July 1915, and reprinted in several newspapers and magazines, the poem became the centre of a silly controversy. First the *Hannoversche Kurier* reprinted 'Feuertaufe' and added a pastiche which suggested that a couple of weeks in the trenches would cure Stramm of his penchant for writing nonsense. Walden reprinted this pastiche in *Der Sturm* (September 1915) alongside the announcement of Stramm's death, thus making further comment superfluous. At the same time an amateur literary legislator by the name of Huth wrote of this 'ridiculous poem' ('die Komik dieses Gedichtes') and declared that the poem could only be regarded as absolute rubbish, if not a public nuisance ('absoluten Blödsinn oder groben Unfug'): that Herwarth Walden did not allow this to pass without comment, may be imagined (see his editorial article 'Die Mücke' in the same number of *Der Sturm*). It was presumably because of this controversy that Walden omitted 'Feuertaufe' from *Tropfblut*. In retrospect this was a mistake on his part, for 'Feuertaufe' is among Stramm's best war poems. Here it is:

Der Körper schrumpft den weiten Rock
Der Kopf verkriecht die Beine
Erschrecken
Würgt die Flinte
Ängste
Knattern
Knattern schrillen
Knattern hieben
Knattern stolpern
Knattern
Übertaumeln
Gelle
Wut.
Der Blick
Spitzt
Zisch
Die Hände spannen Klaren.
Das Trotzen ladet.
Wollen äugt
Und
Stahler Blick
Schnellt
Streck
Das
Schicksal.

The subject of the poem is 'baptism of fire'; since it was written in or after May 1915 the poem might be thought to refer to Stramm's own baptism of fire on the Eastern Front, to which he had just been transferred; but in fact the poem both has a more general connotation and clearly refers back to his own real baptism of fire on the Western Front in the previous year, for ideas in the poem are echoed in a letter written on 12 January 1915. In the poem the 'baptism of fire' has both a passive and an active connotation, for the nameless subject of the poem first shrinks back as he comes under fire and eventually fires back. The first line expresses his shrinking in a vivid, concrete way: Stramm writes that 'The body shrinks its loosely fitting tunic', which is more expressive than it would be to say that the body shrinks inside its tunic, for fear has little in common with logic. Already, then, we have a typical intensification of language. The second line involves a similar technique, for 'Der Kopf verkriecht die Beine' implies both that his head (English: heart) creeps down into his legs (English: boots), and that his head, filled with fear, makes his legs want to creep away to safety. It is his fear which prevents him from firing back: 'Erschrecken würgt die Flinte.' A further expressive feature of the poem is now revealed: Stramm's use of hunting vocabulary (Flinte, äugt, Streck), which underlines the fact that man is hunting down man. Machine-gun fire then opens up; the verb 'knattern', like the similar verb 'zattern' used in 'Abend', is above all onomatopoeic, used to convey the sound of machine-gun fire. All the man's fears are made to rattle away like machine-gun fire, with a shrill sound ('schrillen'), cutting a swathe ('hieben', from the noun 'Hiebe') or battering away, making men stumble in their panic ('stolpern'). The scene is reminiscent of stag-hunting. Throughout the first half of the poem, which ends with the full-stop after 'Wut', the man undergoing his baptism of fire is in a purely passive role, prey to and then overcome by the fears which make his head reel (the neologism 'übertaumeln' is ambiguous and the syntax at this point even more so). The angry shouting (Stramm puts it the other way round, using 'gelle' as an intensification of 'gellende') is a turning-point, for now the man's eyes narrow in anger as a bullet whizzes past ('Zisch' is a bullet sound), making the violence more personal. 'Hände spannen Klaren' means that hands grip their glasses of schnaps; the schnaps, whether real or imaginary, does the trick, for 'Das Trotzen ladet': the man - personified defiance and determination now - loads his rifle, determined to give as good as he has been taking, and so 'courage' is born. He takes aim ('äugen' is again a hunting term) and a flash of steel ('Stahler' intensifies 'stählerner') quickly 'bags' another man's fate ('Streck' is from 'zur Strecke bringen', another hunting term; murder is now passing as sport). In other words, fear is soon replaced by determination, for war is a matter of kill or be killed, with the fact of murder disguised by the euphemistic hunting terminology which the conscience adopts.

Just how personal a poem this is beneath its totally objective surface is shown by Stramm's letters from the front and more especially by his letter of 12 January 1915. We have seen, too, how far removed the poem is from the 'absolute rubbish' for which one stupid reader mistook it; it could be described as a public nuisance only by a totally unintelligent reader or one who wished to see it suppressed because of the unwelcome truths which it contains. The crux of the matter is that the poem not only describes the transition from 'fear' to 'courage' which millions of men experienced; it also reveals how the psychology of survival turns humane men into killers, thus making possible the whole bloody fiasco of 1914-18. In his letters and war poems in general, and in this poem in particular, Stramm shows a finer understanding of this crucial process than any other writer on the German side. Far from being absolute rubbish, the poem is a masterpiece of insight and purposefully controlled language.

Since coming under shellfire was by common consent one of the most traumatic experiences of the war, it is appropriate that this should loom large in Stramm's work and that he should have devoted two carefully differentiated poems to it.

'Schrapnell' first appeared in the July 1915 number of *Der Sturm*; both there and in *Tropfblut* it is entitled 'Granatfeuer'. The quite separate poem 'Granaten' appeared in the September 1915 number of *Der Sturm*. Both poems were written on the Eastern Front, almost certainly in May 1915. Here is 'Schrapnell':

Der Himmel wirft Wolken
Und knattert zu Rauch.
Spitzen blitzen.
Füsse wippen stiebig Kiesel.
Augen kichern in die Wirre
Und
Zergehren.

Stramm first called the poem 'Granatfeuer', but, having sent it to Walden, he subsequently decided that the title was imprecise and inappropriate for the kind of shellfire that he had in mind when writing the poem. On 13 May 1915 he accordingly wrote to Walden asking him to change the title. Like so many of Stramm's war poems, 'Schrapnell' falls into two distinct halves. The first three lines convey the artillery fire in a light-hearted way: the puffs of smoke, the noise and the splinters catching the light – all this is reminiscent of a firework display, and it is from this that the relevant British army slang ('whiz-bang') derives. As the shrapnel lands, however, it is a different story, for a split second later the scene is one of hilarious confusion as everyone dives for cover with flailing feet; but the sparkle of amusement in someone's eye is instantly extinguished as he succumbs to death's ravishment (zergehren). As Stramm says, shrapnel is not without its funny side –

unless, of course, you happen to stop a bit. With heavy shellfire, however, it is quite a different story: that is not funny at all. The poem 'Granaten' is itself a much more heavyweight affair and seeks to convey the deafening, paralysing, overwhelming effect of heavy (high explosive) shellfire, which inevitably ends in shellshock. It is, however, a relatively unsuccessful poem, perhaps because the very subject precludes Stramm's customary precise differentiation of sensations and moments. Be this as it may, the poem's subject matter is more effectively expressed in 'Angststurm'.

'Angststurm' is another of the poems that were omitted from *Tropfblut*; it was first published in *Der Sturm* in September 1917. While it is not known when the poem was written, there is every reason to suppose that it is a very late poem which perhaps only came to light after *Tropfblut* had gone to press in 1915; but it is also possible that Walden at first suppressed it because its honesty might have tarnished Stramm's heroic image as established by *Der Sturm* in 1915. By 1917, when the public attitude to the war had changed very considerably, the poem will have attracted little attention. We have seen that Stramm, for all his personal courage, which is indisputable, never denied the fear that reduced the bravest of men to nervous wrecks in course of time. Indeed, we have seen that fear is one of his main themes; no doubt expressing it in this way helped him to overcome it. The way in which it is described in 'Angststurm' suggests that the poem was most likely written during the worst of his experiences on the Eastern Front, at a time when he was, temporarily, at the end of his tether; that virtually all front-line combatants (or at least the officers among them) reached such a point is a matter of fact.

Perkins has described Stramm's use of the gerundial form in an asyndetic chain or series, rightly pointing out that 'Angststurm'

> consists of twenty-two words, of which fourteen are in the gerundial form; five of the others are the personal pronoun 'Ich' (used substantivally), and the remaining three words are the conjunction 'und'. In the central part of the poem the gerund used in a chain or series can be clearly seen. The second line is the only one with any clear syndetic elements.[20]

This description does not, however, explain the poem and its ultimately overwhelming effect. The poem reads as follows:

Grausen
Ich und Ich und Ich und Ich

Grausen Brausen Rauschen Grausen
Träumen Splittern Branden Blenden
Sterneblenden Brausen Grausen
Rauschen
Grausen
Ich.

The title is ironical, for it shows the unknown soldier on the receiving end of the 'Sturm', being assaulted by horror and terror. The poem starts with 'Grausen' (cf. the 'Elendes feiges heimtückisches Grausen' of which Stramm was writing to Walden by October 1914 already) and ends with the 'Ich' which is alone with its horror. This 'Ich' receives immense emphasis, from the fact that it is capitalised and therefore used substantivally (placed on a par with that by which it is assaulted), from its positions of stress within the poem, and from the fact that this is the *only* war poem proper in which the word appears; Stramm does not use the word 'ich' in the ordinary pronominal way in his war poetry (which must surely be a record). Starting with 'Grausen', and stressing 'Ich und Ich und Ich und Ich', the poem becomes a chain of battle sounds and the reactions they provoke (all equated and therefore personalised through the gerundial form) in individual after individual. 'Grausen' (the leitmotif) is followed by 'Brausen' which appropriately rhymes with it since the 'Grausen' is caused by the 'Brausen', the noise of a shell in the air; 'Brausen' is followed by the near-rhyming 'Rauschen' which denotes a different kind of shell noise, which in turn provokes further 'Grausen'; the au-sound linking them is reminiscent of a cry of pain. The man listening to it all tries to escape by letting his mind wander ('Träumen', linked by vowel gradation), but this is impossible, for there come, in quick succession, a splintering sound as a shell lands close by ('Splittern'), the sound of fire and/or further waves of sound breaking over the cowering listener's mind ('Branden' is a neologistic verbal noun from 'Brand' as well as a conventional form, and therefore has dual meanings), and a blinding flash ('Blenden'). 'Branden' and 'Blenden' are rightly made to near-rhyme because the stages of this 'Angststurm' are virtually indistinguishable, such is the chaos of the experience. The flash as the shell or fragmentation-bomb explodes makes him see stars in the sense of putting the thought of stars into his mind; but, before the mind can wander off on this new escapist train of thought, the horror and fear come flooding back. The last four words mark not just a return to the beginning of the poem and therefore of the whole experience or sensation (what else *could* be real at such a moment?), but an intensification of it, with the 'Grausen' recurring now more frequently; this way neurasthenia lies. Visually the poem moves from 'Grausen' to 'Grausen' to 'Ich', that is, from the idea of horror to the individual whose experience of horror and dread is conveyed by the dense, brutal, overwhelming central section of the poem: we imagine the man crouching in his dugout or crater, shuddering, wincing as each new sound in the terrible orchestra is heard, trying desperately to forget himself and the monstrous experience by which he is being assaulted, but unable to do so, for 'Brausen' rhymes with 'Grausen' and will continue to do so until the end: each shell, and each word, hammers home the horror, from which there is no release save death or madness or poetry. Stramm's own release only came when he was shot in the head soon afterwards.

It is appropriate, therefore, to end with 'Krieggrab', written on the Eastern Front between May and August 1915 and first published in *Der Sturm* in September 1915:

> Stäbe flehen kreuze Arme
> Schrift zagt blasses Unbekannt
> Blumen frechen
> Staube schüchtern.
> Flimmer
> Tränet
> Glast
> Vergessen.

There are two arrangements of the poem: the version published in *Der Sturm* consisted of eight lines, with 'Blumen frechen' and 'Staube schüchtern' as lines 3 and 4 respectively; the version published in *Tropfblut* has seven lines, with the third line reading 'Blumen frechen Staube schüchtern'. In either case the cruciform shape of the poem is appropriate, and, however the poem is arranged, the fact remains that it is, essentially, a single conventional four-beat, four-line stanza rearranged in accordance with what William Carlos Williams was to call 'field composition'. The spelling of the title should also be noted. Stramm uses 'Krieggrab' (as opposed to the usual 'Kriegsgrab', which is also found by mistake); he no doubt uses the appositional form to stress the underlying idea: Krieg = Grab, war leads to death.

The first line, 'Stäbe flehen kreuze Arme', expresses the gesture of praying, with crossed arms, and also describes the simple wooden cross which was used in 1914-18 to mark a grave. The word 'Stäbe' means 'stakes' and refers to pieces of wood used for cross-pieces; to see an allusion to (General) Staffs praying (for more men to continue their war for them), while it might be appropriate in a poem written towards the end of the war, would involve a misreading of the present poem. The neologism 'kreuze' is preferred to 'gekreuzte' because it contains a clearer allusion to the cross. The second line expresses the idea that writing falters before the pale Unknown (Nietzsche's Unknown God?) and that writing loses heart, so that all that is left is the Unknown Soldier. Conventional flowers would be an impertinence in the case of those who 'die as cattle' (Wilfred Owen). The poem ends with words which form the upright of the cross: 'faint light runs with tears', a reference to whatever mourns for man; 'forgetfulness stares' – we are left with forgetfulness, for being forgotten is all that is left. There is nothing here of the eloquence of Owen's 'Anthem for Doomed Youth', but without any pathos whatsoever Stramm too conveys the absolute futility of war: the fate of those who die 'on the altar of the Fatherland' is to be forgotten, for peace has different heroes.

With the blunt honesty of this epitaph we may compare the conventional military pieties accorded to Stramm himself, who was dead by the time 'Krieggrab' appeared:

Nachruf

Am 1. September 1915 fiel bei einem Sturmangriff über einen Kanal an der Spitze seiner Kompagnie

Hauptmann der Reserve
August Stramm

Ritter des Eisernen Kreuzes 2. Klasse, des Oesterreichischen Verdienstkreuzes mit der Kriegsdekoration, und eingegeben zum Eisernen Kreuz 1. Klasse. Seit Januar dieses Jahres dem Regiment angehörend, hat er an den schönen Erfolgen des Regiments zum Teil als Bataillonsführer hervorragenden Anteil. Sein Name ist mit der Geschichte des Regiments, das mit ihm einen seiner tüchtigsten Offiziere verloren hat, eng verknüpft. Als treuer Kamerad und unermüdlich fürsorgender Vorgesetzter wird er uns allen unvergesslich sein.

Im Namen des Offizierkorps
Ahlers
Major und Kommandant des Reserve-Infanterie-Regiments
272

In a letter dated 23 September 1915, in which he referred to the number of *Der Sturm* in which Stramm's death was announced and in which a number of his war poems were printed, the painter Franz Marc wrote:

> Die hier abgedruckten Gedichte machen mir wohl wieder den Eindruck einer *sehr* begrenzten Begabung; aber innerhalb dieser Grenzen des Unvermögens eine grossartige Leidenschaft des Empfindens; die Sprache war ihm . . . Material, aus dem er Feuer schlug . . . *Er war schon am richtigen Wege.*[21]

This remains a very just assessment of Stramm's poetic achievement as a whole. But looking back at the war poems of *Tropfblut* alone and considering them in the context of the other poetry of the war, we can properly go further than Marc. *Tropfblut* is, certainly, one of the two best collections of the war on the German side, the other being Anton Schnack's *Tier rang gewaltig mit Tier*. If poetry depends on originality, mastery of language, concentration of meaning, and insight, then *Tropfblut* contains poetry of a high order. It also contains some of the most original poetry published in the course of the war by a front-line poet; whether Stramm's originality is as important historically as Owen's can be argued either way, but the question certainly arises. Above all, and despite their extreme brevity, Stramm's poems show greater insight into the psychology of war than any other writing (of any length) in the German language.

Notes

1. English translations in *Poet Lore*, XXV, 6, New York, 1914, 499–522.
2. In *Poetry and Drama*, June 1914, 221–8.
3. *Beiträge zu einer Kritik der Sprache*, 1901, I, 108, 122.
4. *The Philosophy of 'As If'*, tr. C.K. Ogden, n.d., 337.
5. Ibid., 68.
6. Cf. Stramm's reference to 'eine nichtssagende, schematische Form' in his letter to Walden of 27 June 1915; like his other letters to Walden from the front, this is to be found in P. Pörtner, *Literaturrevolution 1910-1925*, I, Neuwied, 1960.
7. August Stramm, 'Fünfundzwanzig Briefe an seine Frau' (ed. Lothar Jordan), in *August Stramm: Kritische Essays*, ed. J.D. Adler and J.J. White, Berlin and London, 1979, 148.
8. Ibid., 144.
9. In Pörtner, *Literaturrevolution 1910-1925*, I, 56; most of the passage also in Stramm, *Das Werk*, ed. R. Radrizzani, 1963, 450.
10. See H. Walden, 'Die Mücke', *Der Sturm*, VI, 7/8, September 1915.

11. P. Pörtner, *Literaturrevolution 1910-1925*, I, 55.
12. Ibid.
13. J.M. Cohen, *Poetry of This Age*, 1959, 105.
14. Ibid.
15. *August Stramm: Kritische Essays*, 138.
16. M. Hamburger, *The Truth of Poetry*, 1969, 158f.
17. C.R.B. Perkins, 'August Stramm: The Language of Poetry', *New German Studies*, VI, 3, Autumn 1976, 153.
18. The quotations are from Hamburger.
19. Cohen, *Poetry of This Age*, 106.
20. Perkins, 'August Stramm', 151.
21. Franz Marc, *Briefe aus dem Feld*, repr. Stollhamm (Oldb.) and Berlin, 1948, 90.

4 LICHTENSTEIN, BALL AND KLEMM

In terms of war poetry *Die Aktion* is the most important Expressionist group. Though there were many war poets among the contributors to *Der Sturm*, there were few among the members of the *Sturm* circle in the narrower sense. Indeed, the *Sturm* circle was not interested in the war in the way in which *Die Aktion* was, Herwarth Walden having declared art and politics to have nothing in common.[1] The only outstanding war poet associated with *Der Sturm* was August Stramm, although Peter Baum was also a gifted poet who produced interesting work (*Schützengrabenverse*, 1916) and Kurt Heynicke (*Das namenlose Angesicht*, 1919) deserves to be remembered.

The more politically aware and active *Die Aktion*, which published its anti-war anthology *1914-1916. Eine Anthologie* in 1916, had been opposed to the war even before it broke out. Franz Pfemfert's editorial of 4 July 1914 was a cogent and outspoken attack on the whole idea of patriotism:

> Solange das Volk patriotisch bleibt, solange es an der sentimentalen Vorliebe für das Land, in dem der Zufall es geboren werden liess, festhält, solange wird es auch glauben, dass sein Land sehr viel mehr wert sei, als das danebenliegende; dass es ehrend sei, dafür zu sterben – solange wird es unmöglich sein, den internationalen Kriegen ein Ende zu bereiten... Wenn wir ernstlich der Gründung der 'Vereinigten Staaten von Europa' engegenstreben, d.h. wenn wir den dauernden Frieden der Völker wollen, dann müssen wir uns einzig nur als Europäer, oder besser als Landsleute, als Mitbenutzer der ganzen Erde fühlen.

No less blunt was the editorial of 1 August 1914: 'der Chauvinismus ist die ständige Lebensgefahr der Menschheit. Er, allein er, kann über Nacht aus Millionen Vernunftswesen Besessene machen'. This latter editorial caused the journal to be banned from public sale, though it continued to be distributed to subscribers both at home and at the front. Later in the war the sub-title of the journal made it clear that *Die Aktion* stood for radical pacifism, while the anthology *1914-1916* carried the following note for new readers: 'Dieses Buch (Verse vom Schlachtfeld), Asyl einer heute obdachlosen Idee, stelle ich wider diese

Zeit ... F.P.' War poems appearing in *Die Aktion* were entitled 'Gedichte vom Schlacht-Felde', which made it clear that they were not mere 'war poems' (*Kriegslyrik*), or even 'poems from the battlefield', but 'poems from the field of slaughter'. They were excluded from all contemporary patriotic anthologies. In terms of political and artistic integrity, *Die Aktion* was the most important journal in wartime Germany.

It was typical of Franz Pfemfert's uncompromising stand for humanity and international values that even during the war *Die Aktion* regularly published English writers in translation, including, on 20 November 1915 (col. 597), two poems by Rupert Brooke translated by Hanns Braun: 'The Hill': 'Breathless, we flung us on the windy hill' ('Der Hügel': 'Wir rannten keuchend hügelan im Wind') and 'Sonnet': 'Oh! Death will find me, long before I tire / Of watching you' ('Sonett': 'Mich rafft der Tod, eh ich von deinen Blicken / Satt werde sein'). Others who made a similar (and similarly courageous) stand were George Grosz and Helmut Herzfelde. Member of the German army (until 1916) and then – more appropriately – of Berlin Dada (1917-18), Grosz made a point of regularly speaking English. His *Kleine Grosz-Mappe* (1917), which contained twenty bitingly satirical anti-war lithographs, was published by Wieland Herzfelde, who founded the left-wing anti-war periodical *Neue Jugend* after deserting from the German army on the Eastern Front; *Neue Jugend* was banned in 1917 and subsequently became the Malik-Verlag, publishers of the *Kleine Grosz-Mappe*, itself confiscated by the police. Helmut Herzfelde anglicised his name to John Heartfield as a protest against the chauvinism of the time.

The most important war poets of *Die Aktion* are Alfred Lichtenstein and Wilhelm Klemm.

Alfred Lichtenstein, born in Berlin in 1889, began to attract attention as a poet during his student years (1909-12); his early poems were published in *Der Sturm, Die Aktion* and *Simplicissimus.* Although *Die Aktion*, the leading outlet for radically experimental poetry, published a Lichtenstein number on 4 October 1913, the satirical journal *Simplicissimus* was arguably a more appropriate forum for his work. Known to his friends as a clown, a wit, a man apart, possessed by a profound sense of the absurdity of the world, Lichtenstein admired Wedekind and Rilke and detested Goethe and George. As a poet he can only be compared to Heine.

On 1 August 1914 Lichtenstein was nearing the end of the compulsory year of military service which he had begun in October 1913 and which was to end in his death. The 'Soldatengedichte' illustrate his ironical and finally hostile attitude towards all things military. One of the most remarkable of them, a fragmentary poem beginning 'Doch kommt ein Krieg'[2] shows that he had no illusions about the nature of the coming war:

> Doch kommt ein Krieg. Zu lange war schon Frieden.
> Dann ist der Spass vorbei. Trompeten kreischen
> Dir tief ins Herz. Und alle Nächte brennen.
> Du frierst in Zelten. Dir ist heiss. Du hungerst.
> Ertrinkst. Zerknallst. Verblutest. Äcker röcheln.
> Kirchtürme stürzen. Fernen sind in Flammen.
> Die Winde zucken. Grosse Städte krachen.
> Am Horizont steht der Kanonendonner.
> Rings aus den Hügeln steigt ein weisser Dampf
> Und dir zu Häupten platzen die Granaten.

These lines, written on 9–10 July 1914, a fortnight after the assassination of Archduke Francis Ferdinand and his wife, show that Lichtenstein was not among those who thought that the war would be a piece of cake; he - amost uniquely on the German side - had no vision of glory whether national or personal; he left that to divisional commanders and suchlike. How could the man who only two weeks previously had written of his own 'sonderbare Zivilistenaugen' see glory in war? Clearly he could not. Lichtenstein saw everything with the satirist's eye; his vision was personal, belittling, comic. The pomposity, inflated rhetoric and martial short-sightedness common to most of the poetry being written three weeks later were totally alien to him; he would have been constitutionally incapable of writing most of the outbreak-of-war poems. 'Doch kommt ein Krieg' is written in low-key iambic pentameters; there are no end-rhymes, for even the thought of war does not follow an orderly pattern; but there are sufficient internal rhymes to hold the poem together. Man - the poet himself - is threatened as well as ridiculed by the halo of bursting shells around his head at the end of this poem which strangely anticipates the front-line poems that Lichtenstein was soon to be writing. Word-images like 'Zerknallst' and 'Verblutest' are in line with his curiously refracted vision, for he implies that there is something rather remiss about allowing oneself to blow up or bleed to death; but there is a sharp, mordant edge to his humour here.

Following the Declaration and mobilisation, Lichtenstein was sent to the Western Front with his regiment on 8 August. Before leaving for the front he wrote the poem 'Abschied' which appeared in *Der Krieg. Ein Flugblatt*, ed. Alfred Richard Meyer, 1914.[3] This so-called patriotic pamphlet was banned on account of Rudolf Leonhard's poem 'Franctireurs', but in retrospect it is obvious that Lichtenstein's is the most pessimistic or realistic or honest contribution. 'Abschied' is a remarkable poem and a unique one:

> Vorm Sterben mache ich noch mein Gedicht.
> Still, Kameraden, stört mich nicht.
>
> Wir ziehn zum Krieg. Der Tod ist unser Kitt.
> O, heulte mir doch die Geliebte nit.
>
> Was liegt an mir. Ich gehe gerne ein.
> Die Mutter weint. Man muss aus Eisen sein.
>
> Die Sonne fällt zum Horizont hinab.
> Bald wirft man mich ins milde Massengrab.
>
> Am Himmel brennt das brave Abendrot.
> Vielleicht bin ich in dreizehn Tagen tot.

The simple, naive, honest rhyming couplet form is not so much an implicit reaction against the bombast of many similar poems, most of which Lichtenstein will not have known, as honesty for its own sake. The form, the wording (e.g. that initial 'mache ich noch mein Gedicht'), colloquialism (e.g. 'nit') and trite epithet and phrase ('das brave Abendrot', 'Die Sonne fällt zum Horizont hinab') are all deliberately 'unpoetic'; Lichtenstein presumably feels that high-key poetry at this point would involve the falsification of emotion. Be this as it may, the very simplicity is the making of his poem. There are more rousing poems written in the first week of August 1914, but there is none more impressive in its realism. Clearly Lichtenstein kept his head when others all around were losing theirs. His final forecast was wrong, though: it was to be seven weeks, rather than two, before he was dead.

The next poem, 'Romantische Fahrt', is remarkable for the picture of Kuno sitting on top of an ammunition wagon rumbling through the countryside of this ironically named 'romantic journey', which shows that Lichtenstein is still refusing to take himself seriously. He must have been one of the few men in Europe to do so. He retains the satirist's distance, even when writing about himself; I know of no more memorable picture of a poet going to war than this:

> Hoch auf dem kippligsten Patronenwagen sitzt
> Wie eine kleine Unke, fein geschnitzt
> Aus schwarzem Holz, die Hände weich geballt,
> Am Rücken das Gewehr, sanft umgeschnallt,
> Die rauchende Zigarre in dem schiefen Mund,
> Faul wie ein Mönch, sehnsüchtig wie ein Hund,
> - Baldriantropfen hat er an das Herz gedrückt -
> Im gelben Mond urkomisch ernst, verrückt:
> Kuno.

That the poet knew that he was going to his death is implied by the epithet 'romantic'. 'Romantische Fahrt' and another, weaker poem, 'Kriegers Sehnsucht', both of which follow the pattern of two earlier 'Soldatengedichte' to his mother, were written as his regiment moved forwards on 10-13 August. The regimental historian reported that as the regiment moved forwards, 'Nerven und Phantasie wurden durch die neuen Eindrücke, die auf uns einstürmten, gewaltig angespannt',[4] but his comment seems quite irrelevant to Lichtenstein, whose attitude remains cool and laconic throughout. To find anything comparable to 'Abschied' and 'Romantische Fahrt' one would have to turn to Kurt Tucholsky's 'Unterwegs 1915', which appeared in *Die Schaubühne* in 1917; all that need be said here is that Tucholsky's account, which is written in prose, is hilariously funny and barely mentions the war. There is also Hugo Ball's 'Ich liebte nicht ... '

It was Lichtenstein's remarkable objectivity which enabled him to write a poem that would have created an uproar if it had been published at the time: 'Gebet vor der Schlacht'. The battle to which the title refers is the first large-scale infantry engagement of the war, which took place on 14 August 1914. With the exception of the first and last lines, 'Gebet vor der Schlacht' is written in trochaic tetrameters; it consists of a song said to be sung, *sotto voce*, by every member of Lichtenstein's unit. The song takes the form of a hilariously funny and totally unheroic prayer. The first stanza has an ending worthy of Heine:

> Inbrünstig singt die Mannschaft, jeder für sich:
> Gott, behüte mich vor Unglück,
> Vater, Sohn and heilger Geist,
> Dass mich nicht Granaten treffen,

Dass die Luder, unsre Feinde,
Mich nicht fangen, nicht erschiessen,
Dass ich nicht wie'n Hund verrecke
Für das teure Vaterland.

The ending of this stanza reveals the disparity that underlies the whole poem: the utter disparity between what the poet makes his comrades pray and what the popular ideal of glory demands. The ideals of patriotism and heroism, of sacrificing oneself on the alter of the fatherland, are mocked and debunked by the simple ('cowardly') self-interest of the men. This is a remarkable poem to have been written in August 1914, for it was not really until after the Battle of the Somme that the grandiose patriotic concepts began to be questioned and eventually replaced by other ideals. But Lichtenstein's poem not only mocks the heroic mode in general; it also parodies the expression of that mode in earlier battlefield prayer poems. More particularly, Lichtenstein may well have had in mind two poems by Theodor Körner, 'Bundeslied vor der Schlacht' and 'Gebet während der Schlacht', which appeared, posthumously, in Körner's *Leyer und Schwert* (1814). If Lichtenstein's tetrameters are reminiscent of 'Bundeslied vor der Schlacht', the more interesting comparison is with Körner's other poem. Lichtenstein's 'Gebet vor der Schlacht' is, as its title implies, a kind of parodistic inversion of Körner's 'Gebet während der Schlacht'. The whole point of Körner's poem is that he is willing to die if God wills it.

The second stanza of Lichtenstein's unheroic poem is devastatingly honest and funny, although one can imagine contemporary readers - particularly the armchair warriors - describing it in quite different terms, calling for the damn fellow to be horsewhipped:

Sieh, ich möchte gern noch leben,
Kühe melken, Mädchen stopfen
Und den Schuft, den Sepp, verprügeln,
Mich noch manches Mal besaufen
Bis zu meinem selgen Ende.
Sieh, ich bete gut und gerne
Täglich sieben Rosenkränze,
Wenn du, Gott, in deiner Gnade
Meinen Freund, den Huber oder
Meier, tötest, mich verschonst.

Of course such an attitude (which the poet presumably shared with the

Bavarian comrades-in-arms whom he is satirising) is selfish, cowardly, thoroughly deplorable; but it is also true to life and, at a time when most poets and poetasters were riding a wave of euphoria, it is refreshingly down-to-earth and frank.

The last stanza echoes the first in its shock ending and this time the ending is underlined by a change of rhythm:

Aber muss ich doch dran glauben,
Lass mich nicht zu schwer verwunden.
Schick mir einen leichten Beinschuss,
Eine kleine Armverletzung,
Dass ich als ein Held zurückkehr,
Der etwas erzählen kann.

That last line underlines the whole point of the poem. In August 1914 the word 'Held' normally occurs in the context of 'Heldentod'; to be a 'hero' is almost by definition to be dead. Lichtenstein's ideal is the 'hero' who lives to tell the tale; survival is all. It is not that he was anything so grand as a 'pacifist', although his attitude (and his poetry) does invite comparison with that of Hugo Ball; he was, simply, a realist, and that at a time when realism was practically unknown. 'Gebet vor der Schlacht' is, I think, a remarkable poem, one of the best and certainly the funniest of Lichtenstein's war poems; it is totally and uproariously anti-heroic, and this on the eve of the first great infantry battle of the war. It is a poem which underlines how much German poetry lost with Lichtenstein.

Lichtenstein's war poems reflect his idiosyncratic and ironical vision; war, for him, is an extension of the grotesqueness of life, the consummation of all his fears. All his best war poems show that he is essentially an ironist. As an ironist he writes well only when he has a clear intention.

This he certainly has in his last poem, 'Die Schlacht bei Saarburg'. Both the gap from 22 August to 16 September, when 'Die Schlacht bei Saarburg' was sent home, and the content of this last poem, which did not reach Franz Pfemfert until the end of October 1914, well after Lichtenstein's death, suggest that the poet was involved in heavy fighting at the Battle of Saarburg[5] and subsequently. Saarburg was evidently the baptism of fire which caused his attitude to war to change:

Die Erde verschimmelt im Nebel.
Der Abend drückt wie Blei.

Rings reisst elektrisches Krachen
Und wimmernd bricht alles entzwei.

Wie schlechte Lumpen qualmen
Die Dörfer am Horizont.
Ich liege gottverlassen
In der knatternden Schützenfront.

Viel kupferne feindliche Vögelein
Surren um Herz und Hirn.
Ich stemme mich steil in das Graue
Und biete dem Tode die Stirn.

It is immediately apparent that this last war poem involves at least implicit comment, and here Lichtenstein's real poetic kinship is again revealed. 'Die Schlacht bei Saarburg' is written in *Heine-Strophen*. As with Heine, there is an alternation of feminine and masculine endings, with only the masculine endings rhyming. There is, therefore, not only the same ambiguity and discord as in Heine, but also the added perspective and depth that comes from the deliberate echo of Lichtenstein's great predecessor. The basic tension in the poem is between poet and reality, that is, war. The poem falls into two distinct halves: the first six lines describe external reality, while the last six are devoted, basically, to the poet's reaction to that overwhelmingly hostile reality. The tension between passive poet-victim and aggressive external event is hammered home in those alternating endings, but inevitably the distinction between the two is blurred, for what matters is how reality is seen by the poet and the effect it has on him.

Thus the very first line ostensibly describes the world, at dusk, swimming (Lichtenstein says mouldering) in mist, but from the very fact that he is saying it, and that the line has the feminine ending that denotes victim rather than event, it is clear that it is the poet's sense of reality, even his grip on reality, that is becoming blurred and loosened by the continuous fighting of 18-20 August. The oppressive sense of reality is expressed in the second line: 'Der Abend drückt wie Blei', with the word 'Blei' standing as a reminder that the poet has been under fire for three days. The third line compares the continuous shell-fire to a violent thunderstorm, with the feminine endings suggesting that it becomes a storm in the mind, a brainstorm that reduces the poet to a whimpering, moaning wreck. This reading is reinforced by the ending of the poem.

The second stanza shows the effect of war on the man-made world and on one individual man. The physical wreckage of ruined villages reflects, echoes and helps to cause the way in which the poet is reduced to mental wreck. The poet lies there, God-forsaken ('My God, why hast Thou forsaken me': the biblical question points to the extent of the poet's desolation), while the incessant, nagging machine-gun fire further aggravates his overwrought condition, bringing him to the point where his grip on reality is loosened. The image in the first half of the last stanza ('Viel kupferne feindliche Vögelein / Surren um Herz und Hirn') is not just an obvious poeticism, a simile for all the bullets and shells sawing their way through the air, and not just a typical piece of *grotesquerie*; it is also a parodistic echo of Heine, who himself parodies all those *Vögelein* in folk and Romantic poetry; and the childish image also suggests, finally, that the poet's mind has - at least temporarily - gone. It is because he has reached the end of his tether and can take no more that he ends by writing: 'Ich stemme mich steil in das Graue / Und biete dem Tode die Stirn.' There is nothing else left for him to do but surrender to death, as Lichtenstein did near Vermandovillers (retaken by Wilfred Owen's regiment exactly four years later), just nine days after sending home this poem.

Read in this way, 'Die Schlacht bei Saarburg' can be seen to be the deepest and most personal of Lichtenstein's all too few war poems. It is a poem which shows the inadequacy of Kanzog's assertions that Lichtenstein's war poems read like letters written when he was still close to events and that they were not intended to be anything more than reports of those events.[6] This comment applies only to Lichtenstein's weakest war poems, which are merely descriptive. It is not true of the far stronger poems which go beyond description to render comment ('Abschied', 'Gebet vor der Schlacht', etc.). It is perhaps typical of Lichtenstein that he should have written war poems of two such widely differing kinds and qualities; it is certainly a fact that he did so. It is interesting, too, that in his last poem he returned to the *Heine-Strophen*, which are otherwise characteristic mainly of his early work; but then, as I have shown elsewhere, the variety of his work is greater and the pattern of its development more complex than has been thought.

One of the major innovators of his generation, Lichtenstein might well have developed into a major poet. As it is, he is one of the best and most original of the German war poets, even his war poems being 'self-deprecating, bitter and funny',[7] qualities which otherwise are found only in the work of Hugo Ball and Kurt Tucholsky. Lichtenstein's particular form of irony is, I think, essentially English, and if one thinks of Siegfried Sassoon and the other satirical poets on the English side, it is clear that Lichtenstein's best work falls into one of the major categories of war poetry, that of satire, in which 'human beings seek relief from insupportably nerve-racking experiences... by satirizing them'.[8] It is his war poetry, above all else, that shows how much German poetry lost in him.

Strange as it will seem to those who know his post-war works, and bitterly as he must have regretted it, Hugo Ball was, like most of his contemporaries, carried away by the mass hysteria of August 1914; on the outbreak of war he promptly volunteered for military service. Poetic evidence of his short-lived enthusiasm is 'Glanz um die Fahne':

> Glanz um die Fahne!
> Steh auf! Steh auf!
> Trommler rufen und Hufschlag bellt.
> Lass den Sang und das Mekka der Nacht.
> Alles ist lodernd und hell.
>
> Komm hervor aus den wehenden Schmerzen!
> Schüttle die goldene Mähne.
> Sei mir zerstückte Hyäne,
> Schrei in der Brust und bronzener Aufstand.
> Glühe durchs Land!
> Blute und bete.[9]

The contrast between the glorious lion and the pathetic hyena shows, however, that Ball had his doubts about martial glory. Before the end of his basic training he was discharged for medical reasons. Although the heart condition in question was unimproved, he volunteered a second and third time in quick succession, but was naturally turned down. Impatient to see some action, he travelled to occupied Belgium in November 1914 to see the war for himself. He was horrified by what he saw, as his diary made clear: 'In Dieuze sah ich die ersten Soldatengräber. Im eben beschossenen Fort Manonvillers fand ich im Schutt einen zerfetzten Rabelais... Man möchte doch gerne verstehen, begreifen. Was jetzt losgebrochen ist, das ist die gesamte Maschinerie und der Teufel selber. Die Ideale sind nur aufgesteckte Etikettchen. Bis in die letzten Grundreste ist alles ins Wanken geraten... Alle Welt ist... dämonisch geworden.'[10] His now radically different view of the war is expressed in the poem 'Das ist die Zeit',[11] dating from late 1914:

Das ist die Zeit, in der der Behemoth
Die Nase hebt aus den gesalzenen Fluten.
Die Menschen springen von den brennenden Schuten
In grünen Schlamm, den Feuer überloht.

Die Seelen sind verkauft in Trödelbuden
Um weniges Entgelt und ohne Not,
Die Herzen ausgelaugt, die Geister tot.
Gesträubte Engel gehen um mit Ruten.

Sie dringen würgend in die Häuser ein,
Und ihrem Grimme widersteht kein Riegel,
Sie schwirren ums Gesims der Sakristein

Und reissen mit sich Lattenwerk und Ziegel,
Ihr Atem dampft. Ein schwarzer Sonnenschein
Hängt wie Salpeter überm Höllentiegel.

This relatively weak poem is important as documenting the change in attitude of a man who became obsessed by the 'Weltkatastrophe', as he called the war. He could speak of nothing else at this time; he even went so far as to blame himself for it. His disillusionment came to a head in the spring of 1915, when we find him writing of the 'idiocy' and 'brutality' of the war.[12] In May 1915 he fled Germany for neutral Switzerland because he had become convinced that the war and its so-called 'patriotism' was completely contrary to everything in which he believed. It is to this flight from the war, from the age, in a sense from himself, that we owe one of his two major war poems, 'Ich liebte nicht . . .':[13]

Ich liebte nicht die Totenkopfhusaren
Und nicht die Mörser mit den Mädchennamen
Und als am End die grossen Tage kamen,
Da bin ich unauffällig weggefahren.

Gott sei's geklagt und ihnen, meine Damen:
Gleich Absalom blieb ich an langen Haaren,
Dieweil sie schluchzten über Totenbahren
Im Wehbaum hängen aller ihrer Dramen.

Sie werden auch in diesen Versen finden
Manch Marterspiel und stürzend Abenteuer.
Man stirbt nicht nur durch Minen und durch Flinten.

Man wird nicht von Granaten nur zerrissen.
In meine Nächte drangen Ungeheuer,
Die mich die Hölle wohl empfinden liessen.

Amid the morass of early pro-war verse it is easy to lose sight of a poem like this, which is important because it documents one of the earliest and most decisive reactions against the war and because its depth of feeling gives it a poetic quality which much of the pro-war poetry lacks. Ball subsequently matched his actions to his words by tearing up and throwing into the Zürchersee a notice from the German military authorities requiring him to report again for military service. The sort of thing to which he is taking exception in 'Ich liebte nicht' is Big Bertha, notably apostrophised by Gorch Fock in a poem entitled 'De dicke Berta', which begins:

Dicke Berta heet ik,
tweeunveertig meet ik,
wat ik kan, dat weet ik!
Söben Milen scheet ik

It should be explained that 'Big Bertha', named after Bertha Krupp von Bohlen und Halbach, granddaughter of the founder of the Krupp empire, was the popular name for the big guns (up to 16.5 inches) which could shoot immense distances.[14] 'Gorch Fock' is the pseudonym of Johann Kienau, who served in the German navy and fell at the Battle of Jutland. His war verse stands out because much of it has to do with the war at sea, because it is mostly written in *Platt*, and because of its jocular humour (humour, of a different kind, being mostly found in anti-war verse). 'De dicke Berta', written in the first winter of the war, appeared in Fock's series of *Plattdeutsche Kriegsgedichte* (1914-15).

Meanwhile Ball spelt out in his diary his reasons for being so passionately opposed to the war: the war, he argued, is based on a stupid mistake; men have been mistaken for machines; it is the machines that should be decimated, not the men.[15] His despair over the times in which he was living brought him to the edge of insanity.

It is appropriate that this despair should have led him to write the magnificent 'Totentanz 1916':[16]

So sterben wir, so sterben wir,
Wir sterben alle Tage,
Weil es so gemütlich sich sterben lässt.

Morgens noch in Schlaf und Traum
Mittags schon dahin.
Abends schon zu unterst im Grabe drin.

Die Schlacht ist unser Freudenhaus.
Von Blut ist unsere Sonne.
Tod ist unser Zeichen und Losungswort.
Kind und Weib verlassen wir –
Was gehen sie uns an?
Wenn man sich auf uns nur
Verlassen kann.

So morden wir, so morden wir.
Wir morden alle Tage
Unsre Kameraden im Totentanz.
Bruder reck dich auf vor mir,
Bruder, deine Brust!
Bruder, der du fallen und sterben musst.

Wir murren nicht, wir knurren nicht.
Wir schweigen alle Tage,
Bis sich vom Gelenke das Hüftbein dreht.
Hart ist unsere Lagerstatt
Trocken unser Brot.
Blutig und besudelt der liebe Gott.

Wir danken dir, wir danken dir,
Herr Kaiser für die Gnade,
Weil du uns zum Sterben erkoren hast.
Schlafe nur, schlaf sanft und still,
Bis dich auferweckt,
Unser armer Leib, den der Rasen deckt.

'Totentanz 1916' is a product of Ball's involvement with the cabaret world of Zurich in that it is a parody of a popular cabaret song of the time ('So leben wir, so leben wir'). But it is more than a brilliant parody and satire; it is one of the outstanding anti-war poems of the war and not the less remarkable for being written at least a year before most of the others. If Ball had been living in Germany at the time, 'Totentanz 1916' would have been treasonable; it was one of a number of poems and other literary works dropped over the German lines by the Allies in

August 1918. Also used as anti-German propaganda were Schiller's 'Die unüberwindliche Flotte', Erich Mühsam's 'Die lustige Witwe', Prince Lichnowsky's *Meine Mission in London*, Siegfried Balder's (= Wilhelm Eckstein's) *Das Sturmläuten* and *Zwei Fragen*, as well as writings by Hermann Fernau and others. That this direct use of German war literature as anti-German propaganda worried the Supreme Command is shown by the fact that they offered a reward for each such leaflet handed in and that Hindenburg himself warned the German people in September 1918 against these leaflets 'which are supposed to break our morale'. Ernst Jünger for one found it appropriate that the armies of this 'country of poets' should be bombarded with poems.

In 1917 Ball became assistant to Hermann Roesemeier, editor of the anti-German-nationalist weekly *Freie Zeitung* (Berne). Though bitterly opposed to the war, he insisted that he was no 'pacifist *à tout prix*' (1918). His real position has been best expressed by Emmy Ball-Hennings, who said that he was like a desperate patriot who slowly frees himself from his nationalism and works devotedly and incessantly to open the eyes of his people, with whom he identified himself.[17] The crux of the matter is that Ball retained his love of Germany, although it drove him to despair; this is one distinguishing mark of his anti-war stance; the other is that the war caused him radical personal disillusionment, caused him to reject everything in which he had believed. Turning to the inanities of Dada and sound-poetry was an act of revolt and despair. He had no time at all for the bombastic, Pan-German variety of war poetry; his hatred of 'Kriegslyrik' linked him with most front-line poets. In 1917 he wrote that when things got serious these tub-thumpers would crawl back into their literary dog-kennels.[18] I doubt it was much consolation to him, but they did.

Wilhelm Klemm produced in a few months the work which makes him one of the most interesting poets of the war on the German side. His first and main collection of war poems, *Gloria!* (1915), is said to have been published by Albert Langen after he had read in the foreign press the opinion that Klemm's war poems were the 'only humane utterances' on the German side, a story which I have unfortunately been unable to substantiate. It is known that Klemm published his early poems in the admirably humane 'Gedichte vom Schlacht-Felde' columns of Franz Pfemfert's *Die Aktion* and that Pfemfert wrote to Klemm's wife on 17 October 1914: 'Ich weiss in Deutschland heute keinen zweiten Lyriker, der noch im tiefsten Blutschwamm die höchste Menschlichkeit so rein fühlt, wie Wilhelm Klemm in seinen Kriegsdichtungen.'[19] In another letter dated 12 November 1914 Pfemfert wrote to Erna Kröner-Klemm: 'Die Gedichte haben bis ins Ausland gewirkt - wie mir selbst Redakteure schreiben. In dem Wust von blutrünstiger Brüllerei - ein Mensch.'[20] In his review of *Gloria*, Pfemfert referred to Klemm's work as 'menschliche Gedichte vom Schlacht-Felde', and Klemm himself was to distance himself from the 'war poetry' of the time when he wrote, 'ich habe mich grösstmöglicher Einfachheit befleissigt. Die deutschen Kriegsgedichte sind geradezu entsetzlich. Es ist toll, was in den Tagblättern gedruckt wird. Und immer dasselbe!'[21] On the other hand, Klemm was also to distance himself from Pfemfert's strenuously anti-war stance by having his first collection published by Albert Langen.

Wilhelm Klemm was called up in early August 1914 for service as an army surgeon in General von Hausen's Third Army in Flanders. He left for the front on 10 August. On the eve of his departure he wrote to his wife: 'Ich denke bestimmt, dass es unserem geliebten Vaterland gut ergehen wird und dass auch mir persönlich nichts geschehen wird ... wir wollen und werden siegen.'[22] The earliest letters to his wife, written as his column moved slowly forwards, have the air of carefree unreality that is typical of those early days of the war; it is not until 21 August that he writes, 'Der Krieg hat jetzt für uns begonnen.'[23] It is as well, he writes at about the same time, that he is being kept busy, for 'man macht sich dann keine Gedanken mehr'.[24] There are, at this time too, the almost inevitable signs of enthusiasm: 'Der Krieg ist etwas Grossartiges. Wie ein Ramsch, der alles verändert. Ich glaube fest an eine Massensuggestion',[25] 'Wir leben in einer grossen Zeit'.[26] Enthusiasm is heard for the last time on 5 September, when he wrote to his wife: 'Die Begeisterung ist nach wie vor grossartig.'[27] Then, as the French counter-attack at the Battle of the Marne forced the German First and Third Armies to retreat for the first time, the war began in earnest in the German field hospitals: 'Es waren furchtbar aufregende und anstrengende Tage, dieser fluchtartige Rückmarsch Tag und Nacht. Erlebt hat unser Lazarett schon allerlei ... man gewöhnt sich lächerlich rasch daran ... Das Verwundetenelend ist entsetzlich ... Wir alle hoffen, dass der Krieg mit Frankreich bald zu Ende sein wird, die Franzosen leiden ja noch mehr als unsere Leute.'[28] After that Klemm's remaining letters to his wife (those written after December 1914 were unfortunately destroyed in the Second World War) become strikingly reminiscent of August Stramm's letters to his wife. Klemm makes many of the same points:

— Dies untätige Warten ist schrecklich.[29]
— So leben wir also von Tag zu Tag weiter... der Friede ist etwas Unwahrscheinliches geworden.[30]
— Jeden Morgen denkt man daran, dass doch vielleicht einmal etwas mit einem selbst passieren kann. Es kommt einem beinahe natürlich vor, dass täglich welche verwundet werden und sterben.[31]
— Der Krieg kann so scheusslich sein, dass man sich nach einer Kugel förmlich sehnt, die einen all dieser Aufregungen und Qualen enthebt, das ist z. T. auch das Geheimnis, das den Leuten zu so unsäglichen Leiden Ausdauer gibt.[32]
— Eigentlich ist hier draussen alles gleich. Man kann jeden Tag irgendwie ums Leben kommen.[33]
— Mich überwältigt immer das Milieu so... Die Gestalten der Verwundeten begleiten mich bis in die Träume.[34]
— Du glaubst gar nicht, wie deprimierend es ist, immer in diesem Elend zu waten. Ich gewöhne mich auch gar nicht daran, im Gegenteil, ich werde immer nervöser.[35]

How Klemm was affected by his harrowing experiences as a field-surgeon we shall shortly see. In August 1914 he was 33 and a qualified doctor, so that he was unlikely to be carried away by delusions of glory. In the event his attitude is invariably humanitarian and compassionate. In the Epilogue to the 1961 reprint of Klemm's most representative collection, *Aufforderung* (1917), Kurt Pinthus rightly wrote:

diese Kriegsgedichte sind Anti-Kriegsgedichte; und er wagte es, als andere noch in Schlachtenjubel und Hurrapatriotismus schwelgten, das Grausen des Kriegs in unheimlich dichterischer Übersteigerung zu schildern und im Herbst 1914 während der Schlacht an der Marne plötzlich aufzuschreien:

Mein Herz ist so gross wie Deutschland und Frankreich
                                        zusammen,
Durchbohrt von allen Geschossen der Welt.

Klemm's war poems are found in three collections: *Gloria! Kriegsgedichte aus dem Feld* (1915), *Die Aktions-Lyrik: 1914-1916, Eine Anthologie* (1916), and *Aufforderung* (1917).[36] Some of the poems appeared in all three places. *Gloria* contains the best of his war poetry, as well as an unduly large number of weak poems. The best selection of his war poetry is contained in the anthology *1914-1916*, further evidence of the excellence of Pfemfert's judgement. *Aufforderung* contains the most representative selection of Klemm's work as a whole, but the pages devoted to his war poetry are disappointing. Looking at the dates of his three 'collections', one would suppose the poems to have been written between 1914 and 1916-17, in other words, over a period of two years; one would then expect to find evidence of poetic development. Such a supposition would, however, be entirely mistaken. Since many of Klemm's war poems were first published in *Die Aktion*, the chronology can be checked there, and what emerges is a startlingly different picture. What is revealed is that virtually all his war poems date from a four-month period, 21 November 1914[37] to 20 March 1915. Since these are dates of publication, the dates of composition will be some weeks earlier, but the four-month creative period remains as an extraordinary fact. There is a gap in Klemm's contributions to *Die Aktion* from 20 March 1915 to 9 October 1915 and what appeared then was an extremely weak poem ('Nächtliches Erwachen', not surprisingly omitted from *Gloria*). 'In Pesenchies' appeared on 6 November 1915 and then there is a gap of almost a year, during which time Klemm published non-war poems in *Die Aktion*, until 14 October 1916, when two war poems appeared, the uncollected 'Der Verwundete' and the collected 'Stimmung'. During 1917 he published hardly any war poems, the best of the very few being 'Stellung' (16 June 1917), which was collected in *Aufforderung*. In 1918 he published no war poems as such in *Die Aktion*.

All the evidence suggests that Klemm was unable to write about the war after spring 1915, partly because to have done so would have been to produce weaker and weaker variations on already written poems and partly because in order to keep sane he needed to write about the world of peace. No doubt the everlasting sameness and grimness of his work as an army surgeon meant that he quickly became too exhausted and deadened to be able to recapture any freshness of response once he had written his poems about the wounded and the dying; even in the course of four months he seems also to have become bogged down in an increasingly inflexible poetic method. The evidence shows that not only his most varied and vital war poetry but virtually all of it was written before March 1915. There is some evidence, too, that he was not the best judge of his own work.

Though he was soon to produce deeply felt poems showing his

abhorrence of war, his earliest war poems treat war, in the manner of so many outbreak-of-war poems, as an aesthetic phenomenon, and indeed treat it in the manner of Heym and Rilke. This is true, particularly, of what appear to be his earliest war poems, 'Lichter' (published in *Die Aktion* on 29 August 1914) and 'Anrufung', the latter clearly a poetic response to Mobilisation. 'Lichter' is little more than a five-finger exercise on the theme of 'the lights are going out all over Europe', as the last stanza in particular makes clear:

Lichter verlöschen. Nacht und Verlassenheit
Stürzen herein. Unsre Herzen schauern tiefer -
Blinde Engel fahren verstört empor -
Flügelgeflatter und Wimmern ohne Ende.

There is little sign in the poem as a whole of the exhilaration and euphoria of August 1914, and what there is quickly gives way to foreboding. Like 'Anrufung' the poem is impersonal and unnecessary by comparison with 'Abschied' (see below). The shades of Georg Heym gather more thickly around the opening lines of 'Anrufung':

O du grosses Ereignis, unausdenkbarer Krieg!
Ich seh dich vorüberziehen, gespensterhaft schön,
Auf unzähligen Strassen, auf unzähligen Stirnen -
Ich höre dich rollen und donnern, sterben und schreien.

These lines are also reminiscent of Rilke's 'Fünf Gesänge, August 1914', but, although Klemm evidently admired Rilke's work, he could not have known his five hymns, which only appeared in Insel's *Kriegs-Almanach 1915*. In a general way, however, he was clearly influenced by Rilke. The way in which Klemm poeticises war in 'Anrufung' points forward both to the essentially descriptive nature of his war poetry and to a major weakness of some of it. The use of descriptive adjectives, many of them colour epithets, is a constant and striking feature of his work. A slightly extreme case in point is the first stanza of 'Vorrücken':[38]

Der Himmel glüht fabelhaft. Verwehtes Goldgefieder
Über einem wahrhaft seligen Blau.
Die Purpurstümpfe des zerschossenen Dorfes
Leuchten aus der Bäume Malachit.

It is as a realist that Klemm counts. His realism is always exact and often heightened; it is frequently combined with an ironical vision that allows him to show the grotesqueness of what he is describing. The images he lines up and juxtaposes are essentially realistic; it is the grotesqueness of his subject matter that makes his poetry look expressionistic. Many of his poems are antithetical in structure; war is presented not as the heightened existence for which the jingoists in particular (but not only the jingoists) would have it pass, but as the antithesis of life; he tends to define war by making contrasted definitions of peace; his anti-war attitude is often expressed in this way. His war poems show a remarkable descriptive facility; the warscape is fluently and effectively rendered. And yet he often seems to have little to say, most likely because his feelings are numbed, although it may also be that he is the victim of his own descriptive fluency and poetic method. His method is the 'description-plus' of Alfred Lichtenstein's weaker poems. Like Lichtenstein, Klemm is at his best when he goes beyond description to make an implicit or explicit ironic comment on his subject, in which case the comment normally comes in the last line in the manner of Heine. Perhaps because he tried too hard for telling endings, he appears to have had some difficulty with the endings of his poems and there are some obvious failures in this respect: 'Nächtlicher Vormarsch', for instance, just peters out, and a number of other poems lack any real emotional *raison d'être*, the laconic last half-line tending to be a pseudo-comment only, as though description-plus-comment had become his invariable method. Although he used this method more effectively than most other poets, the fundamental weakness of the method remains. Klemm's very descriptive brilliance is sometimes his undoing, for it led him away from real poetic elaboration. Rilke put it clearly when he said that verbal impressionism has its limits. But the moral of the poem should in any case be organic, not tagged on. By the time he wrote 'Vorrücken', he was sliding into mannerism under the influence of the unchanging nature of his particular experience of war (in the poem 'Gedanken' he wrote that war is always the same) and of the painterly descriptive techniques from which he was unable to extricate himself. His work had, however, tended to mannerism from the outset; this extends to the sometimes rather Rilkean use of simile and his proto-surrealist use of the genitive metaphor.

There also seems to be something mannered about the form and structure of his work. Formally speaking, his poems follow a four-line stanzaic pattern; many of them are near-sonnets; most common is the twelve-line poem. From this point of view Klemm's work parallels Sassoon's. Most of his poems are written in unrhymed free verse, although full rhyme and para-rhyme are also used. There is a good deal of rhythmic variety in a prose-like way (cf. also the number of sentences ending in mid-line); not a little of his work is prose-poetry in stanza form. Within the four-line stanza pattern the grammatical structure is limited to a few basic patterns; in particular there is a tendency to use tripartite constructions, although the use of pairs can also be overdone, as it may appear to be in the last stanza of 'Schlacht am Nachmittag':

>Bis der Regen kam,
>Gegen Abend. Lückenlos fallend auf Freund und Feind,
>Auf das Feld der Ehre und Unehre. Auf Mann und Ross,
>Auf Rückzug und Vormarsch. Auf Tote und Lebende.

In fact there is absolutely nothing of mannerism here. It is not only that the rain does fall, quite indiscriminately, on friend and foe alike, thus reducing all their huffing and puffing to absurdity; the last stanza also reproduces, in more concentrated form, the antithetical structure of the poem as a whole. The series of antitheses, reminiscent of seventeenth-century poetry, both conveys the whole conflict of the war and prompts the reader to ponder the difference between 'Ehre' and 'Unehre', something to which practically no thought was given at this stage of the war. No doubt Klemm's predilection for the four-line stanza form, together with what one assumes to have been his determination to avoid the over-obvious one-sentence-per-line approach of some Expressionists, made the temptation to use tripartite constructions particularly insidious. Many of the succession of weak poems in *Gloria* have a three-sentence form, with one sentence in each of lines 1 and 2 and with the third sentence spread over lines 3 and 4. Another frequent pattern is that of the sentence followed by three qualifications, or three images followed by a comment. Looked at from the point of view of his weaker poems, the rigid adherence to the four-line stanza form was evidently a mistake. The conclusion is inescapable that he does not always avoid the temptation to write poetry for poetry's sake. The best of his poems, on the other hand, avoid the tendency to mannerism or self-pastiche; they are characterised by strong personal feeling which gives the invariably vivid description a real bite.

Although Klemm is probably best known for the high-key realism of his 'clinical' poems, his poem about leaving for the front, 'Abschied', is remarkable precisely for being written in such a *low* key:

>Die Schatten erhoben ihr schwarzes Dickicht,
>Ein schläfriger Lärm kommt unten vom Fluss,

Und die Mondschüssel giesst ihr Licht –
Baum und Stein sind geformt aus Gesang.

Ein Schlösschen steht nah und weiss,
Ganz übersponnen von dunkenl Märchen.
Unschuldig und seltsam blickt ein Turm.
Vom Friedhof schwärmt ein kleiner Totentanz.

Die ganze Landschaft reist in den Himmel.
Die Meile begann. Tief und fern
Tönt der bescheidene Pfiff eines Zuges –
Leb wohl, Agathe. Wir sehen uns niemals wieder!

What a contrast there is between this and virtually all other similar poems except Lichtenstein's poem with the same title. No drums beating, no official farewell (such as normally took place in reality), no visions of glory. Instead there is just the detail that will be remembered and which will acquire more and more of the aura of a fairy-tale as time goes on. If it does go on, that is. Despite the rather histrionic exclamation mark, the last line is merely realistic. Klemm, unlike Lichtenstein, was to return; but many of his comrades did not return. The poem is impressive for the same reason as Lichtenstein's: because honesty replaces the usual histrionics.

Arriving at the front meant coming to terms with death. In the poem 'Sterben', first published in *Die Aktion* on 21 November 1914, the best of a number of poems on this subject which concerned the surgeon more personally than most, precisely observed detail is almost all:

Das Blut sickert schüchtern durch den Rock.
Ruhig welken die schmutzigen, grauen Glieder.
Lippen sind blasser und dünner, Nasen spitzer.
Auf geglätteten Stirnen glänzt der Schweiss.

Augen öffnen sich, alle mit gleichem Blick.
Die sind alle wie blau, alle sanft und gross,
Voll unendlicher Ferne und Güte;
Und vergeben der Welt und uns das höllische Treiben.

Less characteristic of Klemm's work it may perhaps be, but such a relatively simple, thought-provoking poem is more effective than the poems about the wounded and dying in which the clinical detail, factual and true as it is, becomes overwhelming. The problem here is a basic one in war literature and one which has caused many insufficiently perceptive writers to fail, namely the fact that the depiction of too much brutal detail achieves an effect only of brutality. This then brings us to Klemm's 'field hospital' poems. The better of the two poems with the title 'Lazarett', and the one which I wish to quote, is the earlier one (first published in *Die Aktion* on 21 November 1914):

Stroh raschelt überall.
Feierlich stieren die Kerzenstümpfe.
Durch die nächtliche Wölbung der Kirche
Irren Seufzer und gepresste Worte.

Es stinkt nach Blut, Unrat, Kot und Schweiss.
Unter zerrissnen Uniformen sickern die Verbände.
Klebrige, zitternde Glieder, verfallene Gesichter.
Halb aufgerichtet neigen sich sterbende Häupter.

In der Ferne donnert das Gewitter der Schlacht,
Tag und Nacht, grimmig und ernst klagt und murrt es –
Und den Sterbenden, die auf ihr Grab geduldig warten,
Hallt es ins Ohr wie Worte Gottes.

Until that final simile, in which the thunder of battle is likened to the words of God, the poem is starkly realistic. The detail of the scene is grim and unpleasant, but then that is war; all *we* have to do is read the poem, which is saved from becoming overpowering by its relative and necessary shortness and by the final simile, which is a reminder of man's remaining humanity and also points beyond the horror of war's carnage to another order of reality. Without that other order the poem would fail and man would be unable to continue. The case against horrific realism is simply that it impedes compassion and understanding, for after a point the reader will not want to know any more. This is why the shorter poem 'Lazarett' seems to me better and more effective than the longer and later poem of the same title in *1914-1916*. Every detail in the latter poem is no doubt strictly and clinically true, but the poem is overpowering; it leaves no room for imagination and therefore no room for compassion.

The most original of Klemm's war poems is arguably 'Verlassnes Haus'. Here the stark realism of 'Sterben' or 'Lazarett' is transcended in a brilliantly imaginative and successful extended metaphor:

Es öffnen sich der Rippen Flügeltüren.
Schon schwillt das blaue Divanpaar der Lungen,
Der Leber Purpurpolster, grün durchsprungen,
Dazwischen prangt in roten Spitzenschnüren

Ein stiller Baldachin mit vier Kapellen,
Das Herz, aus dessen dunklem Tabernakel
Statt der erhofften himmlischen Mirakel
Nichts als des Blutes schwarze Rosen quellen.

Und in des Hirns totbleichen Labyrinthen,
Und in des Leibes dichtgefüllter Höhle,
Und in dem Wunderschnitzwerk ernster Knochen

Wirst du die Vielgerühmte neimals finden.
Ihr unsichtbares Zeltlein hat die Seele,
Der ewige Nomade, abgebrochen.

Opposite this poem in *Gloria* is a woodcut by the poet's father, showing the 'deserted house' quite literally as an empty room. But the house is the house of life, the body deserted by its soul. Such brilliant extended metaphors are always rare and none more so than this, for 'Verlassnes Haus' is perhaps the most deeply imaginative poem produced on the German side, and it is a matter of historical fact that much of the run-of-the-mill German poetry of the war is lacking in imagination - this is the most obvious of the differences between the German poetry of the war and the English (which is far more deeply rooted in the world of poetry proper). The fact that the poem is a sonnet makes one wish that Klemm had used this form to escape from the monotony of the 12- and 16-line form, although it must be admitted that his only other sonnet, 'Vor dem Krieg', is unremarkable.

One of the best, most characteristic and most clearly committed of all Klemm's war poems is 'Schlacht an der Marne'. Dating, presumably, from shortly after the Battle of the Marne (5-9 September 1914), it appeared in each of his collections of war poems. Written in what was soon to be his favourite 3 × 4-line stanza form, the poem avoids the weaknesses I have described. There is a fruitful contrast between the stanzaic form and the freedom of the predominantly six-beat rhythms with their echo of the heroic mode. This echo is appropriate because, although the poem contains no heroics or exhortations to heroism, which was certainly not Klemm's style, it does point to the need for the basic heroism of survival ('stiff upper lip', we call it):

Langsam beginnen die Steine sich zu bewegen und zu reden.
Die Gräser erstarren zu grünem Metall. Die Wälder,
Niedrige, dichte Verstecke, fressen ferne Kolonnen.
Der Himmel, das kalkweisse Geheimnis, droht zu bersten.
Zwei kolossale Stunden rollen sich auf zu Minuten.
Der leere Horizont bläht sich empor,
Mein Herz ist so gross wie Deutschland und Frankreich zusammen,
Durchbohrt von allen Geschossen der Welt.

Die Batterie erhebt ihre Löwenstimme
Sechsmal hinaus in das Land. Die Granaten heulen.
Stille. In der Ferne brodelt das Feuer der Infanterie,
Tagelang, wochenlang.

In the first stanza all the endings are feminine, fluid, and this, together with the generous sprinkling of dactyls, enables us to *hear* the stones begin to move; after this the first stanza is again basically visual. The next image, 'Die Gräser erstarren zu grünem Metall', is sculptural, while that of the white sky is painterly. The image of the sky as 'das kalkweisse Geheimnis' is suggestive, for 'kalkweiss' has the connotations of plaster of Paris and of quicklime. The most important feature of the second stanza, and perhaps of the whole poem, is Klemm's self-identification with France as well as Germany, a courageous and humane profession of faith in the brotherhood of man which has all too few parallels in September 1914. The last stanza is a piece of straight low-key realism. The last two lines barely amount to anything as definite as a comment; in comparison with some other rather heavily contrived endings this one is admirably understated. But the implications of *incessant* warfare are there for all to realise in their own time. The hung ending, the absence of the final half-line, provides a little time, for a start. A slightly later poem, 'Abend im Feld', shows the non-stop horror and misery beginning to bite:

Jeden Abend in das nasse Zelt
Kommt ein Offizier und erzählt, wer gefallen ist.
Jeden hungrigen Abend, wenn wir frierend uns lang legen,
Sind Tote unter uns, die morgen sterben.

Dem einen riss es den Kopf herunter,
Dort baumelt eine Hand, hier heult einer ohne Fuss,
Einem Hauptmann schmetterte es grade in die Brust,
Und der Regen, der Regen rinnt unaufhörlich.

Durch die Nacht hallen noch immer die Kanonen.
Dörfer brennen fern, kleine, rote Zungen.
O du grosser Gott, wie soll das endigen?
O du suchende Kugel, wann kommst du zu mir?

This is an example of Klemm at his best: no overwriting, nothing laboured, just twelve straightforward realistic factual lines followed by two questions which are fully justified by what has gone before both in the text and in reality. Those for whom the poet speaks are not so much resigned to the 'suchende Kugel', the one with their name on it, as positively wishing for the release that it will bring. There may not be as much psychological penetration as we find in one or two of Stramm's poems - none understood better than Stramm the need to flirt with death - but the poem describes the mood at the end of a bad spell which must have been familiar to legions of the living dead.

When he included Klemm's work in his famous Expressionist anthology *Menschheitsdämmerung* in 1920, Kurt Pinthus remarked on Klemm's 'fantastic vision'. The element of fantasy is a feature, however, only of Klemm's non-war poetry. In his war poetry he uses images which are present all around him and which therefore do not need creating. Indeed, it is, paradoxically, the element of fantasy that we sometimes *miss* in his war poetry, which is fantastic only in the sense that it is a reproduction of a reality which is itself fantastic, grotesque, beyond belief, unreal. It is the unreality of front-line existence which is conveyed in another very early poem published in *Die Aktion* on 21 November 1914, 'Rethel':

Feierlich ragen die riesigen, nächtlichen Schlote,
Aus Pyramiden von Schutt verbrannter Fabriken.
Das geradezu irrsinnig schöne Mondlicht
Prahlt rosa auf Backsteinbergen.

Eine pechschwarze Gasse verschlingt die Kolonne.
Hoch in luftiger Fassade spielt der Mond.
Läuft rasch durch nachtblaue Fensterhöhlen,
Versteckt sich hinter verwegenen Giebeln.

Und nun blankt totenweiss die Trümmerstadt.
Weiss vor Entsetzen - weiss vor Stille.
Und das düstere Heer mit grauen Gespensterhelmen
Zieht dumpf und rollend hindurch um Mitternacht.

The opening word, 'Feierlich', sets the tone for the first half of the poem with its solemn, Hölderlinian rhythms which point back to worlds as different as may be from that of Rethel in autumn 1914. Rethel, a town in the Ardennes, was to be more important in military-historical terms in the Second World War, an accidental accretion of meaning certainly not wished for by the poet. For German readers the name Rethel might well also call to mind the painter Alfred Rethel (1816-59), who was given, appropriately, to conveying historical events in mythological terms, although this connotation too is accidental. What Klemm is trying to do is simply to convey the unreality of the scene and experience, the greyly unreal columns of the living dead passing through the dead town. He first described the town in a letter dated 6 October 1914.

Gegen eins kamen wir hin, der Mond schien leichenklar. Zuerst eine Versammlung von Galgen, die Schornsteine der zerstörten Fabriken. Durch ein Trümmerfeld kamen wir in eine finstere, alte Strasse, ab und zu hohe, ausgebrannte Fassaden, ein halbeingefallenes Haus, ein Keller, der schwarz gähnte. Dazu kein Laut - nur der übliche Aasgeruch und das gedämpfte Lärmen der halbschlafenden Kolonnen. Dann öffnete sich plötzlich eine marmorweisse Ruinenstätte, vielleicht so gross wie Leipzigs innere Stadt, die Ziegelsteinberge rosablass im Mondlicht, die Strassen ausgegraben, schneeweiss, die zerfressenen Mauerreste ... [39]

In prose sketch and poem alike, Klemm's concern is the utter unreality of the ghostly scene with its strange contrast between the crazily beautiful moonlight and the ugly destruction whose outlines it softens and which it bathes in the unreal light of beauty and of the past (for the beauty of moonlight belongs with peace, not war). Ghostly, too, in that the same moonlight plays on 'das düstere Heer mit grauen Gespensterhelmen' whose minds are filled with ghostly memories of the days when life was real and who will soon themselves become shades in the underworld which this whole scene prefigures. 'Rethel' is a poem which does justice to an experience which must have been known to most of those at the front.

One of the best, best-known and most characteristic of Klemm's war poems is 'An der Front':

Das Land ist öde. Die Felder sind wie verweint.
Auf böser Strasse fährt ein grauer Wagen.

Von einem Haus ist das Dach herabgerutscht.
Tote Pferde verfaulen in Lachen.

Die braunen Striche dahinten sind Schützengräben.
Am Horizont gemächlich brennt ein Hof.
Schüsse platzen, verhallen – pop, pop pauuu.
Reiter verschwinden langsam in kahlem Gehölz.

Schrapnellwolken blühen auf und vergehen. Ein Hohlweg
Nimmt uns auf. Dort hält Infanterie, nass und lehmig.
Der Tod ist so gleichgültig wie der Regen, der anhebt.
Wen kümmert das gestern, das heute oder das morgen?

Und durch ganz Europa ziehen die Drahtverhaue.
Die Forts schlafen leise.
Dörfer und Städte stinken aus schweren Ruinen.
Wie Puppen liegen die Toten zwischen den Fronten.

Most of the poem is descriptive, and lines 1-6, 8-10 and 16 are as vivid as the images in a painting. The first stanza is straightforward and economical; it starts with everyone's first and last impression, the waste landscape charted most fully by Wilfred Owen and Anton Schnack. Man features only indirectly, but in a number of significant ways. The unseen man driving the cart or limber is the evil spirit of the landscape, in that he represents those who have destroyed landscape, animal world (the dead horses which formed such an unforgettable feature of the warscape) and man's creation (the roofless house). Man is present in another form too: in the person of the poet whose creative activity represents man's continuing creativity and humanity and whose simile provides the most memorable thing in the first stanza. 'Die Felder sind wie verweint' seems at first very much like a poeticism, a typically Rilkean conceit. In fact there is more to it than that, for 'verweint' can ultimately refer only to God's tears (cf. the poem 'Lazarett'). Formally, too, the stanza avoids poeticism: the predominantly iambic pentameter pattern with alternating line-endings and near-rhyme of lines 2 and 4 is formally understated.

    The second stanza continues with a pattern which is similar but which differs in two related ways. The silent word-painting is interrupted by the onomatopoeia of the third line and the movement of the last line which has to be seen in reality rather than on a canvas; and, as the firing begins, the pattern of the stanza changes, becoming harder and more aggressive (three of the lines have masculine endings).

The pattern changes more radically in the third stanza, which is written, basically, in heroic measure. The clouds of shrapnel flowering and fading continue, in more evanescent form, the painterly imagery. It is with the poor bloody infantry, wet and muddy as ever on whatever side, that man makes his first significant personal entrance into the poem. The indifference to death, which is equated with the rain, is a matter not of heroics, but of heroism as such - the unostentatious heroism of the man-in-the-trenches - hence the basically heroic form of the stanza.

The last stanza moves from the heroic (in the first line) to the commonplace (in the last two lines), via the past in which warfare was a matter of chivalrous heroics; the forts sleeping away represent the past which was outmoded by the Schlieffen plan which involved sidestepping the fortifications. The reality of war in 1914 is very different from that of the heroic age, involving, as it does, wholesale carnage and destruction with the dead lying around between the lines like so many broken dolls (they are at least dead; what about those left wounded between the lines who often took days to die?). Since there is neither rhyme nor reason in what is happening, there is appropriately no rhyming in this last stanza; but there is a kind of vowel gradation or progression which apes the progress in military matters.

'An der Front' is, then, the outstanding single poem in the ironically titled *Gloria*! The other poems by Klemm that seem to me particularly interesting are slightly later ones that come, in one way or another, from *Die Aktion*. One of these is 'Dörfer':[40]

Die Häuser sind wie aus Pfefferkuchen
Und halb abgegessen. Der blaue Himmel hat soviel Platz drin,
Lächelt durch so viele runde Löcher in Trümmerhaufen
Und leere Granaten. Alles, aber auch alles ist zerstört.

Du kannst ruhig gehen durch die helle Strasse,
Rosa und weiss vom Mauerschutt.
Der Feind schiesst ja lange nicht immer
Und der einzelne Mann wird überhaupt nicht getroffen.

Die Kirche ist hohl. Und der Turm, du lieber Gott,
Hat nur noch eine Seite. Darum liegt ein Friedhof
Lauter Soldatengräber. Die weissen Kreuze
Stehen so sauber, als exerzierten sie noch.

Disteln duften süss aus ihren meilenweiten Feldern.
Die Wege sind verwachsen. Mohn blüht wunderbar gross
Berauschendes Rot mit einem Hang ins Purpurne.
Kamillen nicken in riesigen Büscheln.

Though uneven, 'Dörfer' stands out because here the fantasy of Klemm's peacetime poems makes a rare appearance in the first two lines. The houses, looking as though they were made of gingerbread, half eaten up, are straight out of Grimm; the image invites us to contrast the cosy world of childhood and peace with this vile reality. The idea of the blue sky having so much room in it is sheer genius, as well as being both in keeping with the world of the opening simile and exactly observed. The prosy final half-line cannot destroy the world of childlike make-believe which has been created. There is a telling contrast between different kinds of fantasy, the magic and the grotesque, and between fantasy and reality.

It is a far cry from the echoed world of fairy-tale to the slangy, prosy clichés of lines 4 to 8 with their blustering, self-inflating (frightened?) tone. The third stanza marks the beginning of the move away from the grim aspects of reality; the final metaphor is a truism and as such marks, perhaps, an emotional evasion of reality. The wild-flowerscape of the final stanza is no doubt in the first instance realistic; one thinks of the origins of our own Poppy Day and of those fields of poppies beloved of Impressionist painters. But at the same time the wild flowers evoke the world of childhood and peace. The flowerscape is the antithesis of war, a silent condemnation of man's unnatural works and a refuge from horror. The meaning of the stanza, and with it of the poem, is simple: war is unnatural. And this is conveyed not in the abstract, satirist's manner which Klemm mostly employs, but poetically.

So far we have seen Klemm writing in a - for him - relatively low key; this is, in a surprisingly large measure, due to the fact that we have been reading mostly twelve-line poems. With a poet who writes as vividly and concentratedly as Klemm, there is a fairly direct causal connection between the length of a poem and its key. Given that he writes always in the same kind of way, a 20-line poem is likely to achieve a more powerful effect than a twelve-line poem, although concentration is also an important factor. In 'Feuerüberfall',[41] for instance, there is an even greater degree of concentration than before. This is one reason for the success of 'Feuerüberfall', but there are others, including the fact that it does not sag at any point, that it has an effective, unstrained ending and, not least, that compared with so many of Klemm's basically visual poems it has a whole new, acoustic dimension (e.g. 'Es gröhlt, quiekt, rasselt und pfeift, dröhnt wie Bergsturz') which does justice to the confusion of sounds which loomed so large at the time. By comparison, many of Klemm's other poems are like a series of shots from a silent film. In 'Feuerüberfall' he takes advantage of one of the richest parts of the German language, its soundwords, to orchestrate his canvas. The result is impressive and is further enhanced by the rhythmic echoes of Hölderlin. The long lines with their intimations of the heroic mode give an historical perspective to the heroic resignation which waits for the other side to have its breakfast in order to be able to bury its own dead. The regularity of the day's events, whether breakfast or 'frightfulness', was a feature of life in the trenches. The historical perspective reminds us that the Somme valley had been the scene of fierce fighting throughout French history.

The poem 'Somme'[42] names the region in which 'Feuerüberfall' was set. What is in question here is the first Battle of the Somme, which in German military history means the fighting in autumn 1914, not the massacre of summer 1916. The laconic title conceals another very effective set-piece poem with all the descriptive strength of the previous one. The scene in 'Somme' (which, like 'Feuerüberfall', is too long to be quoted) is worthy of a Breughel. Yet all the vivid, concrete detail only serves, finally, to underline the unreality of it all. Quietly, unobtrusively the last line ('Ich gehe hinein, wie ein Zuschauer ins Theater') opens up a new vista and allusive world: the whole *theatrum mundi* theme, dating from the time of the Thirty Years War. There is a thought, in the early months of a war that was supposed to be over by Christmas 1914.

Another similar poem, but shorter and explicitly a poem of protest, is 'Stellung':[43]

Die Maschinengewehre repetieren ihre nächtlichen Rollen.
Manche gurgeln hastig ihren Vers herunter.
Perlen rein, oder verhallen dunkel
Über riesige Bahnen. Knattern ein rasches Terzett.

Eines klopft fünfmal sehr bestimmt.
Fünfmal zirpen die Geschosse über uns weg.
Geisterhaft. Man macht seine Verbeugung.
Aber wie hoch ist der Sternhimmel über den Gräben!

Selig steigen die Leuchtkugeln auf,
Vor zerschossenen Bäumen, schweigsamen Ruinen.

Wie der Novemberwald duftet! Nach Nacht und Nuss.
Wie lange sollen wir noch verzaubert sein!

Concentration on the sounds of the front has here led Klemm to produce one of his most original poems. The metaphor underlying the first stanza - the machine-guns (machine-gunners) are like priests reading their offices - is both imaginative and fruitful, for it points to one of the most deplorable aspects of the whole war: the fact that both sides claimed to be fighting the good fight with the most Christian motivation. The nicely varied first stanza ends with a brilliant burst of onomatopoeia: 'Knattern ein rasches Terzett.' This too is evocative when one thinks of all the 'Kriegslyrik' being fired off at such a grotesque rate. The second and third stanzas end more explicitly with the thoughts that man's genuflexions to Mars remove him as far as may be from any kind of absolute and that it is already high time that people stopped being bewitched by notions of glory or whatever. The penultimate line of the last stanza is a reminder of what life was like and could be like again, a contrasting definition of peace.

The implied message of 'Stellung' is repeated, more explicitly, in what is one of the last of Klemm's war poems, 'Schnee',[44] which first appeared in *Die Aktion* on 20 March 1915:

Nun ist wieder Schnee gefallen.
Das Land liegt weiss wie ein Roman.
Seltsam, unwirklich. Ein Leben ohne Hülle
Wandern unsre Gedanken. Wach auf, mein Freund!

Hörst Du nicht das Schiessen? Es ist Krieg, Weltkrieg.
Überlege es nur, Weltkrieg! Was in Vorträumen gelb
Spukte, ist Wahrheit. Blicke nicht in die Flocken,
Die fallen wie immer und je. Nimm Stelzen der Phantasie.

Jage auf Geisterschenkeln über all die Begebnisse
Entlang die Wege und Umwege Gottes,
Die du nie begreifst. Bis dein atemloses Herz
Plötzlich anhält. Und du dich wiederfindest, unter dem Helm.

This, the most programmatic of Klemm's war poems, was published at the end of his creative spell, although it looks like a poem dating from August 1914. Be this as it may, it is an appeal for people to realise the meaning of the term 'world war' before it is too late. By the time the poem appeared, it was far too late. Imagination is what was necessary if war was to be prevented and what was so tragically lacking.

Klemm's war poems on the whole lack the fantasy of his other work and are written in a lower key; they are in many ways *un*characteristic of his work. Not that anyone can be blamed for finding front-line warfare a sobering experience. Thrown into the horrors of field surgery, Klemm evidently found, first, that he had to write about what he was experiencing and then, a few months later, that he needed to escape from his experiences and to write about the things (love, nature, etc.) which meant most to him. In more senses than one, he found that he could not write about the war, but before that happened he had written the poems that put him among the most effective German poets of the war. Although he continued to write poetry after the war, he did not develop into a major poet.

The outstanding poet of *Die Aktion* is Alfred Lichtenstein. The few poems that he was able to write before his death make him one of the best poets on the German side and confirm that with him Germany lost a major poet. Had he been able to continue writing, he might well have developed into a satirist of Siegfried Sassoon's stature; but he stands out because everything about him - the kind of irony, the underplayed realism, the sense of humour, the refusal to over-react - is totally original. His low-key realism is much more impressive than Klemm's often supercharged realism, which tends to be overdone and therefore to destroy its own effectiveness, although there can be no doubt that Wilhelm Klemm is a brilliant impressionist.

Apart from Lichtenstein and Klemm, the columns of *Die Aktion* included the work of both major and minor poets (I am thinking of Anton Schnack and Alfred Vagts) who only happened to publish some work there. The work of Anton Schnack, an outstanding poet, is discussed in the next chapter. Alfred Vagts, for his part, was more imaginative than Klemm, but never learned to sustain and control his vision. But if for one reason or another the war poets of *Die Aktion* did not achieve their potential, all of them helped Franz Pfemfert to make *Die Aktion* into the most important literary periodical of wartime Germany, the one major periodical which opposed the war from the start and which invariably put literary and humane values first and last.

Notes

1. See Nell Walden and Lothar Schreyer, *Der Sturm*, Baden-Baden, 1954.
2. All Lichtenstein's poems are to be found in his *Gesammelte Gedichte*, ed. Klaus Kanzog, Zürich, 1962. Individual references are therefore not given.
3. Blatt, 12.
4. Otto Staubwasser, *Das K.B. 2. Infanterie-Regiment Kronprinz*, Munich, 1924, 18.
5. The official German designation for the fighting in which Lichtenstein's unit was involved on 18–22 August 1914.
6. Lichtenstein, *Gesammelte Gedichte*, ed. Kanzog, 103.
7. M. Hamburger and C. Middleton (eds), *Modern German Poetry 1910-1960*, 1962, 406.
8. I.M. Parsons (ed.), *Men Who March Away*, 1965, 20.
9. Hugo Ball, *Gesammelte Gedichte*, Zürich, 1965, 11.
10. Ball, *Die Flucht aus der Zeit*, Lucerne, 1946, 13ff.
11. Ball, *Gesammelte Gedichte*, 20.
12. Letter of 10 March 1915.
13. *Gesammelte Gedichte*, 18.
14. That the fashion to which Ball is taking exception is by no means a modern one, is shown by Mons Meg (now in Edinburgh Castle), Mad Marjory (of Ghent) and others dating from the fifteenth century.
15. *Die Flucht aus der Zeit*, 1946, 30.
16. *Gesammelte Gedichte*, 21f.
17. In her introduction to Ball's *Die Flucht aus der Zeit*, 1946, xiii.
18. Ibid.
19. Letter of 17 October 1914, in Hanns-Josef Ortheil, *Wilhelm Klemm*, Stuttgart, 1979, 45.
20. Ortheil, 46.
21. Ibid., 41.
22. Ibid., 30.
23. Ibid., 32.
24. Ibid., 32.
25. Ibid., 33.
26. Ibid., 33.
27. Ibid., 37.
28. Ibid., 38.
29. Ibid., 39.
30. Ibid., 39.
31. Ibid., 39.
32. Ibid., 39.
33. Ibid., 41.
34. Ibid., 41.
35. Ibid., 41.
36. References are given only in the case of poems which do *not* come from *Gloria*.
37. The poems 'Lazarett', 'Sterben' and 'Rethel' appeared (together with two other less impressive poems, 'Schlachtenhimmel' and 'Vormarsch') in the first series of 'Verse vom Schlacht-Feld' in *Die Aktion* on this date.
38. *Aufforderung*, 112.
39. Ortheil, 40.
40. *1914-1916*, 60.
41. Ibid., 66.
42. Ibid., 68.

43. *Aufforderung*, 114.
44. Ibid., 108.

5 ANTON SCHNACK

Anton Schnack, born in 1892 at Rieneck in Unterfranken, is to this day virtually unknown even in Germany. Yet he is one of the two unambiguously great poets of the war on the German side and is also the only German-language poet whose work can be compared with that of Wilfren Owen not only in general terms but also in some detail and who can stand the comparison. The reasons why he never received his critical due are mainly historical. He began publishing poems in *Die Aktion* in 1915, although he was never really a member of the *Aktion* circle as such; until 1917 his poems have no connection with the war. His first war poem is 'Schwester Maria' (*Die Aktion*, 20 January 1917). The next, 'An einem französischen Kamin' (*Die Aktion*, 12 January 1918) is totally unlike the war poems which appeared - and were most likely written - after the war. Four collections by him appeared in the first two years after the war. The first three - *Strophen der Gier* (1919), *Die tausend Gelächter* (1919) and *Der Abenteurer* (1919) - are pamphlet collections.[1] Most important from our point of view is the fourth, *Tier rang gewaltig mit Tier* (1920), published in a limited edition of one thousand copies. This volume, which represents Schnack's collected war poems, contains sixty grandiose sonnets filling 80-odd pages and is immensely impressive. It has rightly been said to contain 'the most inclusive extant image of front-line war as seen by a young man';[2] it is without question the best single collection produced by a German war poet in 1914-18 and contains (in 'Nächtliche Landschaft') the best poem of the war written in German. A book, then, of very considerable poetic and documentary value, of which Schnack said[3] that 'Das Buch enthält keine hurrapatriotischen Gedichte, sondern es ist vielmehr ein Buch des Weinens und der Trauer'. No less than his British fellow-poet Schnack is concerned with 'whatever mourns in man / Before the last sea and the hapless stars'. *Tier rang gewaltig mit Tier* is also, as we shall see, the most stylised book of war poetry in German. The only comparable volume is Eugen Roth's *Der Ruf*, which is, however, stronger in form than in content. The sonnet form, which Schnack uses, is common in war poetry - a number of the better English poems of the Great War are sonnets - but it is typical of Schnack that he does not draw attention to the form of which he makes such brilliant use. Not for him the flamboyance of the *Geharnischte Sonette* (Friedrich

Rückert) of 1814, or of the *Eherne Sonette* (Richard Schaukal) or *Eiserne Sonette* (Josef Winckler) of 1914. But then Schnack was not writing patriotic poems at all, let alone swashbuckling ones.

The poems of *Tier rang gewaltig mit Tier*, with its deliberate and challenging epic title, are dominated by night and death. Schnack writes more vividly and powerfully than any of his German contemporaries; unlike Klemm, he writes in the long rhymed line in free rhythms developed in Germany by Ernst Stadler. His technique is reminiscent of Wilfred Owen, whose work he could not have known. His treatment of war has much in common with the heightened compassionate realism of his British contemporary, and, like Owen, he also frequently uses internal rhyme, alliteration, assonance and reduplication to give his raw material poetic form; it may be that there is an occasional tendency to mannerism in Schnack's deployment of epithets. His work may be described as 'compassionate realism' if one is concentrating on the pity, or as 'heightened realism' if one is concentrating on the poetry. Ultimately almost any war poets worth their salt are realists; the difference between Schnack on the one hand and Klemm or Vagts on the other is more one of poetic quality than of anything else.

If it had not appeared under the heading 'Verse vom Schlachtfeld', there would have been no knowing that 'Schwester Maria' is a war poem. This then is Schnack's first war poem:

Märchen einer scheuen Knabenzeit wachten ihm auf unter dem
    schmalen Glanz ihrer Hände,
Primel sah er gelb im Waldmoos; oh seine Mutter ging lächelnd im
    Sommerlicht
Mit blauen Blumensträussen; klein gingen die Schwestern vorbei mit
    beglühtem Gesicht ...
Bilder ... Bilder ... Süss versang das Fieber Regen ihrer schweben-
    den Worte, kühlend den Stachel der bösen Brände ...
Jubelten Nachtigallen im Maibusch: wenn ihre Stimme köstlich
    vorübersprach,
Waren Veilchen erblüht im Märzabend: wenn sie im Zimmer war? ...
Gold lag irgendwo: neigte sie seitwärts ihr glitzerndes Haar,
Sterne hingen seidig, gingen auf über ihm ihre Augen, im Dämmer-
    gemach ...
Märchen wachten auf, Kinderfeste im Garten. Nachenfahrten im
    Wasserrosensee,
Wilder Kuckucksruf im Wald und banges Versteckspiel mit ihnen,

Den Nachbarskindern; Sterne im Überfluss und der Mond der Julinacht . . .
Unter der Schönheit ihrer Güte milderte süss sich das Feuer im Fieber . . . Mädchen sah er tanzen im Rotklee,
Mutter ging wandeln im Garten; kleine Fröhligkeit flog schmal in die Mienen.
Weit . . . weit im West träumte furchtbar die Schlacht.

Though he chose not to collect it, probably because it is not as directly devoted to the war as the poems of *Tier rang gewaltig mit Tier*, this first poem anticipates the form of Schnack's collected war poems. It is, in other words, a sonnet, albeit of an extraordinary kind. When I say that it is a sonnet, I mean that it is a poem of 14 lines with rhyme scheme (abba, cddc, efg, efg) of the *sonnet licencieux*. It differs from the conventional German sonnet in two main ways: in not being written in iambic pentameters and in that its internal construction does not follow the development of the strict sonnet. Far from writing in a hendecasyllabic line, Schnack uses, in 'Schwester Maria', a long line of varying length and with a varying number of both stressed and unstressed syllables; the feet differ between dactyls and non-dactyls. There is therefore a clear contrast between the external form (14 lines, rhyming in approved fashion) and the internal form (varying number and kind of feet within the end-rhymed lines). This contrast is absolutely basic to the poem, which is based on the contrast between war and peace. The poem describes the regressive childhood vision which the wounded soldier's nurse inspires. The nurse, who takes the wounded man back to childhood magic and peace as his mind wanders deliriously, is an angelic, Madonna-like figure whose name is, one assumes, chosen for its allusiveness. The contrasting hideous reality of war is implicit throughout the poem, although it is referred to directly only in the last line and named in the last word of the poem. War is defined, in the manner of Robert Graves, through a contrasting definition of peace, and is thereby implicitly condemned. It therefore becomes clear that the looseness of the sonnet form is a reflection of its subject matter: the strict discipline of the rhyme scheme is to the freedom within the line as war is to peace. In this vision the notion of the dactylic idyll is elusively allusive.

'Schwester Maria' is a good technical introduction to Schnack's work, for of the 60 poems in *Tier rang gewaltig mit Tier* all but five are sonnets of this kind, and even those five are in effect variations on the sonnet form (two are one line short, one is two lines short and two are one line long). None of them look like sonnets, for the lines are at least as variable as and mostly longer than in 'Schwester Maria'. Such a dense block of words, an epic panorama of war, neither looks like nor behaves like a conventional sonnet. Whereas the sonnet conventionally treats its theme in two moods (octave and sestet), with the octave stating a problem, asking a question or expressing an emotional tension, and the sestet resolving the problem, answering the question or relieving the tension, Schnack's first war poem does not, on the face of it, follow this pattern, although it is in fact an exemplary sonnet in that the whole poem is implicitly aimed at the resolution of its theme. However 'licentious' (in the French definition) they may be in their form, Schnack's sonnets are strictly moral in their ends. They also follow the spirit, if not the letter, of sonnet construction. Thus 'Schwester Maria' has two contrasting subjects and moods; the only difference from the conventional sonnet is that these are spread over and underlie the whole poem rather than being divided off into problem and resolution, tension and relief. Besides, the only real relief will come when peace prevails. For those who take a little trouble in reading it, 'Schwester Maria' is an anti-war poem of the most subtle kind. Though a poem of this kind may appear descriptive rather than reflective, the reflection is there beneath the description; in the poems of *Tier rang gewaltig mit Tier* the description provides a whole additional, epic dimension, as it does in Andreas Gryphius's sonnets on the Thirty Years War. Thus Schnack has a form which enables him to produce a type of poem which is at once epic and moral. His use of this highly effective but idiosyncratic sonnet form, together with the stylised syntax which he was also to adopt, means that his war poetry is more highly stylised than that of any English poet. It is no chance that he and Stramm alike forsake the middle ground of most war poetry and adopt extreme, and brilliantly successful, measures to express what can only with the greatest difficulty and the greatest art be expressed at all.

Of Schnack's range of subject matter there can be no doubt, for his 60 poems cover every aspect of war, including leaving for the front, marching to the forward positions, the dead and death (again and again), every form of destruction, nightscapes, dayscapes, descriptions of particular places and battles, artillery fire, gas, the various routine activities of the front (in the trenches, in a shell hole, observation duty, listening duty, waiting to go over the top, killing duty, etc.), the attack, the retreat, the prisoner, the deserter, etc., as well as more abstract themes. These are some of his themes; the list could be doubled; and of course his long, narrative poems contain countless other incidental themes. His work is epic both in its nature and in its scope. It is true that he writes about every aspect of his single poetic theme in the same way, but before criticising him for this we should remember that war is simply (as Alun Lewis later stressed) a matter of 'Life and Death'. Life or death, kill or be killed — this is what underlies everything: why therefore should he not emphasise this in the way in which he does?

The poems in *Tier rang gewaltig mit Tier* follow an apparently chronological course which suggests that Schnack served first in France and then in Italy. They trace the course of the war, as he experienced it, from departing for the front, through countless experiences to which few other German poets with the exception of Stramm have done justice in more than isolated poems, to retreat and the verge of defeat. The earliest poems show him leaving for the front, marching from railhead to forward position, seeing the first ruined house and church. They are, by his standards, not very remarkable. It is only when he sees the first dead that his imagination and his deepest feelings really come into play. The result is the first outstanding poem in the collection, 'Der Tote':[4]

> Lag da wie eine Einsamkeit, wie ein Gelage Steine, weisslich, hingestreckt, in vielem Regen liegend.
> Warum in der Nacht schrie ihn der Tod an, Nacht hängend voll Mond und warm von Wind? — Stirn noch spülend
> Aus der Zeit jenseits des Rheines Dinge, so: tollen Nachttanz und Heimgang durch die Burggasse; im Blut noch wühlend
> Ein junger Wein oder der rote Lampiongarten, und Abendschwarm der Tauben gegen Untergang hinfliegend ...
> Tanzen werden feierlich Kinder am Strassenrand Ringelrosenreihn, April wird regnen, ein Abend wird voll Käfer sein, doch er ist eine Dunkelheit; Mund
> Voll von Güte, einst heimwärts lallend weiches Wehmutslied in Julidämmerungen. Wer gab ihm Tod?
> Der, der die brütende Hafenstadt durchlief, der glitzernde Nächte sah, weissgewölbt unter dem Altan, südlich, mit Mondviertel, rot,
> Oder der mit den Zirkusen zog in den Lärm der Jahrmärkte, zerfetzt, in grünem Wamse, abenteuerlich und überbunt? ...
> Noch vieles wollte der Mund sagen: vielleicht von Gärten im Herbst durchwandert, vielleicht von Rindern
> Gelblichen Schlags, vielleicht von der Armut der Mutter, grau und ältlich; oder das Ohr, blass und schmal, noch voll von Gewit-

tern, voll dunkeler Tonwellen, so gern noch einmal hörend
Die Frühlingsamsel im Birnbaum, das Wanderfahrtsgeschrei von Städtekindern;
Im Auge dies: ein Netz voll weisser Fische, Gestirne, bläulich, lag in ihm nicht schimmernd gespiegelt voll Efeu ein gotisches Tor?! ...
Nun eine Dunkelheit, ein Tod, ein Ding, ein Stein, zertrümmert über alles Mass, schwer in die Nacht sich über Grausamkeit empörend. –

In the octave 'Der Tote' follows the pattern of 'Schwester Maria', but the sestet differs in that it follows an alternating rhyme pattern until this is broken by the absence of the fourteenth line, which means that the ending of line 12 remains hung, with no echo from beyond the grave. In other words, the poem mirrors the way in which a man's life and expectations are broken by death. The form is used to great effect. Within this form there are notable and even noble lines. Had its pattern (of two similes, the second qualified three times) been repeated, the first line would have smacked of rhetoric; as it is, it shows only the concentration that is uniquely Schnack's. The question 'why' in the second line – why this man? why this time and place? why? – is put in a way, differently stylised, that is noble and humane. Puzzled, mourning alike for slain and slayer, the poet tries to picture their backgrounds, seeking all the time to answer that question ('why?'). The pathos of line 9, the many things that mouth still had to say, has again something of majesty in it. There is majesty, too, in the ivy-wreathed Gothic doorway which the poet fancies to have been reflected in the dead man's eye, just as there is hope that he may not have died in vain and that peace and spirituality may return. We are left with one man's revulsion at another's violent death, the 'eternal reciprocity of tears'. We are left, too, with a noble sonnet memorably mutilated so that it may better express its theme. Like all Schnack's poems, 'Der Tote' has the seriousness and great concentration of feeling and language characteristic of the sonnet form. The length of the line in all his war sonnets means that the rhythm is necessarily slow, giving these 'Gedichte des Weinens und der Trauer' the movement of a dirge.

Other poems – 'Dorf Montfaucon' is a good example – show the poet mourning for ravaged village and landscape. In most of them there are the descriptions of peace's lost idyll which help to define and condemn war. Most memorable of all, perhaps, is the brilliant nightscape of 'Nächtliche Landschaft':

Ein Gestirn wie ein Tag; und dahinter ein Rand, berührt und bezogen von Licht und Geleucht,
Das ging oder kam, das fiel oder stand, unruhig, gespenstisch; und ging es, so war hohe Nacht;
Und kam es, so lag ein Dorf irgendwo, weiss und verhuscht, und ein Wald war gemacht
Und ein Tal voller Schlaf, mit Gewässern, verworrenem Zeug, mit Gräbern und Türmen von Kirchen, zerstört, mit steigenden Nebeln, grosswolkig und feucht,
Mit Hütten, wo Schlafende lagen, wo ein Traum ging umher, voll Fieber, voll Fremdheit, voll tierischem Glanz, wo urplötzlich zeriss
Irgendein Vorhang von Wolken; dahinter wuchs Meer der Gestirne oder ein Reich von Raketen, sprang aus dem Abgrund ein Licht,
Fürchterlich, brausend, rauschte Gerassel auf Wegen, trat einer dunkel ins Dunkle mit einem schrecklichen Traumgesicht,
Sah wandern den Flug von Feuern, hörte Gemetzel im Grunde, sah brennen die Stadt ewig hinter der Finsternis.
Hörte ein Rollen im Erdbauch, schwerfällig, gewaltig, uralt, hörte Fahren auf Strassen, ins Leere, in die geweitete Nacht, in ein Gewitter, schaurig im Westen. – Ruhlos das Ohr
Von den tausend Hämmern der Front, von den Reitern, die kamen, stampfend, eilfertig, von den Reitern, die trabten hinweg, um ein Schatten zu werden, verwachsen der Nacht, um zu verwesen,
Schlachtet sie Tod, um unter Kräutern zu liegen, gewichtig, versteint, Hände voll Spinnen, Mund rot von Schorf,
Augen voll urtiefem Schlaf, um die Stirne den Reif der Verdunklung, blau, wächsern, faul werdend im Rauche der Nacht,
Die niedersank, die weit überschattete, die gewölbt sich spannte von Hügel zu Hügel, über Wald und Verwesung, über Gehirne voll Traum, über hunderte Tote, unaufgelesen,
Über die Unzahl der Feuer, über Gelächter und Irrsinn, über Kreuze auf Wiesen, über Qual und Verzweiflung, über Trümmer und Asche, über Fluss und verdorbenes Dorf ...

What strikes one first is the power, the grandeur, the intensity of the poem. Both the subject matter and the dramatic intensity of its treatment are worthy of the 'devilries' of Bosch. It is no chance that there is so much reaching back to Renaissance precursors in this period; the twentieth century lives as it were under the shadow of the horsemen of the Apocalypse. 'Nächtliche Landschaft' has, too, the grandeur that one associates with Heym's 'Der Krieg', although it is even more impersonal. Heym's poem is dominated by the gigantic, monstrous figure of war personified as Death Triumphant; in Schnack's poem death appears as it does on the battlefield, though there is a distant echo of Heym in the deliberately lower-key 'Schlachtet sie Tod'. Formally the poem is another broken sonnet. The pattern that is broken is that of 'Schwester Maria' (abba, cddc, efg, efg). In 'Nächtliche Landschaft' the sestet rhymes efg, hfg. The octave is absolutely and aggressively regular; all the rhymes are masculine ones; through the enjambments one can *hear* the 'tausend Hämmern der Front'. It is these same hammers that begin the destruction of the sestet; had there been a coda, it would have had to be unrhymed. Lines 9 and 11 do not rhyme, and neither should they; but after 'Ohr', 'Schorf' is as it were a near miss. Line 12 ('Nacht') is a direct hit which shatters the pre-ordained pattern, emphasising the element of Night (so magnificently personified by Heym, we remember) and the death of which it appears to consist. Further attention is drawn to the broken 'Nacht' by the way in which it is surrounded by the only two feminine rhymes in the poem, a dying man held in the nurse's arms. Not a little of the grandeur of Schnack's poem comes from the pronounced and beautifully modulated pattern of alliteration, assonance, vowel-gradation or para-rhyme, and so on. There is no need to rehearse the whole sound-pattern of the poem, it is sufficient to say that this pattern both adds a further dimension to Schnack's war sonnets and orchestrates the sounds of war, helping to heighten the realism of the poem and giving it the inevitability of myth or nightmare. The crescendo of the last two lines is more a matter of rhythm and syntax; it is appropriate because there is no end to it all. The syntax of the poem is typical of Schnack: there is a tendency for nouns to be followed by their epithets, but the constructions are varied in such a way that, although there are recurrent constructions just as there are recurrent themes, at no time does the syntactical pattern run counter to the poem. As always with Schnack the poem contains some memorable images; the most memorable are those describing the dead with their hands full of spiders (line 11), eyes full of bottomless sleep (line 12), minds full of unfinished dreams (line 13). The fact that rhyme-scheme, sound-pattern and imagery combine to give the sestet maximum impact emphasises that his nocturnal landscape is a matter not of rhetoric but of death, the death of countless individuals, the pattern of whose lives has been arbitrarily destroyed. Behind the poem the question 'why?' is still implicit.

This brings us to another of Schnack's great set-piece poems, 'Verdun', which first appeared in the first number of Carlo Mierendorff's socialist journal *Das Tribunal* (Hessische radikale Blätter) in 1919. Not for Schnack the patriotic, conservative socialism of the Socialist Party in 1914 and of the worker-poets; his 'Verdun' appeared in a revolutionary socialist journal because it - like most, if not all, of his war poems - would have been unpublishable in Germany during the war, at least until its latter stages, and at that time Schnack was still at the front. Before reading the poem the English reader needs to know that the Battle of Verdun, which began on 21 February 1916 and lasted intermittently until June 1916, was a desperate affair in which the German losses amounted to almost a third of a million men (hence the penultimate word of the poem). Here, then, is Verdun as seen by the most considerable German poet to be involved:

> Unheimlich, nie gesehn, voll Grausamkeit; an seinem Himmel Feuerschnüre, Säume, pfeilweisse Linien, grüner Wetterschein;
> Sein Name: Schmerz, Verblutung, tausendfacher Tod, Geschwür, Mordstätte, Grab, Gemetzel, böses Labyrinth;
> In Winternächten aufgestiegen, weit hinter Scheiben, ungeheuer, toll, berüchtigt, grollend, voller Eis und Wind
> Und ohne Mond, nur überfallen von den Leuchtern, die aus den Wäldern stachen, gross, gemach, gemein,
> Nur überschwollen von Kanonen, alt, gewaltig, ewig; dick überschwelt von Bränden, Schwefel, Gas und Chlor,
> Von Totenhauch, Traumsternen, Feuerstrahlen, Gold und Nacht, von Wolkenfetzen, Sprengfontänen ungeheurer Art,
> Von Flüchen und Irrlichtern, blendend, mit viel scharfem Glanz, von Schwärmen abenteuerlicher Flieger auf unbeschreiblich hoher Himmelsfahrt;
> Wahnsinnig aufgewühlt durch Streiterei; zerstampft, zertrümmert, rot umlodert von fabelhaften Feuersbrünsten aus einem aufgeflognen Fort ...
> Geworfen in den Schlaf von uns, feindselig, bös, um zu zerstören wunderbarste Träume von Reihern, Veilchenabenden im späten März,
> Von Silbermorgen in dem Tal des Main, von Nachtigallen, Amseln, Mondnächten auf Altanen,
> Von einem Kleid der schönen Margaretha, von südlichen Geliebten, braun und dunkel, von einem Weingelage voll Gelächter ...

Weit hinter Rauch, Dunst, Finsternis, gross, stark und ruchlos,
    voller Tod und Mord, zahllos, gehäuft; und aufwärts,
Am Rand des Himmels immer voller Gold, Rot und voll weissen
    Feuern, grünen Blitzen. - Wer dachte da an Teiche heilger
    Schwanen,
An Liebesworte, schön und rieselnd, wenn vorne standen Tore
    des Feuerofens offen und schweren Todes unzählbare
    Schlächter! . . .

How do you write about a battle in which you are involved which lasts for over three months and in which your side loses some 328,000 men and the other (French) side a further 364,000? What kind of poem can describe the experience of surviving among 700,000 dead?

Three features of 'Verdun' stand out before all others: that this sonnet is more fundamentally ruptured (in the octave), that there is a concentration of abstractions expressing the poet's horror and that the dead man's dreams introduce peace as a straw at which to clutch. 'Verdun' uses the *enumeratio* technique of the poetry of the Thirty Years War, in a now further concentrated and intensified manner. Both Stramm and Schnack felt the need for intensification of language, but how different are their modes, Stramm reshaping individual words, Schnack relying on accumulation. Within their regular abba pattern, the first four lines of 'Verdun' accumulate words which accentuate the poet's horror: 'Unheimlich, nie gesehn, voll Grausamkeit', 'Gemetzel' 'ungeheuer, toll, berüchtigt', 'gemein'. As if to justify the last word of line 4, the next line ends with what was most universally regarded as 'gemein': 'Chlor'. It is this 'Chlor' - chlorine - which causes the sonnet to break down at its most vital juncture, for although 'Fort' nearly rhymes with 'Chlor', it does not in fact do so, for there is an unbridgeable gap between the chlorine of 1916 and the fortifications of 1914, broken tokens of an age of chivalry gone forever. The sestet is perfectly regular (efg, efg, in the manner of 'Schwester Maria'). One feels that this regularity points to the need for self-discipline in order to prevent a total breakdown, but it also links with other features of the sestet. The first and second tercets rhyme perfectly, although their content is totally different. The first contains images of peace in the form of the 'wunderbarste Träume'; the second contains only further images of butchery and horror. Yet these two contrasting sets of images are linked by predominantly feminine rhymes (the first in the poem) which reinforce the dreams of peace and show them continuing even at Verdun. There is, of course, immense emphasis on the two final words of the poem, 'unzählbare Schlächter' (how many men did it take to butcher those 700,000?), but the contrasting image of peace is, in its way, just as clear a condemnation of the war. Clearly 'Verdun' is not a poem which the military censor would have passed, particularly since it is about the battle which marked the turning-point of the war (Schnack's concern is rather the turning-point in history and humanity that has been reached). The burning sky of Verdun represents the destruction of the humanity of the German classical tradition. It is to a famous poem by the greatest poet of that tradition, Hölderlin's 'Hälfte des Lebens', that the 'Wer dachte da an Teiche heilger Schwanen' refers. This is the only sign of hope in the poem. There is hope in the fact that 'Hälfte des Lebens' is remembered at a time like this, although this hope is countered by the fact that Hölderlin's poem, like Schnack's, contrasts images of harmony and discord, only to end in desolation.

Whether 'Verdun' is successful, readers will, of course, judge for themselves. I am sure that Schnack would not have regarded 'Verdun' or any other of his poems as wholly successful, though its power and its humanity are clear to us. Ultimately, however, the problem of Verdun is the problem of what the individual has to endure, day in, day out for what must have seemed like an eternity (even in June 1916 Verdun was only interrupted by the Battle of the Somme, in which Germany lost a further 500,000 men,[5] and dragged on until December). Schnack first wrote the set piece 'Verdun' and, then, knowing that survival becomes a matter of every single day and every single night, he went on to write poems describing a typical day and typical nights: 'Ein Tag', 'Nächte', 'Eine Nacht', and 'Nacht des 21. Februar'. The last of these refers to the *first* night of the Battle of Verdun, when no one, mercifully, could have dreamt what was to come. In poetic terms the most successful are 'Ein Tag' and 'Eine Nacht'. Let us consider first the reality of a single day at Verdun:

Hellgrauer Tag, Fluglärm . . . Haushoher Sprung von Minen; Rauch;
   vergaste Luft; Gewitterabend;
Minutenstille . . . Oh, dass es süsser würde, weisser, bläulicher; oh,
   dass Gestirne schimmernd kämen wie daheim! . . . Es ist so
   weit,
So weit nachhaus zu gehen, so weit zu Kindern, zu der Geliebten
   zarter Lieblichkeit,
Zu hellen Brunnen, tiefen Gärten, Festen . . . Wie? riefe wer, gewaltig, brüllend, und wer in Schächten grabend
Vernähme dies erschreckten Angesichts? - Kanonenfeuer stösst

zum Himmel seine stundenlange Dauer;
Dann widersinnges Schweigen. - Es gab viel Tod. Doch wen noch kümmert Tod.
Tod ist wie dies so häufig, ist so häufig wie Wasser und wie weggeworfnes Brot.
Traf Grabende, traf solche im Gefecht, traf Schlafende, traf Liegende auf spannend fabelhafter Lauer. -
Oh, rauchte nur schon Nacht, oh würde duften Traum, wie würd ich innig beten mein erstmaliges Gebet
Der frühsten Kindheit, wie würd ich schweigen, wenn an den Sternen hin Raketen streifen,
Wie würd ich meine Stirne in Vergessenheit tief niedertauchen, in Schaum, in Trägheit, Heimweh, wunderbaren Sinn,
Wie würd ich steinern sein, da alles draussen unruhig, aufgewühlt wie in viel Winden weht,
Wie würd ich rätselhaft vor diesem Tode bangen und ihn nie erfassen und begreifen! . . .
Dämmernder Tag; Fluglärm . . . Schon ziehen dunkle Geschwader in die Unendlichkeit der nahen Nacht dahin . . .

At first sight it may seem paradoxical that 'Ein Tag' is the most regular of all Schnack's sonnets since 'Schwester Maria'; it follows an unbroken abba, cddc, efg, efg pattern with an equally regular alternation of feminine and masculine rhymes; even the lines (of 10 to 15 stressed syllables) look slightly nearer to convention. There is no break in the pattern because during this and every day there is no respite, just death without end. The alternating feminine and masculine rhymes point to the familiar contrast of idyll and reality, but the wholly conventional external pattern of the poem provides a frame; it is as if the poem were framed as a picture of 'a day in the life of mankind at Verdun'. This certainly is what it is. Schnack is never concerned with his own plight; he is concerned with the plight of the individual as a representative of mankind at large. The use of the shorter line is appropriate because the poem is not a panoramic set-piece; a more personal scale is called for. Although the incessant butchery degrades mankind, it is individual human beings who die. The deliberately commonplace similes of line 7 ('Tod ist . . . so häufig wie Wasser und wie weggeworfenes Brot') express, as more poetic similes could not, the very fact that death *is* so frequent. The poem as a whole is plainer, the diction simpler, because the poet is concentrating on the basic facts. And the basic facts all spell death. If only, line 9 implies, it were night with its dreams and its relative security. But is night in fact any easier to bear than day when it comes to it? This question is answered by 'Eine Nacht':

> Dann es dunkel war um ein Angesicht, beworfen von Brand manchmal, tränend, vorgestiert,
> Lärm im Rauch . . . Ein silberner Vogel schrie dreimal, eine müde Rakete ging zu Wäldern unter,
> Am Sumpfpfad der Einschlag mit Feuerwurf . . . Kroch bestürzt durch den Draht ein Erkunder,
> Lag, blieb liegen, in sich verkrochen, leise. Himmel wurde sechsmal verziert
> Vom Strahl einer glühenden Kugel, flatternd, mit Schweif. – Wenn nur kein Tod kommt, tückisch von vorn
> Oder hinterrücks! Über den Raum der Verfinstrung rauscht Wind; Geschwader ziehen zum Nachtflug,
> Unendlich entrückt ins Hohe. – Weisse Scheinmeere umspülen die Spanne Nacht von Bug zu Bug,
> Von Rand zu Rand, sind da und dort. – Die Herzlosen, wen tötet ihr böser Zorn
> In Schlaftiefe, in sanfter Traumüberblühung?! Doch schon fern sie, Näheres brütet:
> Ein Minenwurf, entsetzlich, spaltend; Näheres lauert dumpf im Erdbauch . . . weiter . . . tiefer . . .
> Bohrende . . . Hämmernde . . . Russ und Grubenlicht . . . Als riefe ein grosser Mund aus einem Schlaf
> Um Mitternacht, zittert es dumpf . . . Um Stirne sinkt alles ermüdet:
> Licht und Fluglärm, Schüsse sind selten geworden; nur Bohrende, Schlagende blau im Schiefer . . .
> Sanftheit, süsse Stille; fast könnte man beten. – Aber dann fiel in Gräben ein Schuss, der Schlafende traf.

'Eine Nacht' starts for all the world like an answer to our question, like a continuation of the previous poem, with a poeticism ('Dann es dunkel war') which is more solemn and more emphatic than the normal form would be. It has the same subject (death) as 'Der Tag' and a similar form. There are again no breaks in the rhyme scheme, and much of what was said about the last poem is equally applicable to this one, for precisely the same reasons. In 'Eine Nacht' there are, however, two impure rhymes (lines 2 and 3, 9 and 12) and there is an irregular pattern of feminine and masculine endings which in the first four lines emphasises the rhyme scheme but thereafter runs counter to it. It is as though after the relief of nightfall the black uniformity of night were interrupted by flares, the sense of security by invasive death. And so of course it is. The pattern of previous poems is repeated in several ways. As in 'Nächtliche Landschaft', which it repeats on a more intimate scale, the flares lighting up the edges of night find their poetic parallel in the brilliant images which leap up at the reader, as in line 2 ('Ein silberner Vogel schrie dreimal, eine müde Rakete ging zu Wäldern unter') and lines 4-5 ('Himmel wurde sechsmal verziert / Vom Strahl einer glühenden Kugel'). As in 'Verdun' - of which, after all, it is a more personal part - there is a literary allusion at the end which gives the poem a sudden further dimension. In the case of 'Eine Nacht', the words 'fast könnte man beten' recall the second stanza of Heine's 'Du bist wie eine Blume'. In Heine's poem the poet withstands the temptation to pray because he knows that it would be in vain. It would be no less vain in 'Eine Nacht', but in this case even the temptation to pray is terminated by the shell which happens to land in a trench and, doing so, kills men in their sleep. In other words, the security of night is an illusion, for the artillery night shift is keeping up the killing and a less frequent shell is no less lethal when it lands. Day ('Der Tag') or night ('Eine Nacht'), it's just the same: war means death.

After poems appropriately devoted to artillery fire in general ('Die Batterien') and heavy artillery in particular ('Schweres Geschütz'), Schnack turns to the trenches in which day and night - often life and death - alike were passed. 'Im Graben' again shows him at his best:

> Alles verweht; nur Tod bleibt übrig, Lauern. Alles ging zur Vergessenheit: Heimat, gelbe Mondnacht, Kirmestanz,
> Alles entschwand. Wir sind Verlorene, wir sind Gezeichnete vom roten Todmund, wir sind so dunkel und alt,
> Klein wie Zwerge. Wir staunen, dass manchmal noch Sterne gehen über den Plan der Nacht hinunter unter den Wald,
> Blau und verwachsen, dass noch eine Blume blüht, keusch, unter den leuchtenden Knochen am Drahtverhau. Wir verrohen ganz,
> Wir verlieren unsre Seele, die süsse, taubenhafte; wir werden gottlos und bös voll Lästerung. In mancher tiefen Finsternis
> Fing einer zu weinen an, erschüttert, gequält. An manchem Sommermorgen, wann in der Heimat blauer Rauch über dem Herd stand,
> Lag der und der erstarrt in der Sappe, mit trockenem Blut am Mund, unter dem Herzen den Schuss. Einer stieg aus dem Stollen, verbrannt,

Gealtert, traurig, mit einem Handstumpf, mancher war nicht mehr
   da, weil eine Mine zur Nacht ihn verriss . . .
Gebete? . . . Oh, manchmal fingen sie an aus dem Munde zu rinnen,
   ungewollt, verworren, stockend, müde,
Wenn die Not zu gross ward, wenn sich alles häufte; Heimweh und
   die Beschiessung, wenn Gas heraufwuchs
Würgend, mit gelbem Gift, wenn einer zu Grunde ging plötzlich
   unter geheimnisvoller Stille, leise, lautlos, ermattet,
Wenn Rauch, grauer, aus Bohrgängen schlug, nach Fleisch riechend
   und altem Tuch . . . Aber wenn eine Rakete ins Nächtliche
   blühte,
Grün, schön und schwebend, dachte (wer?) ich: an seltsame Brunnen, rotmarmorn in Lattich und Buchs,
In fernen Schlössern, südlich; bis unter Flammenschein, hellweissen,
   ich in den Schlaf, ins Stroh hinfiel von Traurigkeit und Schwermut schwarz beschattet. -

'Im Graben' is an important poem because of its powerful, 'Shakespearean' periods and because it describes the dehumanisation of man under the conditions of trench warfare. The deliberate and telling monotony of the familiar sonnet pattern is here further emphasised by the even longer lines. There is one impure rhyme (lines 9 and 12), but it is a matter of no moment. The form as such is unimportant, though appropriate for this reflective poem; the poetry is in the pity. What matters is what is happening to mankind. For the soldiers in the trenches all things come and go, all things pass away, except Death. Everything else, everything that should matter and does matter, is increasingly forgotten, snatched from the memory in a form of living death. They are all marked men, prematurely aged and diminished by incessant degradation, so much so that they are sometimes astonished to see a star or a flower or other reminder of the world before war. They are coarsened beyond the limits of humanity, losing all idealism of whatever kind. They have, increasingly, neither past nor future. They are liable to break down at any moment when the horror becomes too much for them. The sight of a flare, beautiful in the night sky, recalls the real meaning of beauty, the beauty of nature, of woman, of home, the beauty that does not kill. The only way to avoid prostration, and with it the even greater danger of death, is by clinging to the reality of the past, if one can.

An even more transient form of trench is the shellhole, to which the poem 'Im Granatloch' is devoted. The most memorable part of 'Im

Granatloch' is the ending:

> Was sang Ninette? ... Leichtes, Südliches. – Weinen will ich, dass ich lagere in Mord und Stürmen, im blauen Raketenmeer, im Sausen des Windes,
> Unter lärmenden Nachthimmeln, in grünen Wassern voll Schnecken und roten Würmern, in Erwartung des Todes, faul und gross; im Sterbeschrei der Pferde,
> Im Sterbeschrei der Menschen, ich hörte Dunkle rufen aus Dunkelm, hängend in Drähten: so singen Vögel, die sterben wollen, einsam, vertrauert, in Frühlingsjahren.
> Und, über dem Rheine, weit, ging eine knarrende Türe und aus der Öffnung quoll Gebet, das schwerbestürmende, eines vaterlosen Kindes...

There was nothing more harrowing for the yet-to-die than listening to someone from whichever side slowly dying in the wire. It is a subject to which Schnack devotes a whole poem, 'Schreie':

Da waren Nächte ganz zerrüttet von Schreien, von gewaltigen Todesschreien, gebrochen aus der Tiefe kommend, irr und wehklagend,
Dunkle Menschenlaute, in denen Gram sang, rot und nördlich, Schreie, in denen Meere tobten und entfesselte Gewitter.
Riefen sie nach bunter Jugend? Nach heimlichen Waldwegen? Schreie, die Nacht für Nacht kamen, schauerlich, immer zaghafter, immer leiser, tief hervor hinter einem Gitter,
Vor dem der Tod wuchs, langsam, erdrückend und ohne Erbarmen, Tod der Verblutung, Tod der Verhungerung, Tod der Einsamkeit, gross und entsetzlich ragend –
Wer kroch hinaus gegen das Maul, das schrie? Niemand, weil ewig die Gewehre rauschten, von denen, von diesen, weil ewig Tod ritt durch Nacht und Raketenstunde.
Wer brach in Tränen aus vor ihrem entsetzlichen: Helft! Habt Erbarmen! Rettet! Miserikordia! Klang wie Gesang ins Herz herüber von verendenden Vögeln, südlichen, verirrt und fremd –
                                                                    -
Schön überrostete Tod sie, grüner Sumpftod; in ihren Schreien flaggten Wimpel, lagen Sandberge, sprangen Kinderbälle, glänzte der Geliebten Hemd ...
In meinem Ohr alle Abende noch liegt dieses; warum starb ich nicht

Anton Schnack

> daran?, an dem: übermüdeten Nächten, folternden Rufen,
> Rauch über dem Helm, Sterne, brandig, über Halswunde,
> Luft voll Beklagung, da sie hingen verfetzt in Drähten, flatternd, mit
> zerschundenen Schenkeln . . . Wer ersann dies alles? Diese
> Nächte voll Abenteuer,
> Diese Nächte voll Grausamkeit, schändlichen Irrsinns? – Verdarben
> wie Unkraut unter bunten Nachtgewölben, gelb und rot.
> Wem galt ihr Fluch? Wem galt ihr Gebet? Einem Gott, der nicht
> hörte, der auf Wolkenbergen schlief. Nach wem sprang ihr
> Schrei? Herzlosen, die immerfort schossen
> In mächtige Dunkelheit . . . Oh, dass der Himmel nicht zerbarst, dass
> die Erde sich nicht auftat, worauf ihr Schrei quoll, fern und
> immer scheuer,
> Dass die Mütter nicht nahten gramzerfurcht, dass die Kinder nicht
> schluchzten bitterlich aus der Tiefe! Nichts verrückte den Tod,
> Der sie schreien hiess, langgezogen, grässlich, verröchelnd. Silbern
> hingen Sterne dazwischen, weisses Lichtspiel. Hing sich eine
> Stirne vor, war sie von Rauch und Rauschen jäh umflossen . . .

After a poem like that there is little that needs to be said. The poem is, I think, perfect in a number of different but related ways. The unbroken sonnet form again gives it – like 'Der Tag' – the quality of an epitaph or monument. It is a perfect expression of its harrowing subject in the sense of being skilfully controlled, modulated and moderated. It is a perfect example of the compassion that underlies the best poetry of the war (Owen, Rosenberg, Sorley, Schnack and Stramm). It is also a perfect anti-war poem (as opposed to anti-war poetic tracts, which were legion towards the end of the war). It is difficult to imagine a poem which would bring out the tragedy of this war more clearly or more poetically.

There are few poems on either side about the deserter who deliberately made his way to the enemy lines in order to give himself up into unheroic safety. I suppose this is the point: that the action is so patently 'unheroic' as to offend even those of moderate views. The best-known (it is a strictly relative term) treatment of the subject is Wilhelm Lehmann's novel *Der Überläufer* (written in 1925-7, but not published until 1962, which bears out the point). This unpopular subject is, however, treated by Schnack in another powerful poem, 'Der Überläufer':

> Nacht; und darein die Gestirne gesetzt mit zitterndem Licht; ein
> Ton, ein Ruf, ein Geklirr, verstohlen und knapp, unter der

Wolkbank das Meer
Der Scheinwerfer, bleich und gespenstisch; ein Feuer im Grund
　　hinter Wäldern, Flugrauch, der verzog
Mit scharfem Gestank. Ein weites Geschütz anfangend zu heulen in
　　die Finsternis, gross und gewaltig; dann eine Rakete, die flog
In den Raum des Himmels, gewölbt, verschwärzt. Unter ihm lagen
　　sie: tot, zerrissen, verschwiegen mit lauernden Augen, sprach
　　scharf ein Gewehr
Einer Feldwache, unter ihm kroch einer daher, ging einer hinein in
　　die Stollen voll Schlag und kieskollerndem Lärm,
Zerschnitt einer die Drähte, gespannt vor dem Werk... Und da dies
　　so war und die Nacht so warm,
Dacht einer der Brunnen und des Gestühls, wo die Glocken hämmer-
　　ten morgens, dacht er des Weibes und sah seinen Arm
Voll Lehm und Behaarung, und da er dies dachte, starb der und der,
　　lag dunkel ein Toter, verwesend, frassen die Ratten Gedärm...
Stierte er vor, da wachten die dort drüben in Stollen, in Stein und
　　Verhau und warfen Raketen ins Brausen der Nacht.
Sah er denn dies: Eine Süssigkeit - Heimat - die Pflugschar - die
　　Schwestern? Hörte er dies: Das Lied eines Mädchens - den
　　Ruf einer Eule?
Noch lag er im Rauch, sehr tief, noch zwischen Tod, noch wurzelnd
　　in Qual; traf es ihn morgen schweigsam zu sein, erkaltet, mit
　　zerfasertem Leib?
Nebel aus Wald stieg, zog weiss; ein Geroll war hörbar aus Fernen,
　　in steinernen Sappen lag eine verschlafene Wacht...
Kriechend auf Bauch und gezogenem Knie; halbstündig barg ihn ein
　　Loch, bös dunstend von fleischlicher Fäule,
An Wassern vorüber, zwang sich durch Draht und Gestrüpp. Wurde
　　gefangen mit seltsamem Lächeln am Mund, dämmerte Wunder
　　sein Hin; weiss, prächtig, gewölbt, geschenkt war er wieder
　　dem Weib.

'Der Überläufer' follows the familiar formal pattern, so that the deserter appears, paradoxically, in a super-heroic frame. In its way 'Der Überläufer' is one of those poems produced in the latter stages of the war in which the concept of heroism is queried. The arguments for and against desertion are, like the arguments for and against the idea of 'doing one's bit', moral ones. As such they do not concern us directly here. What does concern us is Schnack's *poem*, the psychological insight which enables him to read the man's mind, the total conviction which his words carry. This is not just a poem on its subject, it is *the* poem.

The scene, as in so many of Schnack's poems, is night: night with its panoply of lights: the diadem of stars and then, on the mundane level, the searchlights turning men into moths while distant howitzers howl like wolves. This is the background against which Schnack portrays the would-be deserter slowly cutting the wire while all around him men go on dying and rats go on gorging themselves on the guts of the dead: such, such is death. The living and the dead are cheek by jowl, which is why the rhymes in lines 4–8 are practically indistinguishable; the distinction between living 'Arm' and rotting 'Gedärm' can scarcely be heard, just as the chance bullet or piece of shrapnel or whatever that kills a man may scarcely be heard by his neighbour. Meanwhile the man crawls on, half-crazed, thoughts of his own body lying there in the open on the following morning, torn to shreds, alternating with confused thoughts of home, until at last he is captured, a strange secretive smile on his lips, the thought that now he might see his wife again after the war invading his mind like a miracle. It is all superbly done.

We have seen that Schnack's real subject is man, whatever mourns in man. His poems are very properly impersonal in that he is not concerned about his own plight. Practically the only 'personal' poem is 'Ich trug Geheimnisse in die Schlacht':

Ich trug Geheimnisse in die Schlacht bei Arras: septemberlichen
    Mövenflug in Silbergrau, den roten Mond von Franken.
Ein hohes Gesicht, das ich einst hinter Fenstern sah, Bootfahrten in
    der Mitternacht, eine andalusische Nonne im Frühlicht und
    Heloisens sehr schmalen Leib in Seide.
Ich trug noch mehr: Volkslieder aus den Höfen, von Mägden in der
    Dämmerung gesungen, den Dom von Bamberg, Grabmäler in
    der Pikardie und eine Spessartheide,
Trompeten in Konzerten von Beethoven, Samt einer Stirne, Feuer-
    meteore über Norddeutschland, holländischen, gewaltig
    süssen Schnaps, den wir mit Dirnen tranken.
Dies trug ich in den Rauch, emporgewölkt, in einem Hirn, sehr irr
    und jung. Dies trug ich gegen Tod, zu Flammen, tausendfach
    gezackt und wusste dies: dass ich zehn Wochen lag
In einem Kloster Bayerns hinter hundertjährigen Folianten, dass ich
    zu Gott Verworrenes hochschrie, ihm dunkel fluchte und den
    Satan pries,
Dass ich mich ganze, wunderbare heisse, sehr blaue Nächte über den

Silberleib von Annunziata liegen liess,
Dass ich durch Böhmen zog, dass ich die Haare lang trug in den Sommerwinden, dass ich im Wahnsinn schrie an einem Julitag ...
Oh, diese Zeit wie war sie fein und reich
Von tänzerischen Spielen, Landpartien, Licht aus Fenstern, Feuernacht, von Jagd auf Schmetterlinge, Grillen, grauen Vögeln, wie stieg sie märchenblau
Aus Meer und Ferne, Himmelsbögen, Seen, daliegend in den abgemähten Wiesen, den Blick in die Unendlichkeit der Dämmerung geschossen,
Und hörend rote Pfeifer in uralter Stadt und sehend rührend-herbe Nacktheit Sechzehnjähriger im Frühlingsbad in gelbem Rosenteich,
Im Ohr Gelächter der Cafés, das goldne Geigenspiel aus italienschen Opern, die Flöten hell und süss, oh, ging ich einmal noch mit einer Frau
Den Morgengang durch das erwachte Gries, mit Kindern in die Sternnacht von Apulien, mit Freunden quer durch Landschaften in Sachsen, ich war einst von den Wassern weissen Mains umflossen.
Raketen fallen nun ermüdet in den Wind, grün und gespenstisch, verklärend Mitternacht. Aus Dunkel leuchten Tote weiss und bleich.

But even here the poet is at once himself and a representative human being made of memories. The poem, which refers to the Battle of Arras in September 1918, has a memorable title and opens superbly in a way which shows that it is to be one of the most vivid of all Schnack's poems. Both the 'Silbergrau' against which the gulls reel and the red moon of France are straight out of Impressionist painting. The vivid, visual imagery continues throughout the poem, which is composed of the memories of which the poet consists, to which he must cling and the very vividness of which he must preserve if he is not to be lost. 'Ich trug Geheimnisse' follows the normal pattern of the *sonnet licencieux*, with an important variation in the form of an extra line. After the initial reference to the Battle of Arras, the first quatrain is given over entirely to the internal, remembered reality which is denoted by the feminine rhymes. The second quatrain opens with a further reference to the battle ('Dies trug ich gegen Tod'), after which internal reality again takes over. But the external reality of the battle can now be heard, insistently, in the background: all the rhymes in the second quatrain are masculine. This pattern, once established, dominates the poem. The sestet as a whole describes the poet's memories but contains a preponderance of masculine rhymes representing the threat of actuality. There is, therefore, a tension between the vivid, visual images and the increasingly aggressive sound pattern through which we can hear those memories fading. The sestet is given added weight by the addition of an extra line to the orthodox interlaced rhyme pattern (efg efg e). There are two odd lines out: lines 9 and 15. Line 9, which reads like a kind of pre-pendant to the following line, stands out by reason of its shortness, which emphasises the attractiveness of the memory which is to be described. Line 15, on the other hand, stands beyond the harmony of the sonnet pattern proper, and brings the poet or combatant back to the battle which in driving away his memories threatens to overcome the man.

Every one of Schnack's poems deserves to be read and remembered, but it is impossible, as well as unnecessary, to discuss them all. I wish to end my discussion with a final variant on the sonnet form which is devoted to that which alone endures at the front: death. From several possible poems I have chosen 'In Bereitschaft':

Ich werde eingehn in den Tod wie in ein Tor voll Sommerkühle,
    Heuduft, Spinnweben; ich werde nie mehr wiederkommen
Zu bunten Schmetterlingen, Blumen, zu den Frauen, zu einem Tanz
    und einem Geigenspiel,
Ich werde irgendwo zu Steinen niedersinken mit einem Schuss im
    Herzen zu einem andern, der schon müde niederfiel,
Ich werde durch viel Rauch und Feuer wandern müssen und schöne
    Augen haben wie die Frommen,
Nach innen blickend, sammetdunkel, unbegreiflich heiss ... Was ist
    der Tod? Das lange Schlafen? Das Ewige tief unter Gras und
    Kraut
Bei alten Kieselsteinen? Tand. Vielleicht komm ich zu Gott und
    werde eingehn in die weisse Schneenacht seiner Sterne, in
    seine seidnen Gärten,
In seine goldnen Abende, zu seinen Seen?! ... Ich werde unter
    freiem Himmel liegen, seltsam, uralt, gewichtig,
Im Hirn noch einmal alles: Lusttage in Tirol, Fischfangen an der
    Isar, Schneefelder, Jahrmarktstrubel
In reichen Dörfern Frankens, Gebete, Lieder, Kuckucksrufe, Wald
    und eine Bahnfahrt nachts entlang dem Rhein.

Dann werd ich abendlich, verschlossen, eine Dunkelheit, ein Rätsel,
    ein Geheimnis, eine Finsternis, dann werd ich sein wie Erde,
    wesenlos und nichtig,
Und ganz entrückt den Dingen um mich her: den Tagen, Tieren,
    Tränen, tiefblauen Träumen, Jagden und dem Jubel,
Ich werde eingehn in den Tod wie in die Türe meines Heimathauses
    mit einem Schuss im Herzen, schmerzlos, seltsam klein.

The title, the plainness of which stands in contrast to the splendid opening line, is in fact ambiguous. 'In Bereitschaft' means both 'standing to' and 'being in a state of preparedness (for death)'. Schnack's point is that the one must mean the other. But what *is* death? The crux of the whole poem is that question in line 5: 'Was ist der Tod?' It was to ask and seek to answer that question that the poem was written, and it is that question that explains the form of the poem. One has only to consider the nature and formal arrangement of the poem, and to compare it with those that have gone before, for it to become clear that 'in Bereitschaft' is the opposite of a tailed sonnet, that is, a curtail (though not of the Wordsworthian variety). It opens memorably - 'Ich werde eingehn in den Tod wie in ein Tor voll Sommerkühle, Heuduft, Spinnweben' - and quickly slips into a conventional abba pattern as the poet begins to list what he will see no more (line 2 evidently lists his major loves). But he realises, as we do, that he is taking death for granted, which is hardly surprising since it has been his constant companion and only lover for so long. But what *is* death? There is nothing to rhyme with the definition of death in lines 5 and 6, because there is no idea to chime with this. The question is unique and must stand alone; to allow it to become the subject of a rhyme would rob it of its significance. The first answer is conventional and tentative, so that line 6 also rightly remains unrhymed. But then, in the middle of line 7, the poet begins to elaborate a rather different answer. It is to this that the fully rhymed sestet is devoted. The sonnet is - most unusually - broken and curtailed in the second quatrain, although the most extraordinary part of the sonnet is not the second quatrain but the sestet. In part Schnack is agreeing with Charles Sorley, who, in the second of his 'Two Sonnets' in June 1915, rejected the sentimental attitude to death in favour of a realistic one:

Such, such is Death: no triumph, no defeat:
Only an empty pail, a slate rubbed clean,
A merciful putting away of what has been.

Schnack, for his part, is rejecting the idea of a triumphant entry not into Valhalla, but into the gardens of the Hesperides. And he is rejecting the idea for the same reason as Sorley, in other words, because he knows death (cf. especially the first and last lines of the sestet). The extraordinary thing is that death is described in precisely the same images as life (as opposed to front-line existence). In part the poet is forced into this view by sheer logic; in part it is a matter of hope. The last line ('Ich werde eingehn in den Tod wie in die Türe meines Heimathauses mit einem Schuss im Herzen, schmerzlos, seltsam klein') is dignified, realistic and resigned, but also hopeful: not all die so painlessly. There is no illusion, no vision of death leading to some kind of glory. Schnack knows very well what happens to the dead. He makes effective use of the image of death's door, both in 'In Bereitschaft' and in the more rhetorical 'Am Tor des Todes'. In the former poem we have just seen him writing of death as a kind of homecoming, a 'putting away of what has been' as the child's toys used to be put away. Other poets have attempted to come to terms with death by defining it in other ways, but Schnack surely spoke for all when he wrote, in 'Am Tor des Todes':

> Nur der Tod ist ewig, nur die Erde und die Glocke des Himmels darüber.

Anton Schnack is, then, one of the outstanding poets of the war, a poet of the same order as Owen and Rosenberg. On the German side his only peer is August Stramm, and Stramm's work is limited by the severe verbal constraints within which he chose to write. Schnack knew as much about war and the pity of war as Stramm and wrote about it in a single collection which for sheer poetic power is unequalled by any other collection on either side. The fact that all his war poems are broken sonnets in no way detracts from his range and power. Nor does it excuse the scant recognition which he received in his lifetime. Here is poetry of the very highest order.

Notes

1. Details are as follows: *Strophen der Gier* (Dresden, 1919, 15 pp.: Das neueste Gedicht, Bd 22); *Die tausend Gelächter* (Hannover, 1919, 16pp.: Die Silbergäule, Bd 16); *Der Abenteurer* (Darmstadt, 1919, 18pp.: Die kleine Republik, Nr 7).
2. See *Ohne Hass und Fahne*, ed. Deppe, Middleton and Schönherr, Hamburg,

1959, 177.
   3. In a letter to the author dated 1 November 1960.
   4. In the case of poems from *Tier rang gewaltig mit Tier* no further reference is given.
   5. England also lost 500,000 men, and France 200,000. In other words, Verdun and the Somme together accounted for 2 million deaths.

6 LERSCH, BRÖGER AND ENGELKE

After the work of such dyed-in-the-wool patriotic poetasters as Walter Flex and Walter Heymann, the poetry of 'worker-poets' like Heinrich Lersch and Karl Bröger was among the most popular and widely read of the war. Much of the work produced by such poets was 'popular' poetry written in an over-simplified lyric vein, often based on the folk ballad, which was bound to lead to the expression of an over-simplified view of the war. This happened in countless cases, though Lersch at least was able to find new modes of expression for the experiences that affected him so deeply. At this stage it is worth recalling I.M. Parsons's comment:

> They [the Georgians] belonged to a ... poetic generation, whose inherited tradition and technique were utterly at variance with the material which they suddenly found themselves trying to handle ... What men ... were experiencing and feeling, after the holocaust of the Somme if not before, could no longer be given poetic expression by writers whose ... poetic conventions were out-worn even before the war started.[1]

This is a valid point and one which applies to most of the German poetry of the war, which was written in precisely that 'over-simplified lyric vein' of which Parsons writes. Looking back two generations later, I simply cannot see that the folk ballad, say, can under any circumstances be an adequate means of expressing one's reaction to modern warfare; it may in some – few – cases have been adequate for expressing an enthusiastic initial response to what was, after all, expected to be a short-lived cavalry war,[2] but it was totally inadequate for expressing any valid poetic, as opposed to satirical, response to the sort of war that developed. As the war itself changed out of all recognition, different modes of poetic response were necessitated. By and large these modes were forthcoming only from the more advanced and therefore independently minded poetic circles. Confirmation of this is provided by the fact that so many poets wrote one or two outbreak-of-war poems which became quite well known, but then fell silent. There was, of course, little room left for unthinking enthusiasm after the first six months or so of the war, but the real point in the present context is that the vast majority of those who appear in all the anthologies and who are still widely regarded as the main war poets simply lacked the poetic means to respond to the war of mid-1915 onwards. Most of the 'traditional' poets, it must be emphasised, produced work that was totally naive, to say nothing of disastrously pathetic.

One of the most important and interesting exceptions to this rule is Heinrich Lersch, whose letters written during the war show him to have been fully aware of these problems. This chapter is accordingly concerned with the work of Heinrich Lersch and his fellow workerpoets Karl Bröger and Gerrit Engelke. The work of all three shows that in the right hands conventional realism and naive poetic forms can be made to express modern warfare as effectively as more modern and sophisticated styles, although such honourable exceptions only serve, ultimately, to prove the rule that naive forms spell naive thoughts.

On 2 February 1915 Lersch wrote to Alphons Petzold (another of the more interesting worker war poets): 'Ich glaube, dass meine Entwicklung stehnbleibt; ich finde es in meinen Gedichten, deren ich mich im Herzen fast schäme, obgleich die Leute daran Gefallen finden. Ich mag sie nicht mehr sehen.'[3] It is true that at this time Lersch's work was not developing; but it was to develop considerably in the course of the war - he would have been incapable of writing 'Massengräber', say, in 1914, and one of his next letters shows that he is very conscious of the poetic challenge posed by the war. On Easter Sunday 1915 Lersch writes to Petzold again complimenting him on the poetic power of one of his poems; he adds: 'ich hätt's mir ja nicht *so* vorstellen können, - keiner kann's, denn so etwas ist so neu, dass es nie zum Kriegsein gehört hat'.[4] Writing to another fellow-poet, Josef Winckler, on 16 January 1916, he points to one of the many difficulties facing the poet at this time: 'Ach, die armen Leut wollen das Schreckliche schön verziert und verbrämt, gezähmt und halb lauwarm auf einem Präsentiertellerchen haben, um in Stimmung zu kommen. Wollen das Riesigste grad so klein haben, wie sie selber sind. Als wenn Kunst etwas andres wäre als geformtes Leben!'[5] One of the forms which this poeticisation takes is for 'das Riesigste' to be trivialised by being cast into folk-ballad form. His letters make it clear that his attitude to the war changed radically; this is most fully expressed in his letter to Max Barthel of 25 February 1918:

Für mich als Mensch und Dichter ist die Zeit bis 1917 überlebt . . . Die Idee meines Dichtens war alt und hat sich ausgelebt, weil sie nur Überlieferung waren. In Wirklichkeit existiert z.B. so ein 'preussischer

Musketier' überhaupt nicht. In Wirklichkeit ist ja das Gefühl, fürs Vaterland zu kämpfen, nur im ersten Kriegsjahr lebendig gewesen. In Wirklichkeit bin ich von der Idee abgekommen, dass der Zweck des Menschen grösser sei als das Sein. Bisher war mir wirklich der Staat höher als der Einzelne, die Gemeinschaft mehr als das Individuum, und so konnte es garnicht anders ausbleiben, dass ich ein guter und getreuer Staatsbürger war. Nun, da ich aber sehe, dass der Staat von der ihm durch seine Mitglieder gegebene Kraft Missbrauch treibt, kann ich nicht länger mehr mittun.[6]

However, more eloquent than anything Lersch wrote in abstract terms is the development of his war poetry, for the way in which a conventional attitude, conventionally expressed, gives way to an individual attitude, quite differently expressed, is there for all to see. Looking back in 1930, Lersch wrote that his experience of war was diabolical, horrendous ('das, was mein Erlebnis durch die Schlacht war, war satanisch und grauenhaft').[7] There is not less a gulf between his early and later war poetry than there is between this attitude to war and that which he had embraced so enthusiastically in August 1914.

Heinrich Lersch (1889-1936) was one of the 'Werkleute auf Haus Nyland', the group of so-called 'worker-poets' founded by Josef Winckler, Wilhelm Vershofen and Jakob Kneip. He was made famous practically overnight by the poem 'Soldatenabschied' written in August 1914, the decisive turning-point in his life. Because of ill health he was unable to volunteer until the end of November 1914; he reported to the basic training depot of the 65th Reserve Infantry Regiment on 1 December 1914. He therefore missed the early German advance. By February 1915, when he was posted to the front, the static trench warfare had begun. He arrived at the front just in time to experience the final stages of the unsuccessful French advance in the Champagne. At the end of May he was buried alive during an artillery bombardment; coming on top of his already damaged lungs, this caused him to suffer from ill health for the rest of his life; it also explains the horror of war which is soon seen in his work. On 2 June 1915 he was posted home as unfit for active service and spent the next three months at Hadamar. Released from hospital in October 1915, he had to spend another year officially on garrison duty but in fact unfit much of the time, before finally being invalided out.

His development from patriot to pacifist to communist to nationalist was typical of his generation. A Catholic, he was brought to the edge of religious despair by the war: 'Gott starb am Menschen, im Menschen,' he wrote in 1931. His war poetry, in which he speaks for the common soldier, is filled by an ever deeper compassion; he is indeed the 'Feldpostsänger des ersten Weltkrieges' (Julius Bab). He produced the best popular poetry and the best genuinely religious poetry of this war in which pseudo-religion loomed so large. Having said this, his achievement as a war poet can now be seen to be more limited than it seemed in 1934, when Ronald Peacock wrote that 'in truth of all the war poets he is the most powerful through a consistent and uniform body of work'.[8] This title, we can now see, unquestionably belongs to Anton Schnack, whose *Tier rang gewaltig mit Tier* Peacock appears not to have known. When we have read some of Lersch's best poems, we shall be in a position to return to this subject. Whatever his poetic stature, he was certainly one of the most prolific of the German war poets. His war poems appeared, first, in the form of a series of ten pamphlets published at München-Gladbach by the Sekretariat Sozialer Studentenarbeit between 1915 and 1918.[9] These pamphlet collections are given the collective title of *Kriegsgedichte*.

Partly because of the ephemeral nature of paperbacked pamphlets, Lersch's war poetry is more often associated with the two collections in book form in which it also appeared. These two major collections are: *Herz! Aufglühe dein Blut. Gedichte im Kriege* (1916; contains the poems he wrote on active service) and *Deutschland! Lieder und Gesänge von Volk und Vaterland* (1918; contains retrospective war poems). An earlier collection, *Abglanz des Lebens* (München-Gladbach: Verlag der westdeutschen Arbeiterzeitung, 1914) contains his pre-war poetry. A selection of his poems appeared in 1935 under the title *Deutschland muss leben*; reprints in 1940, 1941, 1943 (*Feldpostausgabe*) and 1944 (*Wehrmachtausgabe*) brought the edition to 95,000. His *Ausgewählte Werke* appeared in two volumes in 1965-6; the first volume contains many of his war poems, while the second contains letters dating from the war years.

Like the great majority of poets on either side, Lersch was, initially, very much the patriot. It is the enthusiastic, unquestioning patriotism of the hour that informs his first and most famous war poem, 'Soldatenabschied',[10] which begins:

Lass mich gehn, Mutter, lass mich gehn!
All das Weinen kann uns nichts mehr nützen,
denn wir gehn, das Vaterland zu schützen!

The poem consists of five six-line stanzas rhyming abbacc. The predominantly trochaic rhythm is varied, as is the number of feet per line; trochees and feminine endings (on the bc lines) represent soldiers and mothers respectively. The real naiveté of the poem appears in its sentiments and diction, which make it no longer quotable as a whole, although the final stanza is an exception:

> Nun lebt wohl, Menschen, lebet wohl!
> Und wenn wir für euch und unsere Zukunft fallen,
> soll als letzter Gruss zu euch hinüberhallen:
> Nun lebt wohl, ihr Menschen, lebet wohl!
> Ein freier Deutscher kennt kein kaltes Müssen:
> Deutschland muss leben, und wenn wir sterben müssen!

It was, I suppose, those last two lines that made the poem so famous at the time. In retrospect one sees only that the poem as a whole is spoilt by its whimsical diction and that Lersch as yet clearly lacked the language to match his idealism, which is itself as yet unoriginal; it is only when his idealism develops in a personal direction and he finds the visionary language to match it that his work becomes more remarkable. At the time, however, it was a different story. First published in the *Westdeutsche Landeszeitung* for 4 August 1914, the poem reappeared the following day in the *Kölnische Volkszeitung* and was then reprinted countless times in newspapers, periodicals and anthologies. Like Bröger's even more famous 'Bekenntnis', 'Soldatenabschied' represents an instinctive, emotional reaction to the war and the threat which it brings to his country. English readers need to remember that Germany felt just as innocent and just as indignant as England did. Whether either side should have felt differently is not the issue here. The point is the poetry which the simple, patriotic response brought forth.

Most of Lersch's other early war poems express a similarly uncomplicated view of things in an even more naive form. A good example is 'Ballade', which begins:

> Die Nacht ist so dunkel, der Sturm geht so laut,
> all die Sterne sind tot und verweht.
> In Deutschland steht eines Soldaten Braut
> am Fenster und sinnt ein Gebet.

The poem, which ends with Heaven reflected in the dead soldier's eyes, is an unhappy attempt to recapture the directness and naiveté of the folk ballad. Implicitly the poem glorifies war and death by using the heroic ballad form. The dead soldier, who at the end looks like nothing so much as Millais' 'Ophelia', has clearly gone where all good heroes go. As a treatment of death and grief in the 1914-15 context it is inadequate, and, besides, Lersch himself later wrote that death is not the worst; worse than death is a living death.[11] More relevant still is what Lersch wrote to Petzold on 13 February 1915, that since being in the army he had not needed to go on writing poems.[12] His 'Ballade' was written at the beginning of October 1914, at a time when he had no way of knowing what he was talking about.

Now although his active service, which ended so horribly, caused Lersch to change his simplistic view of war, the balladesque form remains a permanent feature of his work. It is modified, true, and his best poems tend to be written in other forms, but the ballad remains the basis of his war poetry, as it does of Karl Bröger's. This is, ultimately, his great weakness as a war poet. The naive, ballad form is, I think, only compatible with the realities of this war when ironised by a poet like Brecht; otherwise the naive form either leads to or prevents the poet from going beyond naiveté of thought. Lersch is not an ironist and is not sufficiently sophisticated to use the ballad form successfully. This is shown by one of his better-known poems, 'Im Schützengraben', which was first published in 1916, but which dates from his period of service in the trenches in spring 1915. The poem is informed by a compassion and sense of brotherhood which is more fully developed and much more convincingly expressed in the famous poem 'Brüder'. The trouble with 'Im Schützengraben' is that it is cast in a form which positively encourages the poet in his naive, unconvincing attitude. The heroic ballad form and heroic diction are unsuited to the expression of real compassion. The poet's remorse - 'Mein Kamerad Franzos, dich traf ich gut! / Du musst nicht böse sein, dass ich dich schoss' - remains on a puerile level and in any case seems false because of the inappropriate echoes of Uhland's poem, long become a folk ballad, 'Ich hatt' einen Kameraden'. The remorse is therefore a matter of words merely and the words simply do not ring true, despite the fact that the poet identifies with the dead and indeed expresses the worker-poet's international idealism in the final stanza:

Wir hören's nicht. Wir liegen kalt und tot.
Uns weckt kein Singen, keines Friedens Gruss,
auf unsern Leibern steht der Menschheit Fuss:
Sie schaut hinein ins neue Morgenrot.

Though a new attitude to the war on Lersch's part is clearly struggling for expression, the tension between incipient internationalism and time-hallowed heroic-patriotic form is grotesque. In the case of 'Der Kriegsinvalide', discussed below, it is a different matter.

Simple but honest and also courageous is Lersch's second best-known poem, 'Brüder'. First published in the *Westdeutsche Arbeiterzeitung* for 26 June 1915 under the title 'Der Tote', 'Brüder' is impressive in its simplicity:

Es lag schon lang ein Toter vor unserm Drahtverhau,
die Sonne auf ihn glühte, ihn kühlte Wind und Tau.

Ich sah ihm alle Tage in sein Gesicht hinein,
und immer fühlt ich's fester: Es muss mein Bruder sein.

Ich sah in allen Stunden, wie er so vor mir lag,
und hörte seine Stimme aus frohem Friedenstag.

Oft in der Nacht ein Weinen, das aus dem Schlaf mich trieb:
Mein Bruder, lieber Bruder – hast du mich nicht mehr lieb?

Bis ich, trotz allen Kugeln, zur Nacht mich ihm genaht
und ihn geholt. – Begraben: – Ein fremder Kamerad.

Es irrten meine Augen. – Mein Herz, du irrst dich nicht:
Es hat ein jeder Toter des Bruders Angesicht.

As Sir Maurice Bowra remarked in his Taylorian Lecture for 1961,[13] Lersch 'comes close to what many men felt' as he tells of a dead man hanging on the wire in front of his trench. He fancies the man is his brother and imagines that he can hear him crying out. It is only when he has crawled out to bring him in for burial that he sees that it was not his brother; no matter, for all the dead are joined in brotherhood – as the living should be. Because it is a matter not of subtlety of argument or response, but of the natural wisdom of the heart, the simple rhyming couplets are entirely suitable. Precisely because of its simplicity 'Brüder' remains in its way a classic, a true reflection of what most of the combatants came to feel. The point underlying 'Brüder' was expressed more abstractly and sophisticatedly in a poem by Bruno Frank, 'Dort, wo der Tod am nächsten droht', which was also written in 1915:

Dort, wo der Tod am nächsten droht,
Dort ist nicht Hohn und ist nicht Hass,
Bereitschaft herrscht ohn Unterlass
Und Schweigen vor dem Tod.

Ein Schicksal tötet, nicht der Feind,
Und einmal muss die Sense ruhn.
Und die sich schuldlos Arges tun,
Sie werden doch vereint.

In his early war poetry Lersch uses three forms: the folk ballad, the poem in ballad form with extended lines (e.g. 'Nachtlied'), and - more occasionally, but also more successfully - poems in free verse. His first use of free verse immediately produces a poem that stands out from his previous work in conveying a more original, personal vision. The poem is the second in the three-poem cycle entitled 'Im Artilleriefeuer':

Wir haben uns eingewühlt in der Erde Tiefen,
im Dunkel der Höhlen wähnen wir Schutz,
wie Kinder verbergen ihr Gesicht im Schosse der Mütter.
O, Mutter der Erde, dass deine Tiefen
nicht tief genug sind uns zu verbergen.
Wir wünschen, es täte ein Abgrund sich auf,
schaudernd tief,
wir ersehnen stürzende Urwälder über uns.
In allen unsern Herzenstiefen rast das heisse Verlangen:
Ströme und Meeresflut müssten den heiligen Leib der Erde zerreissen
zwischen uns und - drüben.
Unser armes, zerquältes Herz bettelt und bittet um Erdbeben und
    tiefe Nacht,
um so grosse Not, die allem Streit und Hass
zwischen den Menschen ein Ende macht.

Interestingly enough in view of the totally different form (the other two use the 'modified ballad' form), this second poem in the cycle was first published together with 'Brüder'. Like that poem, 'Im Artilleriefeuer II' expresses an attitude which was shared by many - it is also the subject of Karl Bröger's better-known but weaker poem 'Der Soldat an die Erde' - and which had not been expressed before. The poem is successful because it uses, with imagination, the unconventional form necessitated by its subject, because it expresses without any unnecessary elaboration a reaction (clinging to Mother Nature) that is as old as the human nature that the war is ultimately about, and because it ends with a dignified idealism appropriate to its subject. It is one of the first of Lersch's poems to show something of his real imagination. It is vastly superior, as a poem, to Bröger's 'Der Soldat an die Erde', which suffers from a fatal archness of diction. It is a great pity that Lersch was so rarely able to recapture the power of this poem.

The one poem in which he unquestionably does this and more is 'Massengräber':

MASSENGRÄBER

liegen in der Einsamkeit der Heide im Niederland. Dunkle Tannenwälder stehen von ferne, die Heide ist braun und der Sand ist weiss. Der hellblaue Himmel steht hoch über zerschossenen, verlassenen Dörfern.

Aber Wolken ziehn tiefer vorüber, weisse und graue Wolken, segeln vorbei. Ihre Schatten huschen herab, als grüssten sie die Toten darunter von Kameraden, die im Meere auf den Wellen treiben oder liegen hergetrieben am einsamen Strand.

Massengräber liegen verstreut über Land. Vögel seltener Art, mit langen, schwebenden Flügeln, kreisen darüber, Vögel mit schwarzem Gefieder und roten Brüsten, trauernde, liebende, suchende Sehnsuchtsstunden einsam Liebender in der Heimat.

Sie singen das Klagelied der Mütter und Bräute, der Männer und Kinder um die stolzen Helden, die Helden der Liebe und Pflicht. Singen es, suchend von Massengrab zu Massengrab, ohne Unterlass, Tag und Nacht.

Kaum berühren ihre unmächtigen Füsse, schmale untüchtige Füsse der Sehnsucht, die Erde; zum Rasten sind sie nicht geschaffen.

Schwarz sind die Augen, glänzen wie Perlen, die von Tränen geworden sind.
Aus ihrer zerrissenen Brust leuchtet das rote zuckende Herzchen aus dem Metall der Federn.

So fliegen und kreisen sie über die Länder, über die Meere.

Selten, nur selten klingt ein silberner Schrei auf, schmerzlichen Glückes voll: Ein Vogel findet seiner Liebe Ziel; wenn das Blut aus dem Herzen quillt, weiss er, da, wo es quoll, liegt seine Liebe.

Noch einmal singt er das Lied zu Ende, das Lied der Unbekannten, der vielen; immer roter rauscht der Blutstrom aus dem Herzen und dringt in die trockene, geborstene Erde hinein.
Ein schwarzes Kreuz, liegt der sterbende Vogel mit breiten Schwingen, den Kopf erhoben, auf dem Grabe.

Leiser wird das Lied, nun singt es von Wunden und Sterben, von Wiedersehn und Auferstehn, bis das Lied und der Vogel erstirbt.
Und in der Heimat trocknet eine schmerzgestärkte Mutter die letzten Tränen ab.

This is not only the most powerful poem in Lersch's first main war collection; it is, incomparably, his best war poem. Nowhere else does his work have the visionary depth and sheer poetic power that it has here. This is strange because he is reported to have been a highly imaginative person. He was also, as poems like 'Die Mutter Gottes im Schützengraben' (from *Deutschland*) show, a visionary. It may well be that this last-named poem contains the explanation for Lersch's failure to realise his full poetic potential. The explanation is, I think, that his mind was basically too conventional, so that even his 'visionary' poems tend to operate within a conventional religious framework or, occasionally, to go off the rails altogether.

'Massengräber' is a truly remarkable poem. It is like no other poem by Lersch or by any other poet. It makes marvellous use of the long line to which Schnack owes not a little of his impact. But it is not just that; Lersch had written in the long line before, though not as long as this. More crucial is the fact that his imagination never flags; here he is truly inspired, able to maintain his vision until it has been expressed. None of his besetting weaknesses are seen here (I am thinking of the usual inability to sustain his imagination, of the tendency of his diction to go flat or fall into abstractions and of a certain lack of poetic control). In 'Massengräber' the lines are not only freer than any he has deployed before; they are also beautifully controlled: modulated in rhythm and length to avoid any risk of woodenness. But this again is ultimately incidental; it is the sustained power of the imagery, never to be repeated, which makes the poem. It is time now that we forgot about Lersch the 'Feldpostsänger' and remembered and celebrated him as the writer of one of the most remarkable poems of the war. Here, fleetingly, is imaginative power of the same order as Wilfred Owen's.

After 'Massengräber', Lersch's most imaginative poem is 'Wenn es Abend wird' (from *Herz! Aufglühe dein Blut*), the first half of which deserves to be quoted:

> Wenn die letzten Strahlen der sinkenden Sonne über das Kampffeld streichen,
> steigen aus Gräbern und Grüften die toten Soldaten herauf;
> aus Gräbern in Wäldern und Schluchten, aus Gräbern in Heide und Sand;
> stehn vor ihren Hügeln betend, der Heimat zugewandt, auf fremder Erde.
>
> Es singt der Vogel in der Nacht.
>
> Da lösen sie sich, steigen auf, schweben heimatwärts,
> über zerschossene Städte, über verwüstete Felder,
> über noch kämpfende Heere,
> an blinkenden Flussläufen vorbei, hin, hin, in ihre Heimat.
>
> Dort schweben, wenn es Abend wird, Schatten heran
> von den Grenzen des Vaterlandes, von Gebirgen und Meeren,
> Schatten wie von abendroten Wolken
> senken sich, senken sich wie singende Lerchen in ihr Nest.
>
> Allüberall.
>
> Dort: am Rande des Waldes,
> wo zwischen den reifenden Feldern ein Pfad,
> von Mohn und Zyanen gesäumt, hügelan steigt,
> Gestalten:
> Selige Bewegung ausbreitender Arme; segnende Hände
> streicheln nickende Ähren, beugende Nacken senken Gesichter,
> schmerzlichen Glückes voll, in die Flut der Halme,
> führen wildblühender Blumen leuchtendes Rot und Blau
> an ihre blassen Lippen.
> Knien, die Arme gestreckt dem goldenen Reichtum des Lebens,
> im blühenden Klee.

In its way this poem is more characteristic of Lersch than 'Massengräber' was, for it shows both his strength and his weakness. This first half is only slightly less powerful than 'Massengräber' and equally concrete, equally well sustained. The trouble is that the second half of the poem tails off disastrously. Although the imagery in which the spirits of the slain are visualised in the first half of the poem is perfectly clear, Lersch now proceeds to explain it, unnecessarily and in language that is both too abstract and contains too many conventional patriotic pieties, which in the context represent an embarrassing lapse of poetic taste. Had it ended with 'im blühenden Klee', 'Wenn es Abend wird' would have been a remarkable poem; as it is, it goes on to become a remarkable failure.

Lersch's second major collection, *Deutschland. Gesänge von Volk und Vaterland*, came out in 1918; it consisted almost entirely of war poems written after he had been invalided out. The most powerful poem in the collection is 'Der Krieg und die Sinne', to which I have already referred. There is, in general, something pathetic about the volume with its sub-title that would have been more appropriate in 1914 and which seems to give the lie to the first poem in the book, an epigram entitled 'Soldaten':[14]

Granaten haben die Lieder erschlagen,
nicht Worte mehr singen das Heldentum aus.
Dem Dichter berstet das Herz von Gesängen,
sein schweigendes Staunen ist mehr als sein Lied.

It is to the 'Kriegslieder' of 1914 that Lersch's sub-title harks back. It is puzzling, to say the least, that the man who had written in 'Rückkehr aus dem Kriege' that 'Jeder, der heimkehrt vom Kriege, der ist im Meere der trauernden Menschheit eine leuchtende Insel von Glück' could go on to write such a blood-and-thunder ballad as 'Der eiserne Hauptmann', but then Lersch would not have been Lersch had he not done so.

The outstanding poem in *Deutschland* is not to be found among those which vie, unsuccessfully, with 'Massengräber'. It is, rather, one of the simplest poems in the whole book, a poem which takes us straight back to 'Soldatenabschied': 'Der Kriegsinvalide':

Ihr könnt mein Lächeln, Leute, nicht verstehn?
Ich lächle, wo ich immer geh und bin.
Ich darf noch einmal in das Leben gehn.
Für mich hat alles andern Sinn.

Ob auch mein linker Arm sich nach dem rechten sehnt
(der irgendwo verfault), das brennt wie Gift;
und doch, der linke, der sich mächtig dehnt,
der packt das Leben, wo er es nur trifft.

Ich weiss ein Land, das voll von Toten liegt.
Einst lag ich mitten unter ihnen - wund.
So oft mein Auge rückwärts schauend fliegt,
schmeckt mir die Zung wie Blut im Mund.

Noch gräbt man täglich tausend Tote ein -
ich sah sie fallen, Stück um Stück.
Ich aber lebe und die Welt ist mein.
Es gibt auf Erden ja kein grössres Glück,
als nicht Soldat, als nicht im Krieg zu sein!

This is not, of course, the poem to which Lersch referred in a letter to his brother Leo in 1916, when he said: 'Ich habe ein ganz gemeines Gedicht auf den Krieg geschrieben, das heisst der "Invalide", es ist sehr lang und enthält allen Hass auf den organisierten Völkermord, der manchmal in mir so bitter wird, das [sic] ich weinen möchte vor Wut über die Menschheit.'[15] The poem 'Der Kriegsinvalide', dating, presumably, from 1915-16, makes the same point more compactly; I find this an impressive poem because its anti-war sentiments are expressed in a form which appropriately recalls all those uncritically enthusiastic pro-war poems of 1914, including, as Lersch clearly admits, his own. Having thus come full circle, Lersch was then, in 1916-17, to describe himself as being opposed to lyricism ('lyrik-feindlich').[16] His last words on the war, however, were not written until 1930, when he said quite bluntly that his experience of war had been diabolical, horrendous.[17]

At the time, and for some time afterwards, Lersch's poetic achievement seemed greater than it actually is. It is impossible to read his work now without coming to the conclusion that he wrote very few uniformly strong poems. Few of his later poems escape from the naiveté of the earlier ones. As one would expect, *Herz! Aufglühe dein Blut* is on the whole a stronger collection than *Deutschland*; the experience of war is better not recollected in tranquillity, unless for presentation in non-lyrical (notably epic) form. In the case of Lersch, as of Bröger, it is the least characteristic poems that are the best. It could be argued that both made a serious error of poetic judgement in not stretching their wings more. The folk-ballad form which characterises Bröger's work even more than it does Lersch's has little to be said for it. It is extraordinary that Lersch, known for his imagination, should have shown such a signal failure of imagination when it came to his own poetry.

My own view is that of all Lersch's war poems 'Massengräber' alone can stand beside the best of, say, Anton Schnack. He is an honest man and an honest poet, which makes him pretty exceptional, but it is no use being blinded either by sentiment or by morality: his permanent poetic achievement is extremely small, far smaller than it should have been. Lersch and Schnack both grafted a Whitmanesque long line on to a conventional form (ballad and sonnet respectively), but Schnack alone succeeded in achieving the intensification of effect which they both sought. Lersch's images are short-winded. His long-line poems are too often naive in concept, flat in diction and slack in outline. They nearly always lack the concentration that characterises the most poetically convincing work of whatever kind. Compared with Stramm's, Lersch's rendering of an artillery bombardment falls flat, or at least falls short of the target; it has nothing of the explosive impact of Stramm. It is impossible to avoid the conclusion that Lersch is more important in the context of attitudes to war than in the context of war poetry as such.

Karl Bröger (1886-1944), who served on the Western Front throughout the war, is comparable to Heinrich Lersch in a number of ways. Worker-poet, Catholic and socialist, he wrote, in 'Bekenntnis', what became the most famous of all outbreak-of-war poems when it was quoted in the *Reichstag* by Chancellor Bethmann-Hollweg. Bröger produced three collections of war poetry: *Aus meiner Kriegszeit. Gedichte* (1915), *Kamerad, als wir marschiert. Kriegsgedichte* (1916, an extended reprint of the previous title) and *Soldaten der Erde. Neue Kriegsgedichte* (1918). He continued to produce poetry prolifically after the war. *Sturz und Erhebung. Gesamtausgabe der Gedichte* (1943 [= 1944]) purports to be his collected poems, but includes only a fraction of his war poetry (to wit: 25 poems). Together with Lersch, Bröger produced the most memorable war poetry of any 'worker-poet' proper; his work remains even more closely tied to the popular ballad. Much of what has been said about Lersch in general terms applies also to Bröger. His vividly realistic and much-reprinted war novel, *Bunker 17. Geschichte einer Kameradschaft* (1929; in English, *Pillbox 17*, translated by Oakley Williams, London, 1930), shows his political naiveté. He also wrote an autobiographical novel, *Der Held im Schatten* (1920).

In an autobiographical foreword specially written for the English translation of *Bunker 17*, Bröger gave a conveniently brief retrospective account of his war:

[Having previously spent two years, from 1906 to 1908, as a Bavarian infantryman,] I was mobilized as a militia man in the 7th Company of the 6th Bavarian Reserve [Infantry] Regiment, and was wounded in the early fighting for the Loretto heights. I can still see the First Aid label through the second buttonhole (from the top) of my tunic; its single red edge indicated urgent treatment. The French splinter was embedded in back of my head, but had been considerate enough to give the artery a miss. In any case the wound was serious enough to put me out of action. I spent the rest of the war, as no doubt every sentient and thinking human being, whether at home or on active service, spent it, in realizing it to be the greatest disaster that has ever overtaken the human race. My most noteworthy feat of arms lies in the fact that throughout my whole course of active service I did not fire a single shot from my rifle, model 98. This was not due to any deliberate intention on my part. In action I was a runner orderly, constantly in the front line, but I was not allowed to fire because my functions were those of a postman rather than a rifleman. The number of times I missed being shot is evidence that Heaven had a purpose in view for me.

Any account of Bröger's war poetry must begin with the poem that made him famous, 'Bekenntnis',[18] which illustrates, as perhaps no other German poem did to the same degree, the simple, almost inarticulate patriotism of the man in the street in the first days of the war:

Immer schon haben wir eine Liebe zu dir gekannt,
bloss wir haben sie nie mit einem Namen genannt.
Als man uns rief, da zogen wir schweigend fort,
auf den Lippen nicht, aber im Herzen das Wort
    Deutschland.

Unsre Liebe war schweigsam; sie brütete tiefversteckt.
Nun ihre Zeit gekommen, hat sie sich hochgereckt.
Schon seit Monden schirmt sie in Ost und West dein Haus,
und sie schreitet gelassen durch Sturm und Wettergraus,
    Deutschland.

Dass kein fremder Fuss betrete den heimischen Grund,
stirbt ein Bruder in Polen, liegt einer in Flandern wund.
Alle hüten wir deiner Grenze heiligen Saum.
Unser blühendstes Leben für deinen dürrsten Baum,
    Deutschland.

Immer schon haben wir eine Liebe zu dir gekannt,
bloss wir haben sie nie bei ihrem Namen genannt.
Herrlich zeigte es aber deine grösste Gefahr,
dass dein ärmster Sohn auch dein getreuester war.
    Denk es, o Deutschland.

Bröger's lack of subtlety is compensated by his transparent honesty and lack of rhetoric. His poem is an immediate response to the emotional pressure of the time in both a general and a particular sense. In a general way the poem shows the awakening of national consciousness in response to an external threat. At such a time people 'are suddenly aware that they belong to something much larger than themselves and have towards it obligations which they cannot shirk ... For the moment, the emotional pressure is so strong that it hardly allows analysis of what it means.'[19] Events themselves showed that this was an occasion when people acted first and thought a good deal later. It was the same on both sides. A more reasoned and sophisticated poem would not have been a true reflection of the national mood in the way in which this one was. We can, however, be more specific about the national mood and the particular way in which 'Bekenntnis' was a response to it, for Bröger's poem is in fact an elaboration of the words of the Social Democratic Party leadership in the *Reichstag* on 4 August 1914: 'Wir lassen in der Stunde der Gefahr das Vaterland nicht im Stich!' It was with these words that the Socialists, hitherto regarded as 'enemies of the Reich', announced their decision to vote for the war credits, a decision which was immensely popular (quite apart from anything else). On 27 February 1917 Chancellor Bethmann-Hollweg alluded to Bröger's 'Bekenntnis' in the *Reichstag*, his reference to 'ein Volk, von dem ein ergreifendes Wort eines feldgrauen Dichters sagen konnte, dass sein ärmster Sohn auch sein getreuester war' provoking lively applause from the left of the house.[20] An obvious parallel to Bröger's 'Bekenntnis' being quoted in the *Reichstag* is Rupert Brooke's 'The Soldier' being quoted from the pulpit of St Paul's by Dean Inge on Easter Sunday, 1915. Vastly superior as they are as poetry, Rupert Brooke's outbreak-of-war poems do not voice much more subtle sentiments. Bröger's poem was also quoted with approval by a later German Chancellor, Adolf Hitler, in his address to the First Congress of German Workers on 10 May 1933.[21]

In justice to Bröger it must be stressed that he, unlike some other 'worker-poets', resisted Hitler's blandishments. That his 'collected' poems came out in 1943 is hardly surprising; nor is it surprising that a selection of his poetry appeared in a *Feldpostausgabe* (of 45,000) under the title *Volk, ich leb aus dir* (1940-41). The title of this selection explains its appearance: the patriotism which Bröger discovered in August 1914 was to remain with him. 'Bekenntnis' is an important poetic document; it is also a better poem than Lersch's comparable 'Soldatenabschied', to say nothing of the thousands of similar poems. Lersch, incidentally, also wrote a patriotic poem entitled 'Bekenntnis' (the key line is 'Ich glaub an Deutschland wie an Gott'), which appeared in his *Deutschland*, while Bröger also produced a work with the title *Deutschland* (Ein lyrischer Gang in 3 Kreisen, Rudolstadt: Greifenverlag, 1923).

'Bekenntnis' reappeared in due course as the opening poem of Bröger's *Kamerad, als wir marschiert*. The poems which followed it were essentially folk ballads; for the most part they lacked the descriptive poetic quality of the conventional narrative poems produced by the English minor poets. An exception to this rule is 'Nachtmarsch':

Schwer wuchtet der Tornister auf dem Rücken,
ein Spaten klappert manchmal, ein Gewehr –
Die müden Schultern vorgestemmt, entrücken
wir Glied um Glied ins graue Ungefähr.

So seltsam wesenlose Dinge gleiten
an unsrer langen Marschkolonne hin.
Des fremden Landes fremde Dunkelheiten
umgaukeln schwankend den gespannten Sinn.

Aus geisterhaft verhängtem Grunde heben
Gesichte sich, umballt von Nebelrauch,
und wenn sie nahe uns vorüberschweben,
streift jeden süsslich dumpfer Totenhauch.

Am tiefen Himmel widerzuckt ein Scheinen.
Weit drüben stehen Dörfer loh im Brand.
In sich gekrümmt wie lang verhaltenes Weinen
liegt endlos weit das stahlbesäte Land.

Nur selten, dass in dies gedehnte Grauen
ein breiter Schwall blühweissen Lichtes fällt,
als wollte einen Weg des Friedens bauen
der Mond herüber in die blutige Welt.

'Nachtmarsch' stands out because here Bröger is responding to his subject both humanly and poetically, which he does not always do. The description is sensitive and exact. The regular alternating rhymes unobstrusively echo the marching column; there is no sign here of the arch doggerel into which this type of poem all too easily degenerates. The poem starts with the most obvious and tangible ('Schwer wuchtet der Tornister auf dem Rücken'), goes on to the less tangible but no less real (the strange unreality of the nightscape) and ends with a poeticism that is totally justified in that it both transcends the scene and constitutes a sensitive implied comment on it. It is not a 'powerful' poem, but it is one which shows Bröger at his best. It invites comparison with Carl Zuckmayer's 'Morituri':

Truppen marschieren bei Nacht.
Alle Gesichter sind gleich:
Fleckig und bleich,
Helmüberdacht.

Mancher hebt sein Gesicht
Jäh aus dem Mantelkragen:
Hörte er eben nicht
Laut seinen Namen sagen?

Ins Auge runnt Schweiss,
Schweiss beisst im Genick.
Wohl dem, der nichts weiss
Von fremdem Geschick.

Zuckmayer's poem was written in 1917 and appeared first in *Die Aktion* and subsequently in his collection *Der Baum* (1926). Bröger's poem, written in iambic pentameters, is - as one would expect - the more conventional. Zuckmayer's rather more 'expressionistic' poem is written in mixed two- and three-beat dactylic lines which give a more laconic, taciturn and tense impression; his title is much more explicit than Bröger's simple descriptive title. Two very different but equally effective ways of treating the same subject. Carl Zuckmayer, who served on the Western Front throughout the war, went on to make his name as a playwright with the anti-militaristic comedies *Der fröhliche Weinberg* (1925) and *Der Hauptmann von Köpenick* (1931). His war story *Engele von Loewen* (1952) was filmed under the title *Ein Mädchen in Flandern* in 1955. He also wrote an adaptation of Hemingway's *A Farewell to Arms*. His early poetry is virtually unknown.

The other outstanding poem in Bröger's first collection is 'Sang der Granaten':[22]

> Eiserne Vögel des Krieges stossen wir aus der Luft.
> Unsern Aufgag umwittert Gefahr, unsern Niedergang Gruft.
>
> Unsichtbare Schwingen dicht an den Leib geklappt,
> stählerne Fänge zu tödlichem Griff gekappt,
> lassen wir uns auf Menschen und Dinge schmetternd nieder
> und entspreiten das hundertzackige Stahlgefieder.
> Fliegen wir dann von der bebenden Erde wieder auf,
> wirft unser Flügelschlag Bäume und Häuser zuhauf.
> Alle Stille erstirbt, jeder sanfte Klang
> vor unserm erderschütternden Donnergesang.
> Immer, ob wir schwirren aus Ost oder West, aus Süd oder Nord,
> heult vor uns her das grausige Lied vom Mord.
>
> Raubvögel des Todes stürzen wir aus der Luft.
> Unsern Aufgabe umwittert Gefahr, unsern Niedergang Gruft.

Quite unlike any other of his poems, except perhaps the weaker 'Zug der Verwundeten', 'Sang der Granaten' shows Bröger producing a piece of more or less pure poetry; presumably this is why it was not included in *Sturz und Erhebung*. The nature of the poem is shown by its title and form. It is written in rhyming couplets in lines which carry intimations of the heroic mode and therefore of the days when war was a matter of chivalry and chivalric-heroic poetry; the preponderance of dactyls reinforces this 'poetic' impression. Bröger elaborates nicely on his initial metaphor. But there is more to the poem than this; it is more than a poetic exercise, more than an elaboration of the 'poetry of war'. Immediately before the near-refrain, which shows the next round of shelling beginning, Bröger drops a bombshell into what has seemed to be the placid pool of his poem. Long after we have read the poem that word 'Mord' remains in the mind. It brilliantly justifies what might otherwise have seemed an unjustifiable piece of aestheticism. As in 'Nachtmarsch', Bröger is again in complete control of his poem.

This is not always the case, although it is true that Bröger is unfortunate in that some of his poems invite comparison, to their disadvantage, with similar poems by other poets. Thus 'Patrouille in der Nacht' is feeble when compared with Stramm's 'Patrouille'; 'Zug der Verwundeten' is less impressive than any of Klemm's comparable poems; and the opening poem of his second collection, 'Der Soldat an die Erde', is abstractly and archly weak in comparison with Lersch's 'Im Artilleriefeuer, II'. But it is not just that. Bröger is in fact, like Lersch, a poet with very obvious limitations. Their strengths are complementary; Lersch has, at his best, greater imaginative power, while Bröger is better able to see a poetic conception through to the end. Both are, however, liable to lapse; neither has the consistency of Stramm, Schnack and Trakl, or even of Klemm and Lichtenstein.

Bröger's second collection of war poems, *Soldaten der Erde*, is not unnaturally both more varied and rather more war-weary than his first. In terms of poetic quality there is little to choose between them. The new collection also contains few really outstanding poems. The two most interesting are 'Das rote Wirtshaus' and 'Die Gärten des Todes', which stand out by reason of their vividness.

This certainly applies to 'Das rote Wirtshaus':

Drüben, wo sich die schmalen, weissen
Bänder der Strasse zum Knoten verweben,
steht - einst "cabaret rouge" geheissen -
ein Trümmerhaufen ... zerscherbtes Leben ...

Sparren und Giebel ausgebrannt,
geschwärzt und zerborsten die rötlichen Mauern,
starrt es mit toten Augen ins Land,
umweht von Herbstwind und Nebelschauern.

Drinnen sitzt ein hagerer Gast
allein und schweigend am runden Tisch.
Der seit Monden hier zecht, seit Monden hier prasst.
Deutsche sein Fleisch, Franzosen sein Fisch.

Manchmal erhebt sich der einsame Zecher
und streckt die Knochenarme ins Licht,
dass ein Strahl sich in dem beinernen Becher,
sich im blutig funkelnden Weine bricht.

> Schattet Abend die Wiesen und Bäche,
> die Nacht zieht vorbei in silbernem Boot,
> dann torkelt über die flimmernde Fläche
> trunkener Tod.

Vivid, gruesome, increasingly predictable: the poem is all these. But it is also an excellent example of the genuinely successful modern popular ballad. The ballad form is in this case the only possible one; it harks back to the oral tradition in which 'war poetry' has its distant origins and ultimately to the nature of human nature. It recalls too, of course, the medieval dance of death and is far more effective than the following poem in the collection, which actually bears the title 'Totentanz'. However great the differences between kinds of warfare at various times in history, war has always been about death: death on the rampage, ravishing men's minds and bodies alike. Bröger's personification of death, prefigured in the dead-eyed house, belongs on all the battlefields of history; it has the same kind of mythical dimension as Heym's figure of Death Triumphant. Bröger's final image of Death, drunk with success, reeling over the battlefield, points to man's absolute subjection to death. Popular ballad, yes, but a triumphantly successful one which transcends actuality as relatively few more sophisticated poems do.

No less vivid, but completely different in form, is another poem with a similar theme, 'Die Gärten des Todes':

> Aus Millionen zerspaltener Herzen glüht
> die kalte, duftlose Pracht.
> Nie haben die Gärten des Todes reicher geblüht,
> nie haben Erde und Meer so in seinen Farben geglüht
> wie diese Nacht.
>
> Beet bei Beet
> stehen die Blüten dicht gedrängt.
>
> Der Herr der Gärten geht
> durch die langen Zeilen, sinnend die Arme verschränkt.
> Aus dem Tränenstrom, der durch die Gärten fliesst,
> schöpft er Wasser, wenn er die Furchen begiesst,
> und wendet stumm
> neue Erde für neuen Samen um.
> Dann mit leeren Blicken auf seine Harke gelehnt
> folgt er der Flucht der Gärten, die sich in den Himmel dehnt.

Gehen die Sterne noch immer den alten Gang?
Die Gärten des Todes prahlen in ihrem blühendsten Überschwang.

The figure of gardening death is as different as may be from the figure of the drunken reveller in the previous poem. This is reflected in the form of the poem. The poem is short, as it needs to be, for the gardens of death could easily have become boring; the endless varieties of death and endless deaths are suggested, initially, by the variety of the rhyme pattern (this variety is replaced by a constant pattern in the second half of the poem, because what is in question are different varieties of the same thing) and then by the way in which the end-rhymes and the number of stressed syllables per line are played off one against the other, giving the impression of an almost endless variety of permutations. Given the simplicity and shortness of the poem, both necessitated by the subject, all the different deaths and manners of dying represented by the serried ranks in Death's garden are suggested with considerable skill. Whether Bröger's starting-point was those simple crosses to be seen everywhere, or the poppies made more abundant by the unburied dead, or something else, does not matter, for he has produced a memorable poem. We now know that death flowered from some 10,000,000 hearts.

With the exception of these two poems, *Soldaten der Erde* seems to me to contain no poems that are not flawed in one way or another; something similar applied to his previous collection, just as it applied to the work of Heinrich Lersch. Bröger's achievement as a war poet is different from Lersch's, but in its way just as limited. He wrote nothing on a level with 'Massengräber', and there is no reason to think that he had it in him to do so. But he did produce, in 'Nachtmarsch', 'Sang der Granaten', 'Das rote Wirtshaus' and 'Die Gärten des Todes', four poems which are successful on a humbler level. What is surprising is not that both poets did not produce more poems on this imaginative level, but that they produced these poems at all.

Other worker-poets wrote war poetry. One thinks above all of Alfons Petzold (author of *Krieg*, 1914; *Volk, mein Volk*, 1915; *Der stählerne Schrei*, 1916; *Dämmerung der Herzen*, 1917). But the other important poet in this context is Gerrit Engelke.

Gerrit Engelke (born 21 October 1890), the most original of the 'Werkleute auf Haus Nyland', began writing poetry at the age of 20, by which time his parents had emigrated to the United States. He was helped into print by Richard Dehmel, by then a respected poetic elder statesman, who later said straight out that Engelke was a better poet than he was himself. At the outbreak of war Engelke was at Faarborg in Denmark, beginning to write his novel *Don Juan*. He was tempted to stay in neutral Denmark to continue writing - after all, the war was not expected to last long - but his conscience drove him home. He joined up in Flensburg in October 1914, as a private soldier, and in December was posted to Landwehr-Ersatz-Battaillon 85 in Sonderburg. From February 1915 onwards he served in the trenches near Langemarck, on the Yser, at the Somme, in Champagne, near Dünaburg, outside Verdun and at St Mihiel. He won the Iron Cross while serving on the Yser. For nine months he belonged to a permanent patrol. In winter 1916 a selection of his poetry appeared in a volume entitled *Schulter an Schulter*, which also contained work by Heinrich Lersch and Karl Zielke. This anthology, which sold well enough for a reprint to be called for, brought Engelke into touch with Heinrich Lersch, whom he eventually met in April 1918, when he was recovering from a wound. In May 1918 Engelke returned to the front after an absence of six months. In the last months of the war Heinrich Lersch did everything he could to have Engelke taken out of the front line and, despite Engelke's indignation, almost succeeded. But not quite. Engelke fell on 11 October 1918 near Cambrai (his last letter was addressed from Cannières). He was picked up the following day and taken to an English dressing station, where he died on 13 October 1918. He is buried in the military cemetary at Étaples, the base from which Wilfred Owen set out for the front line following his return to Flanders in 1918. Owen fell two weeks later, crossing the nearby Sambre canal. Owen and Engelke may very well have faced one another in the trenches, as did Ernst Stadler and Charles Péguy almost 10 million deaths earlier. Of all the worker-poets Engelke was quite the least enthusiastic about the war, which he hated. Some 400 of his letters from the years 1912 to 1918 have been preserved; his *Gesamtwerk* includes many wartime letters. His collected poems appeared in 1921 under the appropriately Whitmanesque title *Rhythmus des neuen Europa*. His collected works (*Das Gesamtwerk*)[23] appeared in 1960.

From the very beginning Engelke took a keen interest in the poetry of the war, most of which he detested. Within a month of war breaking out he was asking for some war poems to be sent to him.[24] One of the few early war poems of which he approved was Dehmel's 'Lied an Alle'.[25] In general he found most such productions feeble ('matt'),[26] commenting on the way in which many writers were simply rehashing earlier war poetry. By 10 December 1914 we find him writing of the wretchedness of most of the war poetry being written at the time (his own word is 'Kriegslyrikmisere');[27] he knew that too many people were writing too much too fast - he included Rilke in that category[28] - and that most of what was being produced was rubbish. He found particularly tiresome the poetry-writing gentlemen sitting at home by their firesides.[29] For Engelke it was a matter of pride that he did not produce any 'Kriegslyrik' himself.[30] He wrote relatively few poems about the war and was mostly not satisfied with what he had written. An exception was the poem which he sent to Richard Dehmel on 15 December 1914, referring to it as a contribution to the current epidemic of war poetry, but adding that he reckoned it to be one of his best poems;[31] he does not name the poem, but it seems most likely that it is 'Im Marschieren'. At various times he spoke of a projected 'faustische Kriegsdichtung'[32] - mercifully the project was shelved - and of his plan to write a verse epic not about any national war, but about war as such,[33] which might well have turned out better than most. On several occasions he wonders whether the right time to write about the war will not be when it is over. He had strong views not only on the war and the nature of war as such, but on how war should be depicted. Thus he wrote to Jakob Kreip on 12 April 1917: 'Das ist auch meine Ansicht, dass eine Darstellung der Krieges ins Übersinnliche steigen, alles örtliche und zeitliche Geschehen (Schlachten) aber frei verwalten muss. Mir persönlich ist nur ein Gewaltiges vor allem anderen herauszuheben: Tod: Massentod, Schrecken.'[34] One of the side-effects of war was to sharpen literary judgements: at such a time literary works were immediately seen to be either necessary or unnecessary.[35] Most of them were the latter. While Engelke himself was a fairly shrewd judge in such matters, others clearly were not, for at no other time in history have so many totally superfluous works been produced in such a short time.

Engelke's immediate reaction to the war was to hope it would go away again. When it did not, he first wrote a war sketch ('Die Festung') to salve his conscience and, when that did not work, he returned to Germany to enlist. In retrospect he said that he should have done so at once. The 'Tagebuchblätter aus dem Kriege',[36] dated 24 December 1914, show that at that time he took a positive view of the war, which he, like so many others, hoped would have a purifying, revitalising effect on the nation. He was, however, less committed to the national idea than either Lersch or Bröger. Though a provincial North German, Engelke was spiritually a citizen of the world; his reading alone shows this. Notwithstanding the uncharacteristically silly 'Tagebuchblätter aus dem Kriege', written on Christmas Eve 1914, clearly in a moment of patriotic sentimentality, if not of outright inebriation, his letters show that he was opposed to the war from the beginning. To Jakob Kneip he wrote on 18 November 1914 that he was still instinctively opposed to the war;[37] his letters show that he became increasingly fed up with it. On 29 April 1918 he said that as soldier and serviceman he had the feeling of being buried alive.[38] His most striking comments on the war bring us back to how the war can be expressed:

> Ich glaube, dass der Krieg als solcher sich überhaupt nicht gestalten lässt. Dieser Krieg nicht. Erstens, weil er so ungeheuer kompliziert ist . . . und zweitens, weil ihm doch eigentlich die Seele fehlt . . . Der eine grosse Ton der letzten Not, wie er so manchem der früheren kleineren Kriege die Seele war, fehlt dem unseren.
>
> Dieser Krieg wird in der Gestaltung durch die Kunst wohl immer nur als zeitbestimmte, so grossartige wie wahnsinnig blutige Geschehensunterlage wirken. Krieg ist die Verneinung oder doch mindestens Verkümmerung des Seelischen und Erweiterung der Macht des Materiellen.[39]
>
> Alle Kultur, und dazu gehört ja auch die jetzt so berüchtigte 'Literatur', entspriesst dem Frieden. Dem Frieden, den sie halten hilft und dem sie dient. Krieg ist *immer* Vernichtung, mag er noch so heilig sein. Krieg fördert die Kultur nicht, sondern hindert sie am Wachsen oder gar am Leben. Wir hier fühlen den Krieg mit all seinen Wirkungen am eignen Leibe als den *Krieg an sich*! So will auch meine Auffassung vom Kriege in diesem Sinne als eine *allgemeine*, nicht als deutschnationale verstanden sein. . . . Meine bisherige Dichtung besonders dient dem Frieden, der Menschenbrüderlichkeit.[40]
>
> Unser Krieg ist bluternst und tragisch - nicht so theaternd-pathetisch und hurra-optimistisch wie man ihn vom Schreibtisch aus sieht oder konstruiert.[41]

These passages show that Engelke thought about the war in a way in which Bröger and probably Lersch did not. They show too - the two things go together - that he is unlikely to be found composing narrowly or thoughtlessly patriotic poems. Had he done so his work would hardly have been published in the United States (in newspapers in Port Blakeley and Seattle) in October-December 1915.

Engelke's work is as sincere as his language is powerful. He was influenced by Walt Whitman, with whom the 'modern attitude' to war of 'compassionate realism' has been said to originate. From 1914 Whitman's work was widely translated and he was hailed as the 'singer of war'; later, towards the end of the war, be became the 'poet of democracy' in the new, revolutionary sense which the word 'democracy' had by then acquired; finally, following the armistice, he became the 'poet of peace'. In a letter dated 11 July 1918 Engelke wrote: 'Ich habe den guten grauen Walt Whitman, der wird mir draussen Trost sein.' On 25 July he wrote of 'mein lieber Vater Walt Whitman', adding: 'Er ist immer in der Herztasche meines Rockes. Dieser Dichtermensch ist unendlich . . . Du musst ihn kennen! Ihn kennen und lieben, ist nur die einzige Möglichkeit.'[42] The last book that he read, shortly before his death, was a monograph on Whitman. Remembering Sassoon's and Rosenberg's acknowledgement of their indebtedness to Whitman, the tragedy of this war in which poet fought poet is again brought home. The volume of Whitman that Engelke carried around with him will have been either Franz Blei's selection from *Leaves of Grass, Hymnen für die Erde* (Insel Bücherei, 1914), which he received from a friend of Heinrich Lersch on 30 June 1918, or the volume that he much preferred, Johannes Schlaf's translation of *Leaves of Grass* (*Grashalme*, Reclam, 1907). A number of references in his published letters[43] show his veneration for Whitman.

In his diary Engelke wrote, apparently in 1918, that in the face of death all talk of 'heroism' pales into theatrical insignificance.[44] Though the horrors of the battlefield deaths were still to come, his poem 'An den Tod',[45] published in spring 1914, reads like a war poem:

Mich aber schone, Tod,
Mir dampft noch Jugend blutstromrot, -
Noch hab ich nicht mein Werk erfüllt,
Noch ist die Zukunft dunstverhüllt -
Drum schone mich, Tod.

Wenn später einst, Tod,
Mein Leben verlebt ist, verloht
Ins Werk - wenn das müde Herz sich neigt,
Wenn die Welt mir schweigt, -
Dann trage mich fort, Tod.

The naked subjectivism of this poem is the very opposite of the wartime exhortations to die a heroic death 'on the altar of the Fatherland'. Engelke's poem, although written before the war, is a simple prayer ('spare *me*') that must have been silently voiced by countless members of his generation. We have already seen Lichtenstein's jocular yet wholly serious 'Gebet vor der Schlacht'. Before the war death was for the young poet the absolute antithesis of life. By the time he had suffered the living death of the war for four years, death had come to be regarded rather differently:

Tod ist Leben
Leben - Schweben,
Angstvoll schön -
Immer Wolken in den Höh'n
    Überall . . .

These lines are the last stanza of a poem entitled 'Saaten säen', which, although not dated by Engelke's editor, appears to have been written in mid-1918. These lines in particular seem to have pleased Engelke; he quoted them two or three times in his letters. Though romantically ambivalent, they do clearly suggest that life and death may have changed meanings in the poet's mind. It is not the first time we have met this reaction.

One of the first and best of Engelke's war poems is 'Im Marschieren':

Sie treten alle stramm im Marsch,
Die Feldtornister sind nicht schwer,
Sie schultern kräftig ihr Gewehr
Und singen kunterbunt und barsch.
Linker Tritt, linker Tritt, marsch . . .

Ich sing nicht mit, weil ich nicht mag;
Die Knarre drückt, ich gehe krumm,
Ich bin im Kopfe stumm und dumm -
Man singt von Müllers Taubenschlag.
Linker Tritt, linker Tritt, marsch . . .

Sie haben all' ein Herz zu Haus,
Ein Weib, ein Liebchen oder zwei -
Bekommen Wurst und allerlei,
Tabak und warmes Unterflaus -
Linker Tritt, linker Tritt, marsch . . .

Ich denk an eine (die ist schlecht),
Die schweigt, die gar nicht an mich denkt, -

Ich bin allein und unbeschenkt
Und soll doch auch bald ins Gefecht!
Linker Tritt, linker Tritt, marsch . . .

This was written on 16 November 1914, exactly a month after he had written home from Faarborg to say that he was about to return to Germany to enlist. On 16 November he had been in the army about three weeks. Presumably marching loomed large in his basic training. Be this as it may, he has written a poem which, if it has little to do with war in terms of fighting, is an excellent expression of its subject; we have already seen how Bröger and Zuckmayer treated the night march. Basic to Engelke's poem is the 'left-right' pattern. The poem consists of a series of contrasts. The first four lines of each stanza are four-beat iambic; the fifth line, being three-beat dactylic, breaks into or counterpoints the established rhythm. The fifth line represents the refrain of the song which the recruits will be singing. The regular rhythms and regular abba rhymes of the first four lines of each stanza express the men's thoughts while marching, these thoughts being interrupted in the fifth line by the sergeant's voice shouting 'Linker Tritt, linker tritt, marsch' ('Left right left, left right left, left'). There is therefore a repeated contrast between internal and external reality, individual and army – which at this stage are still opposites; after all, basic training is about turning individuals into cogs in the military machine. This is underlined by the further contrast between the first and third stanzas on the one hand and the second and fourth on the other. The contrast in attitudes is not only presumably true to life, for some are more susceptible to military discipline than others, but provokes the reader to further thought. Some of the men are evidently potential 'heroes', others are distinctly 'unheroic'. Are these valid concepts? What *is* 'heroism'? The question, so little asked in November 1914, is implicit in the poem. Though there is no proof that this was the case, it seems reasonable to assume, in view of the quality of 'Im Marschieren', that this was the one early war poem with which Engelke was satisfied.

Since his letters show Engelke to have been a thinking and sensitive writer with strong and humane views on the war, it is perhaps surprising that he did not write more and better war poems or begin writing effectively earlier. That he did not do so may be due both to the physical circumstances of his existence and to his characteristic slowness of response. At all events, it was not until 1917-18 that he wrote the Whitmanesque hymns that constitute his most distinctive contribution to the poetry of war. The first major poem in this new style is 'Buch des Krieges':

Mein Freund du, gebrochenes Auge nun,
Gebrochener Blick wie der des erschossenen Hasen
Oder verächtlichen, kalten Verräters –
Zwölf Jahre gemeinsam sprang uns der Zeitwind entgegen,
Schweigsam teilten wir Bücher und Brot,
Teilten im Schulhaus die Bänke,
Des Lebenshindranges rauschende Not,
Einigen Sinnes Erkenntnis und Lehre,
Freund, dein Auge ist tot.

Darum deine Mutter im Kummer nun geht,
Harmvoll, seufzend, doch schlicht in der Menge,
Darum Klein-Schwester, Klein-Brüder zu frühe schon spüren
Verfinsternd qualmendes Schicksalgewitter
Und mächtiges Mähen des Todes.
Leer ist dein Bett in der ärmlichen Kammer
Und dein Platz am Tische des Mittags.
Und darum, dass niemand mehr wartet auf dich,
Geht grau deine Mutter im Kummer.

Du wärst eine Wurzel, ein Saatkorn,
Ein trotzender Keim in den Furchen des Lebens,
Ein bärtiger Vater von freundlichen Kindern geworden.
Ein schmerzenzerpflügtes Ackerland frass dich,
Ein blutbedüngter Acker verdarb dich,
Der weise und ewige Säer zertrat dich.
Wer hadert und redet von Schuld?
Doch wärst du ein Saatkorn und wärest ein Vater!

Du wärest das Saatkorn – und wurdest doch Opfer;
Ein tausendstel Gramm nur, ein blutendes Fleisch
Fielst du auf blutleerer Leichen unendlich Gebirge.
Ist auch dein Tod nicht mehr denn ein anderer Tod.
Marschierten doch Tausend und Tausende rhythmischen Schrittes
Hinweg in das qualschwarze Nichts,
Regiment und Brigade, Armee und Armeen
Ins blutigbefleckte Ruhm-Reich des toten Soldaten.
Du wurdest ein Opfer.

Der Brimont ist kahl und sein Wald ist zerschroten,
Keine Fichte verschont, dir daraus ein Grabkreuz zu schlagen.
So liegst du stumm in zertrümmertem Boden,
In brustbedrückendem, traumlosem Schlummer.
Nicht Held, noch Führer – Soldat nur, unbekannt.
Gebein im Wind der Verwesung.
Doch des gewaltigen Friedens unzählbare, selige Glanzlegionen,
Wenn ehern und klirrend sie über dein Grabfeld marschieren,
Wirst du erschauernd einst hören,
So horche und harre darauf.

'Buch des Krieges' was written between 27 and 30 October 1917, in response to the news that his best friend, August Deppe, was missing assumed dead; it was apparently intended as the beginning of the 'grosse rhythmische Kriegsdichtung' dealing with 'der Krieg an sich' which Engelke told Jakob Kneip he wished to write.[46] On sending the poem 'Buch des Krieges' to Kneip on 30 October 1917 Engelke wrote: 'da hältest Du den Anfang des Kriegsbuches! Ich denke, er ist gut, und in diesem (*Form-*) Stil müsste es weitergehen.'[47] The title of the poem shows that it was intended as part of a 'Buch des Krieges' as such. The poem shows that Engelke has finally found *his* style and that this style is indebted to Whitman. It was obviously the shock and sorrow that he felt on hearing of Deppe's death that caused this poem and indeed this form of poetry to be released. There are no other poems in German that are written so freely (Anton Schnack uses a far more stylised long line and uses it in a stylised way) and with such depth of personal feeling. No other poems by other poets, that is, for 'Buch des Krieges' is transcended by another poem written in memory of August Deppe, 'An die Soldaten des Grossen Krieges (In memoriam August Deppe)':

Herauf! aus Gräben, Lehmhöhlen, Betonkellern, Steinbrüchen!
Heraus aus Schlamm und Glut, Kalkstaub und Aasgerüchen!
Herbei! Kameraden! Denn von Front zu Front, von Feld zu Feld
Komme euch allen der neue Feiertag der Welt!
Stahlhelme ab, Mützen, Käppis! und fort die Gewehre!
Genug der blutbadenden Feindschaft und Mordehre!

Euch alle beschwör ich bei eurer Heimat Weilern und Städten,
Den furchtbaren Samen des Hasses auszutreten, zu jäten,
Beschwöre euch bei eurer Liebe zur Schwester, zur Mutter, zum
    Kind,

Die allein euer narbiges Herz noch zum Singen stimmt.
Bei eurer Liebe zur Gattin - auch ich liebe ein Weib!
Bei eurer Liebe zur Mutter - auch mich trug ein Mutterleib!
Bei eurer Liebe zum Kinde - denn ich liebe die Kleinen!
Und die Häuser sind voll von Fluchen, Beten, Weinen!

Lagst du bei Ypern, dem zertrümmerten? Auch ich lag dort.
Bei Mihiel, dem verkümmerten? Ich war an diesem Ort.
Dixmuide, dem umschwemmten? Ich lag vor deiner Stirn
In Höllenschluchten Verduns, wie du in Rauch und Klirrn;
Mit dir im Schnee vor Dünaburg, frierend, immer trüber,
An der leichenfressenden Somme lag ich dir gegenüber.
Ich lag dir gegenüber überall, doch wusstest du es nicht!
Feind an Feind, Mensch an Mensch und Leib an Leib, warm und
 dicht.

Ich war Soldat und Mann und Pflichterfüller, so wie du,
Dürstend, schlaflos, krank - auf Marsch und Posten immerzu.
Stündlich vom Tode umstürzt, umschrien, umdampft,
Stündlich an Heimat, Geliebte, Geburtsstadt gekrampft
Wie du und du und ihr alle. -
Reiss auf deinen Rock! Entblösse die Wölbung der Brust!
Ich sehe den Streifschuss von fünfzehn, die schorfige Krust,
Und da an der Stirn vernähten Schlitz vom Sturm bei Tahüre -
Doch dass du nicht denkst, ich heuchle, vergelt' ich mit gleicher
 Gebühr:
Ich öffne mein Hemd: hier ist noch die vielfarbige Narbe am Arm!
Der Brandstempel der Schlacht! von Sprung und Alarm,
Ein zärtliches Andenken lang nach dem Kriege.
Wie sind wir doch stolz unsrer Wunden! Stolz du der deinigen,
Doch nicht stolzer als ich auch der meinigen.

Du gabst nicht besseres Blut und nicht rötere Kraft,
Und der gleiche zerhackte Sand trank unsern Saft! -
Zerschlug deinen Bruder der grässliche Krach der Granate?
Fiel nicht dein Onkel, dein Vetter, dein Pate?
Liegt nicht der bärtige Vater verscharrt in der Kuhle?
Und dein Freund, dein lustiger Freund aus der Schule? -
Hermann und Fritz, meine Vettern, verströmten im Blute,
Und der hilfreiche Freund, der Jüngling, der blonde und gute.
Und zu Hause wartet sein Bett, und im ärmlichen Zimmer

Seit sechzehn, seit siebzehn die gramgraue Mutter noch immer.
Wo ist uns sein Kreuz und sein Grab! –

Franzose du, von Brest, Bordeaux, Garonne,
Ukrainer du, Kosak vom Ural, Dnjestr und Don,
Österreicher, Bulgaren, Osmanen und Serben,
Ihr alle im rasenden Strudel von Tat und von Sterben –
Du Brite, aus London, York, Manchester,
Soldat, Kamerad, in Wahrheit mitmensch und Bester –
Amerikaner, aus den volkreichen Staaten der Freiheit:
Wirf ab: Sonderinteresse, Nationaldünkel und Zweiheit!
Warst du ein ehrlicher Feind, wirst du ein ehrlicher Freund.
Hier meine Hand, dass sich nun Hand in Hand zum Kreise binde
Und unser neuer Tag uns echt und menschlich finde.

Die Welt ist für euch alle gross und schön und schön!
Seht her! staunt auf! nach Schlacht und Blutgestöhn:
Wie grüne Meere frei in Horizonte fluten,
Wie Morgen, Abende in reiner Klarheit gluten,
Wie aus den Tälern sich Gebirge heben,
Wie Milliarden Wesen uns umbeben!
O, unser allerhöchstes Glück heisst: Leben! –

O, dass sich Bruder wirklich Bruder wieder nenne!
Dass Ost and West den gleichen Wert erkenne:
Dass wieder Freude in die Völker blitzt:
Und Mensch an Mensch zur Güte sich erhitzt!

Von Front zu Front und Feld zu Feld,
Lasst singen uns den Feiertag der neuen Welt!
Aus aller Brüsten dröhne *eine* Bebung:
Der Psalm des Friedens, der Versöhnung, der Erhebung!
Und das meerrauschende, dampfende Lied,
Das hinreissende, brüderumarmende,
Das wilde und heilig erbarmende
Der tausendfachen Liebe laut um alle Erden!

Whereas 'Buch des Krieges' was, despite its title, a poem of sadness and mourning addressed to his dead friend, this last poem, written in July 1918, is much more. This in Engelke's testament as man and poet alike. It is important because it is the only poem he was to write that does justice to his view of war and his vision of brotherhood and because it is a poem which no one else could have written. It is the only fitting end to this consideration of the work of a great human being who, had he survived the last few weeks of the war, might well have written the greatest retrospective book of poetry about the war.

Notes

1. I.M. Parsons (ed.), *Men Who March Away*, 1965, 14.
2. Cf. the popularity of the *Reiterlied*.
3. H. Lersch, *Ausgewählte Werke (AW)*, II, 394.
4. Ibid., II, 396.
5. Ibid., II, 401.
6. Ibid., II, 418.
7. Ibid., I, 52.
8. R. Peacock, 'The Great War in German Lyrical Poetry 1914-1918,' *Proceedings of the Leeds Philosophical and Literary Society*, May 1934, 212.
9. The pamphlet collections are as follows: [1:] *Die heilige Not. Gedichte aus der Kriegszeit*, 1915, 16pp.; [2:] *Mit Herz und Hand fürs Vaterland. Gedichte eines Soldaten*, 1916, 23pp.; [3:] *Champagneschlacht. Gedichte aus dem Kriege*, 1917, 16pp.; [4:] *Die toten Soldaten. Gedichte*, 1916, 18pp.; [5:] *Rückkehr aus dem Kriege. Gedichte*, 1917, 18pp.; [6:] *Hauptmann und Soldaten. Gedichte*, 1917, 20pp.; [7:] *Die arme Seele. Gedichte*, 1917, 19pp.; [8:] *Der preussische Musketier. Drei Gestalten*, 1918, 16pp.; [9:] *Schulter an Schulter. Gedichte von Krieg and Arbeit*, 1918, 16pp.;[10] *Das Land. Gedichte aus der Heimat*, 1918, 19pp.
10. Page references are not given to poems in *AW*, which contains an index.
11. Letter to his brother, 1915: *AW*, II, 399.
12. Ibid., II, 393.
13. C.M. Bowra, *Poetry and the First World War*, 1961, 23.
14. It is also expanded into a poem entitled 'Das neue Lied'.
15. *AW*, II, 404.
16. Ibid., I, 50.
17. Ibid., I, 52.
18. Most of Bröger's poems, including 'Bekenntnis', will be found in *Sturz und Erhebung (SuE)*, to which page references are therefore not given.
19. Bowra, *Poetry and the First World War*, 8f.
20. See: *Bethmann Hollwegs Kriegsreden*, ed. F. Thimme, Stuttgart and Berlin, 1919, 194.
21. *The Speeches of Adolf Hitler*, ed. Norman F. Baynes, I, 1942, 847f., 864.
22. *Kamerad, als wir marschiert*, 1916, 37; the poem was not included in *SuE*.
23. Abbreviated *GW* in the references that follow.
24. GW, 372.
25. Ibid., 378.
26. Ibid.
27. Ibid., 382.
28. Ibid., 383.
29. Ibid., 446.

30. Ibid., 478.
31. Ibid., 384.
32. Ibid., 415.
33. Ibid., 469.
34. Ibid., 450.
35. Ibid., 316.
36. Ibid., 313.
37. Ibid., 377.
38. Ibid., 558.
39. Ibid., 420f.
40. Ibid., 425.
41. Ibid., 465.
42. Ibid., 579.
43. Ibid., 486, 490, 498, 579, 581, 582.
44. Ibid., 320.
45. All Engelke's poems are to be found in *GW*.
46. See letter of 25 September 1917, ibid., 469.
47. Ibid., 472.

7 EPILOGUE

In war poetry, imagination, direct experience and moral indignation come uniquely together. It is this combination of qualities which underlies one of the last and most remarkable poems of the whole war: the young Bertolt Brecht's 'Legende vom toten Soldaten'. Brecht was studying medicine at Munich University in the spring of 1918 when the 17-year-olds and the over-age were called up. He was called up himself and placed in a hospital in Augsburg as a medical orderly; he later commented, 'I saw how they patched people up in order to ship them back to the Front as soon as possible.' When the over-age were called up, it was popularly said that they were digging up the dead ('Man gräbt die Toten aus'). The starting-point for Brecht's poem, which takes the form of a wicked parody of an heroic ballad, was partly this saying and partly George Grosz's drawing 'KV' of 1916-17.

The poem tells of a soldier who 'got the message' that the war didn't look like ending and therefore died a hero's death, death being the only way out for an honourable man ('Und als der Krieg im vierten Lenz / Keinen Ausblick auf Frieden bot / Da zog der Soldat seine Konsequenz / Und starb den Heldentod.'). The Emperor, however, finds himself running out of cannon fodder, so the dead body is dug up, pronounced 'ka-fau' ('kriegsverwendungsfähig': 'fit for general service'), cleaned up a bit ('to stop it stinking', for that would be unheroic), painted in the national colours and marched through the streets. The patriotic excitement is such that in the end nobody even notices the dead soldier, 'Doch der Soldat, so wie er's gelernt / Zieht in den Heldentod.' Written in the mixed four- and three-beat lines in four-line stanzas of the ballad as adapted for his own satirical purposes by Heine, the poem's form matches its intention. Just as the notion of glory is ruthlessly guyed, so too is the ballad form; those outrageous, preposterous rhymes (used by Heine in his most wickedly satirical moods), which deliberately reduce the poem to doggerel, reinforce the satirical intention, for it is the military machine which those now regular, now broken march rhymes represent. But however powerfully reinforced by rhymes, diction, etc., it is what is said (both directly and indirectly) that ultimately matters: the scorn poured on the idea of dying an heroic death on the altar of the Fatherland. This ballad is uniquely good at translating the contrast between brave (or culpable) pretence (the camp follower; Weihrauch; Farben) and gruesome reality (the corpse; Verwesung; Kot) into garishly and often grimly concrete terms. It is a poem which perfectly illustrates Brecht's statement that truth is concrete, to say nothing of showing that poetry is triumphantly able to have the last word on human folly.

Much less well known than the 'Legende vom toten Soldaten' is another striking anti-heroic ballad, Karl Kraus's 'Der Sterbende Soldat', published in 1919:

Hauptmann, hol her das Standgericht!
Ich sterb' für keinen Kaiser nicht!
Hauptmann, du bist des Kaisers Wicht!
Bin tot ich, salutier' ich nicht!

Wenn ich bei meinem Herren wohn',
ist unter mir des Kaisers Thron,
und hab' für sein Geheiss nur Hohn!
Wo ist mein Dorf? Dort spielt mein Sohn.

Wenn ich in meinem Herrn entschlief,
kommt an mein letzter Feldpostbrief.
Es rief, es rief, es rief, es rief!
Oh, wie ist meine Liebe tief!

Hauptmann, du bist nicht bei Verstand,
dass du mich hast hieher gesandt.
Im Feuer ist mein Herz verbrannt.
Ich sterbe für kein Vaterland!

Ihr zwingt mich nicht, ihr zwingt mich nicht!
Seht, wie der Tod die Fessel bricht!
So stellt den Tod vors Standgericht!
Ich sterb', doch für den Kaiser nicht!

It may be that there is less poetic imagination at work in Kraus's ballad, which is typical of the last two years of the war, when the various patriotic, nationalistic and militaristic concepts which had been accepted without question in 1914 were debunked one after the other. What matters at this stage, however, is that here again we see an heroic form being turned against the very virtue which that form might be expected to express. This is a point to which we shall return.

156   Epilogue

It is imagination that is the great strength of Peter Baum, who was born on 30 September 1869 at Elberfeld and served as a medical orderly on the Western Front (at 45 he was too old for anything else). He fell on 5 June 1916, wounded by a stray piece of shrapnel, and died the following day. As a writer he belonged to the Peter Hille circle (Else Lasker-Schüler, Paul Scheerbart, Julius Hart), and was then introduced into the *Sturm* circle - with which he had little in common - by Else Lasker-Schüler. Among the war poets of the *Sturm* circle he is second only to August Stramm, albeit a poor second; he has little in common with Stramm except his conscientiousness, his mysticism and the concentrated nature of his (very different) poetry. As well as poetry he wrote prose in the tradition of E.T.A. Hoffmann and E.A. Poe. What concerns us here is his *Schützengrabenverse* (1916), which was reprinted under the not very appropriate title *Und alles war anders* (Köln: Luthe Druck) in 1955. I say 'not very appropriate' because Peter Baum - a gentle, charitable soul - was infinitely far removed from the disillusioned patriot that the 1955 title suggests. He was an imaginative writer with a strong sense of the grotesque, which comes across in his war poetry. His plan to write a 'Grabenbuch' in prose came to nothing, but then he knew that it would in any case be unpublishable since it would encourage the Allies. His unpublished letters from the front speak of the progressive demoralisation of the German army. A passage from an undated letter, dealing with the *Schützengrabenverse*, speaks of the way in which it is possible to smuggle a good deal of one's experiences into unwarlike lines.

This is a point to which we shall return. Certainly there is nothing warlike about Peter Baum's verses from the trenches. He is a poet to whom Wilfred Owen's words 'The Poetry is in the Pity' apply. He was, ultimately, more concerned with truth than with poetry, and this sometimes shows in his poetry in the form of archness or gaucheness. In his best work poetic feeling (Owen's 'Pity') and poetic expression are evenly matched. One of the more interesting of his war poems, written in 1915, concerns the way in which the war has gathered momentum:

Am Beginn des Krieges stand ein Regenbogen.
Vögel schwarz vor grauen Wolken schnitten Kreise.
Silbern glänzten\Tauben, wenn auf ihrer runden Reise
Sie durch einen schmalen Streifen Sonne bogen.

Schlacht grenzt hart an Schlacht. Sie himmlisch logen.
Viele Reihn geklaffter Stirnen grausen.

Oft kracht der Granaten Kopf,
Wenn sie schon schwänzelnd leiser sausen.
Immer wachsen der Granaten Wehebogen.

Harrend zwischen Tod und Friedensbogen,
Fester krampfen sie den Lauf, das Heim zu schützen,
Speien auf den Feind, sich wankend stützen,
Über Hügel stürzend, Meereswogen,
Schwanken sie heran, vom Tod magnetisch angezogen.

Despite the six-beat trochaic lines, the 14-line poem starts by looking very much like a sonnet. The regular abba rhyme pattern of the quatrain reflects the rainbow of the opening lines and the opening optimistic months of the war; the perfect harmony of the spectrum and of national unity is broken by those black birds of war, harbingers of death, to whose circling, vulture-like movements the trochees point.

The poem proceeds from the image of optimism (even the black birds are offset by the silver dove representing 'peace by Christmas') to the inevitability of death. If the opening quatrain was in some ways ominous (the black birds, those aggressive trochees), this was nothing compared with what should have been the second half of the octave, where things almost immediately begin to go badly wrong. The formal and metrical patterns and the rhyme scheme are all broken: there are five lines instead of four, the acdca rhyme pattern is grotesque, as is the pattern of 55446 accented syllables, which runs directly counter to the rhyme scheme. What started as a sonnet with a difference is being blown apart - a perfectly proper indication of the violence of the war in its post-euphoric period. Much the same points apply to the five lines of what should be the sestet; the aeeaa is surely unparalleled in any peacetime sonnet. If the acdca of the first quintain was odd, the aeeaa of the second is very odd indeed. This is the point. The 'sonnet' is made to reflect its subject matter, the war, in getting right out of control. The war, like the 'sonnet', started 'regularly', but then things started to go wrong. And there is no getting away from the war: the 'sonnet's' end is in its beginning (those a rhymes). Those who are the subject of the violence tearing the poem apart - all the combatants - are caught between death and the mirage of peace; but it is death towards which they are irresistibly drawn, like so many moths towards a light. What makes this violently impressive poem so interesting is the way in which the form of the poem exactly reflects the subject matter.

Both the last poem and another, 'O Deutschland, grosses Muttervolk der Erde', make clear Peter Baum's conviction that the war can only end badly and that Germany needs to change its anachronistic values ('wandelst dräuend mit dem [Donner-] Wetterschwerte'). The memorable thing in this poem is, however, the reference to 'Tigeraugen, die dich hassumglühn', for here – in expressionistically neologistic form – is the animal imagery in which Peter Baum's view of the war receives its most characteristic and impressive expression. It may have been Anton Schnack who used the title *Tier rang gewaltig mit Tier*, but it is the war poetry of Peter Baum which actually illustrates this theme. The opening poem of *Schützengrabenverse* contains as full a treatment as any:

> Leuchtkugeln steigen hoch hinauf,
> Nachtweitend Feuerwerk und Lichtgebraus
> Zerfallenden Monds. So starr ragst du dahin
> Bei deinem Büchsenlauf, wie die erhellten Häuser.
>
> Leuchtkugeln aus gesträubtem Tigerhaar.
> Jeder erhellten Regung lauert auf ein Hahn
> Bei Späherblick, als blute noch der Tag,
> Wo einer noch des anderen Wild,
> Mund lag bei Kehle,
> Bis man vernahm des andern Orgelton.
>
> Mit aufgerissnen Augen staunst Du auf die Pracht
> Des bunten Raubtiers, funkelnd aus der Finsternis.
> Bis wieder tief vergräbt mich Nacht und Schneien,
> Graugrüne Augen halten wach die wilden Melodeien.

Peter Baum's message is conveyed through the imagery. He does not use Stramm's hunting vocabulary, which denotes a human (though not humane) activity. He sees the war rather as a fight to the death between wild animals. There are some extraordinary and striking images, e.g. 'Leuchtkugeln aus gesträubtem Tigerhaar'; whether the image was suggested by the barbed wire, or by the bristling guns, it is impossible to tell, but the image – the predator with its hair standing on end in anger – speaks for itself, as does that of the green predator's eyes, ever watchful in the darkness.

The imagery of beasts of prey spans the whole collection, recurring in a notable form in the final poem:

> Wo Wölfe durch die blanke Schneenacht liefen,
> Mit jährm Hunger war die Nacht geladen:

Luftwildem Heulen. Die Granaten
Und die Schrapnells mit langen Hälsen riefen.
Eiserne Zähne ohne Lippen.
Hungerten heiss nach meinen Rippen.

Früh uns im Schneelichtfieber überschwimmen
Von neuem die vom Tod zerdehnten Stimmen,
Mit gellem Knallen nach uns grimmen.

The final line contains an incidental borrowing from Stramm - 'gell' as an intensification of 'gellend' - perhaps intended as a tribute. Now had Baum served on the Eastern Front, the wolves might have been supposed to be real, but as it is they are identical with Trakl's 'wilde Wölfe' (*homo homini lupus*), although Baum's starting-point is the howling of shells through the air. The shells themselves are animalised (they have long necks and lipless iron teeth), and the whole of 'Wo Wölfe . . .' is dominated by those 'vom Tod zerdehnten Stimmen' of men baying for blood. One can only assume that Baum's work was not understood by the military censor; seen in retrospect it could hardly be much more clearly 'anti-war'. This is perhaps where poetry has the edge on satire. Satire is always liable to be banned; poetry, as Brecht knew so well, may get away with it. But Baum does not always leave it to do so, and in another poem the characteristic imagery is combined with a bitterly clear comment:

Viele Tiere dräuen, Vielzeller, die Granaten,
Einzeller bohren nur ein kleines Loch.
Zu einem Mythenfest bin ich geladen.
Harpyien suchen tief und schweifen hoch.
Im ganzen mild. Sie könnten furchtbar schaden.
    So mancher Arm vermisst den Körper doch,
    Den armen Kopf, der eben lenkte noch.
        O Sturm, o Ruhm
        O Heldentum!
Schön glänzt auf weissem Feld die süsse rote Blum.

Nothing could be clearer, or more apt, or more courageous than the typographically accentuated 'O Sturm, o Ruhm / O Heldentum!': what price 'glory' now? In June 1916, when this harmless, gentle soul died, it was a good question.

Unlike Peter Baum, who was an original, all too many poets of the war were *Epigonen*, unoriginal writers expressing prejudiced feelings in other men's words and forms; at best writers whose poetic conventions were worn out before the war had even started. Such men lacked the poetic and even the moral qualities that would have enabled them to respond adequately to the destruction of their world. No less essential than imagination, which cannot exist without it, is *real* feeling, which in turn demands individual expression.

As a reflective form ideally suited for the expression and resolution of a conflict, the sonnet would seem, in theory, most appropriate for use in this most problematical of wars. Effective conventional sonnets were produced by, among others, Siegfried Schlösser (author of *Sonette aus dem Schützengraben*, 1916) and Karl von Eisenstein.

Karl Eisner Reichsritter von und zu Eisenstein, born into the Austro-Hungarian nobility in 1889, held a regular army commission and served as a lieutenant on the Southern Front. His ancestors had been military men for generations. Like Julian Grenfell he was both a natural soldier and a natural war poet. Among the German-language poets of the First World War he was the only real successor to the major poet of the previous (Franco-Prussian) war, Detlev von Liliencron. His volume of war poems and prose sketches, *Lieder im Kampf* (1916), deserves to be remembered, for it has real quality and is unique of its kind.

In Eisenstein's 'Sonett an den Tod von Anno 14', the skill of the poet and his knowledge of the tradition within which he writes is combined with the courage of the professional soldier and his knowledge of the tradition to which he belongs. We have seen that the real leitmotif of the war, the one constant amid so many vicissitudes, is death. On one level or another, visibly or invisibly, this is the theme of most of the poetry of the war. As might be expected, Eisenstein tackles the problem head on, in his 'Sonett an den Tod von Anno 14':

Einst kamst auf leisen Sohlen du geschlichen,
heimtückisch harmlos, völlig unscheinbar:
Da hassten wir dich, Sanften, Bürgerlichen,
vor dessen Willkür keiner sicher war.

Gedämpft sprach man von deinen Sensenstrichen.
Du warst die Furcht in jeglicher Gefahr.
Du wolltest mehr! – Nun ist dein Ruhm erblichen.
Er welkt und schrumpft mit deiner Opfer Schar.

Nun kauerst du hinter Kanonenrohren
grossmänlig, wütend, brüllst vertausendfacht
uns deine Furchtbarkeit in taube Ohren.

Feig und verächtlich ist die Übermacht.
Wer zuviel lärmt, mein Freund, erweckt Verdacht!
Gevatter Tod, dies Spiel hast du verloren!

This is an excellent sonnet of a more traditional kind than most of the others that have been discussed in this context. Tradition is not only the poem's but the poet's great strength. The title takes the reader straight back to the seventeenth century, to the Thirty Years War, the time when sonnets to death were almost as commonplace as death itself. Another poem, 'Der wilde Tropfen [Blut]', reveals that Eisenstein's forefathers fought at the Schlacht am Weissen Berg (1620), at Lützen (1632) and Jankau (1645). In his sonnet Eisenstein is showing a fortitude in the face of death that was not only typical of the seventeenth century, but must also have been sustained by the knowledge that members of his family had for centuries been in his present position. And of course over and above this the poem is expressing an attitude that became widespread as the very ubiquity of death robbed it of its unknown quality and therefore of some of its terror.

On the whole, however, there are relatively few successful straight sonnets among the German poetry of the war. The major reason for this is clear: however ideally suited for the expression and resolution of a conflict, the sonnet could only be properly used by those who both recognised the moral conflict in question and saw a way of resolving it, and there were few indeed of the latter. The sonnet therefore tended to be abused, particularly in the early days of the war, by being used as a vehicle for simplistic, chauvinistic rhetoric. The most interesting and successful sonnets are very free indeed. The broken sonnets of Anton Schnack are among the outstanding productions of the war and their most eloquent feature is the way in which the traditional form is so barbarously broken to match the content. We have seen something similar happening in the work of Peter Baum. This brings us back to the whole question of the myriad problems facing the poets who were sufficiently sensitive to realise that they existed.

This book has had to do with the question of how to find the objective correlative for a uniquely horrific, terrifying and degrading experience. Leaving aside the underlying human paradox (men under shellfire, intent on killing one another, writing poems), the first question is whether *any* form can be appropriate. Does not form as such conflict with the bitter formlessness of reality? Does not form falsify? In Stramm's 'Sturmangriff', for instance, there is a seeming conflict between a horrific reality and a frankly artificial poetic device (the lay-out of the poem is reminiscent of seventeenth-century figure poetry). The *visible* form of this poem seems to raise in an extreme form the whole question of turning horror into aesthetically and morally acceptable poetic artefacts. The point about the form of 'Sturmangriff' is, however, that it is an intrinsic and indispensable part of the concentrated expressiveness which makes the poem so successful. Art for art's sake would be intolerable; art for truth's sake is another matter. It is the truth of the poem that strikes us and therefore justifies its aesthetic form. The Poetry, that is to say, is ultimately in the Pity.

More generally, there can be no doubt that the best poets are those who allow their depiction of war to speak for itself (Stramm, Trakl, Schnack, among others), provided the tone is right. It is the same, later, in the war novel; Renn's *Krieg* is more effective, in its objectivity, than Remarque's more strident and explicit *Im Westen nichts Neues*. What this means, in terms of poetry and morality, is that a well-written poem ending in a well-meant moral is no more an adequate war poem than is a brutally realistic poem with a tagged-on moral. Poetic good intentions are not enough. The road to Hell is paved with them. The poetry and the morality need to be fused together. Then, and only then, does form become moral; otherwise it is immoral.

The basic problem facing all front-line poets was how to express their experience in valid terms. It is now clear that it was not until they had come to terms with the irrelevance of the heroic mode that they were able to produce valid work. Coming to terms with it meant either ignoring it or ironising it by emphasising the gulf between heroic ideal and tragic reality. Heine, because of the calculated dissonances of his poetry, was the one potentially useful model; but unfortunately his example was ignored by most poets, with the notable exception of Lichtenstein, Brecht, and, on a different level, Tucholsky.

Satire is one of the main poetic modes of the war and would have been a far more important one on the German side if Heine's work had not been so neglected because it was thought to be unpatriotic and 'un-German'. Always more explicitly concerned to make a moral point than lyric or elegiac poetry, satire became, in the latter stages of the war, increasingly concerned only with the morality or politics of it: the poetic expression eventually tended to become a mere means to a non-poetic end. Tucholsky, for instance, unlike Lichtenstein, doesn't give a damn about 'poetry'. The poetry doesn't matter to him because, by the time he came to write his war poems in 1918, poetry had, by and large, been obliged to leave the field to satire. There was nothing to celebrate; most of the elegies had been written. Many of the best poets were dead (Lichtenstein, Trakl, Stramm, Engelke) or had long since fallen silent (Klemm), giving in to the unsayable. The bitterness and revolution in which this war for a 'botched civilisation' ended, could, it seemed, only be expressed satirically, often by angry inversions of outbreak-of-war hymns.

Recognising the false charms of the heroic mode and its forms for what they were, was, however, only a necessary first step. There remained the question of whether poets should seek to express the chaotic horror of their experience through an appropriate dislocation of form, or by means of a deliberately inappropriate harmony of form. Logic would suggest that the expression of a totally new experience calls for a new or dislocated form, and the dominant role assumed by poets associated with Expressionism seems to confirm that the war necessitated new forms of expression. In fact Expressionism came triumphantly into its own. Traditional forms and modes of expression worked less well, and there will be a number of reasons for this. Naive forms, unless used by a poet of genius, spell naive thoughts, which in the present context lead to failure. There seems to have been no German equivalent to the exception to this rule in the form of the anti-heroic soldiers' jingles which circulated in the trenches and even found their way into *Punch*. Those who employ conservative forms are, on the whole, likely to profess conservative ideas, and the traditional notions to which such forms are tied have little to do with a war which called for the rethinking of traditional notions and values. Forms which go together with the traditional idea of heroism could not be used, unless ironised, once that idea had been perceived to be no longer tenable. More generally, established poetic forms are (again, unless ironised) inappropriate because this particular war has little to do with previous conventions of war and therefore with the modes and forms of previous war poetry. Normal, peacetime poetic forms may be useful for making contrasted definitions of peace, but they must be allowed to create no false idylls. Modern war implicitly invalidates existing poetic forms and will therefore tend to be best expressed by means of a shockingly new form (Stramm, Owen) or by the no less shocking rupture of an old form (Schnack). Although the pitfalls of empty rhetoric and of brutal realism have to be avoided, the grotesque and ghastly intensification of experience at the front necessitates an intensification of language of one kind or another (neologisms, reduplication, etc.). This is the rule. Exceptions prove it. But given the objective correlative, the poetry is, in the last analysis, where Wilfred Owen declared it to be: in the Pity. Pity alone does not make poetry, but without it there can be no war poetry worth the title.

TRANSLATIONS OF GERMAN QUOTATIONS

1.   'Modern Warfare': In this war I find it most difficult to reconcile gas-mask and pennon. How can that be? Those who do not yield an inch to the enemy, [who] deal him death with chemical means, and who remain chloriously at their posts even though the sun is shining overhead – why were they not dismissed from the army for highly commendable cowardice in the face of the enemy?

3-4.   'Five Hymns, August 1914, I': For the first time I see you rising, hearsaid, remote, incredible War-God. How very thickly terrible action has been sown among the peaceful fruits of the fields, action suddenly grown to maturity. Yesterday it was still small, needed nurture, now it is standing there tall as a man: tomorrow it will outgrow man. For the glowing god will suddenly tear his crop out of the nation which gave it roots, and the harvest will begin. At last a god. Since we were often no longer able to grasp the peaceful god, the god of battle suddenly grips us, hurling his brand: and over the heart full of homeland screams his crimson heaven in which, thunderous, he dwells.

4-5.   For three days now, what has been happening? Am I really singing the terror, really singing the god in whom I believed, admiring him from afar as one of the early gods now barely remembered? Like a volcanic mountain he lay in the distance. Sometimes flaming. Sometimes crowned by smoke. Sad and godlike. Perhaps only a nearby, adjoining place trembled. But we raised our scathless lyre to other, to what gods of the future? And now he uprose: stands: higher than standing towers, higher than the breathed air of another day of ours. Stands. Stands supreme. And we? Glow together into one, into a new creation which he animates with death. Thus I too *am* no more; out of the common heart mine beats its heart-beat, and the common mouth forces mine open.

5.   Up and appal the appalling god! Dumbfound him. Joy of

165

battle pampered him in former times. Now let grief, a new, astounded Grief of Battle impel you ahead of his fury. Though a heritage in your blood overcome you, a blood coming from your forefathers on high: let your mood still remain yours. Do not ape earlier, former moods. Test whether you are not grief. Grief in action. Grief has its triumphs too. O and then the flag will be flung open over your heads in the wind which comes from the foe! Which flag? Grief's. The flag of Grief. The heavy, flapping cloth of Grief.

6-7. 'War': What grips you now has long been familiar to me. I have long sweated the red sweat of anguish when people played with fire ... I have wept my tears in advance ... today I can summon no more. The greater part had happened already, and no one realised ... The worst is yet to come, and no one realises. You are allowing yourselves to be driven by forces from without ... These are the flaming characters on the wall, not [mere] foreknowledge. I take no part in the struggle as you experience it.

7. The prophet is never thanked ... To *him* what is the murder of hundreds of thousands compared with the murder of life itself?

7. *His* office is praise and blame, prayer and penance ... He is gripped by a deeper dread.

7. There is no call for rejoicing: there will be no triumph, only many deaths without dignity ... Escaping from its maker's hand, the monster of lead and tin, bars and barrels, careers about out of control. When false, once-heroic perorations are heard, he laughs grimly who saw his brother fall, a mass of pulp, who lived in the shamefully ravaged earth as vermin do ... The old god of battle is no more. Diseased worlds are raging to their fall in that frenzied uproar. Holy is alone the blood which is spilled innocently, a great river.

8. In both camps no thought [or] inkling of what is at stake ... Here: merely concern to act like a shopkeeper where another is already acting like one ... to become what one

despises in the other and to deny oneself – 'A nation is dead when its gods are dead.' Over there: bragging of former prestige of pomp and tradition, while the mercenary desire to exploit seeks to breathe its last in comfort ... In the realm of clearest insight no faint glimmer of understanding that the tabooed are destroying what was ready to fall, that perhaps a people 'hated and abominated by the human race' may once again bring it salvation.

But my song shall not end with malediction. Many an ear already understood my praise of stuff and stock, of kernel and core ... Already I see many hands stretched out towards me when I say: O land too beautiful for foreign feet to ravage: where the flute sounds among willows, Aeolian harps murmur in groves, where the dream still stirs indelibly in the presently faithless heirs ... Where the fair mother of the [now] degenerate white race first revealed her true countenance ... Land in which much promise still resides – which therefore shall not perish!

11. War has never been properly depicted. Usually only partial aspects or consequences of it are shown. The terrible thing about war, however, is the disintegration of all existing certainties and conventions. The animal [in man] runs riot and stifles everything spiritual. It is like a cancer. Man no longer lives for years, months, days, [or] hours, but only for moments. And even these he no longer lives. He just becomes aware of them. He exists merely.

11. 'Loretto': To immerse oneself in silence one whole day long! One whole day long to cool your head in flowers and let your hands drop, and dream: this black velvet, dulcet dream: Not to kill one whole day long.

12–13. 'On the Pathetic': The same object can displease us if we judge it from a moral point of view, and be very attractive to us from the aesthetical point of view. But even if the moral judgement and aesthetical judgement were both satisfied, this object would produce this effect on one and the other in quite a different way. It is not morally satisfactory because it has an aesthetical value, nor has it an aesthetical value because it satisfies us morally.

21-22. 'War': He is arisen who was long asleep, arisen from vaults deep down below. He stands in the dusk, immense and unknown, and crushes the moon in his brute black hand.

Into the nightfall noises of the cities there falls far off the chill and shadow of an alien darkness. And the maelstrom of the markets solidifies into ice. Silence falls. They look around. And no one knows.

In the streets something touches their shoulder lightly. A question. No answer. A face turns pale. In the distance a peal of bells trembles thinly, and beards tremble round their pointed chins.

On the mountains he is beginning to dance, and he shouts: All you warriors, up and at them! And there is an echo when he tosses his black head, round which hangs a loudly rattling chain of a thousand skulls.

Like a tower he stamps out the last glow, where the day is fleeing the rivers are already full of blood. Numberless are the bodies already laid out in the reeds, covered white with death's strong birds.

Into the night he drives the fire across country, a red hound with the screaming of wild mouths. Out of the darkness springs the black world of nights, its edge lit up dreadfully by volcanoes.

And with a thousand tall pointed caps, flickering, the dark plains are strewn, and what is fleeing in swarms on the roads below, he casts into the forests of flame, where the flames roar.

And the flames, burning, consume forest after forest, yellow bats clawing jaggedly at the foliage, like a charcoal-burner he strikes his poker into the trees to make the fire roar properly.

A great city sank in yellow smoke, threw itself soundlessly into the belly of the abyss. But gigantic over glowing ruins he stands who brandishes his torch three times at the wild heavens

above the reflection of storm-torn clouds, into the cold wastelands of dead darkness, to dry up the night far away with the conflagration, he pours fire and brimstone down on Gomorrah.

26. 'Mankind': Mankind lined up in front of fiery gorges, a roll

of drums, sombre warriors' brows, footsteps through a haze of blood; black metal grinds; despair, night in sorrowing minds: here [is] Eve's shadow, hunting, and red coin. Cloud which light pierces, the Last Supper. In bread and wine a gentle silence dwells. And they are assembled, twelve in number. At night they cry out while asleep under olive-branches; Saint Thomas dips his hand into the stigmata.

29. 'Trumpets': Beneath pollarded willows, where brown-skinned children are playing and leaves blowing about, trumpets sound out. Blood runs cold. Scarlet pennons rush through the sadness of the acorn, cavalrymen riding past rye fields and empty mills.

Or shepherds sing at night and deer join them round their fires, the age-old sadness of the woods. Dancers get up from a black wall. Scarlet pennons, laughter [or: pools of blood], madness, trumpet-calls.

30. 'On the Eastern Front': The people's dark wrath is like the wild organ notes of a winter storm, the crimson wave of the battle, of defoliated stars.

With shattered brows, with silver arms night beckons to dying soldiers. In the shade of the autumn ash the spirits of the slain are sighing.

Thorny wilderness engirdles the town, the moon chases terrified women from bleeding steps. Wild wolves broke through the gate.

32-33. 'Lament': Sleep and death, the ghastly eagles all night long whirl around this head: the golden image of man may be consumed by the icy wave of eternity. On terrible reefs the purple body shatters. And the dark voice laments above the sea. Sister of stormy sadness see how a fearful boat sinks down beneath the stars, the silent countenance of night.

33-34. 'Grodek': In the evening the autumn forests ring with deadly weapons, the gold plains and blue lakes, over which the sun more darkly rolls; night embraces dying warriors, the wild lament of their broken mouths. Yet in the willow-grove a red cloud gathers, in which an angry god resides, shed blood gathers, moonlike coolness; all roads end in black decay.

170 *Translations of German Quotations*

Beneath the golden bough of night and stars the sister's shadow sways through the silent thicket to greet the ghosts of the heroes, their bleeding heads; and in the reeds the dark flutes of autumn softly sound. O prouder sorrow! You brazen altars, a mighty grief today feeds the hot flame of the spirit, the unborn grandchildren.

35. 'The Storm': Magnetic coldness surrounds this proud head, glowing sorrow of an angry god.

35. 'Evening': With the figures of dead heroes, moon, you fill the silent woods.

42. It's odd, life and death are the same ... Both the same ... Battles and privation and death and nightingales are all the same. The same! And fighting and sleeping and dreaming and being busy: all the same! There's no distinction! Everything boils down to the same thing, merging and unmerging like sun and horizon. It's just that now one thing gains the upper hand and now another. So we fight go hungry die sing. All of us! Private and commanding officer alike. Night and day. Bodies and blossom. And over me a hand appears. I drift through everything. Am everything. Me!

42. I'm standing here as though convulsed, with nothing to hang on to, no anchor, clinging to nothingness, fixed and frozen in a grimace of determination and defiance.

42. Where have I got to? ... I'm living in a deep, deep frenzy. Inwardly. Not outwardly. Not that. They call me brave. And I am brave too and have to clench my teeth when tears threaten to unman me. Not for myself, not for anything that I know of. I don't know for what.

43. What can I say. There is so much death in me death and more death. Inwardly I weep and outwardly I am hard and tough ... Everything is so contradictory, I cannot find a way through the enigma ... I cannot read or think any more. Words fail me with horror ... I have no faith. I belong to the living dead and yet am healthy and strong as a hard-shelled empty nut. I need to murder murder then I shall at least be

at one with the murder all around then I shall again be standing on firm ground then I shall not be so horribly alone floating in the air without wings. Where is the preacher of murder who preaches the gospel of murder of the murder you have to commit. Murder is duty is heaven is God. Where are words to express what we are going through . . . I'm no longer writing poems, everything all around here is a poem. Wretched cowardly, insidious horror, and the air cackles cynically the while and comes thundering down from the mountains . . . Everything is untrue, everything a lie.

43-44. 'Battlefield': Clod softness lulls iron off to sleep, bloods clot ooze patches, rusts crumble, fleshes slime, sucking ruts around decay. Child eyes blink murder upon murder.

45. My country?! The idea is too narrow, would not excuse me in my own eyes! No! I am murdering in order to put an end to murder. I am murdering and inciting others in order that incitement may no longer hold sway. I am brave, an up-and-at-them type, I've heard it said. Not for the sake of it, not out of brutality and wanting to be brutal! No! Out of anger, out of hatred of the indescribable brutality going on, the unbelievable brutality which is unworthy of humanity. I'm squandering my powers because I am raging against the squandering of all man's power for good. I am not brave in the crude sense in which I am said to be, in which the men look up to me, I am cowardly, unutterably cowardly, because I want to do away with that kind of crude bravery altogether. And the idea of my country comes into it because everything that I hold dear is to be found there, but also because when all is said and done my country is for me the positive embodiment of whatever higher and nobler things I am striving for and, as the only nation which currently guarantees the way forward, can and *must* prevail!

46. 'Wounded': The earth bleeds beneath the helmeted head. Stars fall. Space gropes. Terrors roar. Lonelinesses swirl. Mists weep far off your look.

47. 'Assault': From all corners yell fears. Steeling oneself. Scream! Life lashes along before it gasping death. The heavens are cut to shreds. Blindly horror butchers out wildly.

172   Translations of German Quotations

49. Words fail me with horror ... I have no faith [cf. 'the heavens are cut to shreds'] ... Where are the words to express what we are going through?

49. 'War': Grief graves. Waiting stares aghast. Labour shatters. Giving-birth tenses the limbs. The hour bleeds. Question raises its eye. Time gives birth. Exhaustion renews death.

51. 'Patrol': The stones menace, window grins treachery, branches strangle. Loomy bushes rattle leaves, shriek death.

53. 'Baptism of Fire': His body shrinks its loosely-fitting tunic. His head creeps down into his boots. Fear throttles his gun. Fears rattle, shrill, rattle, swathe, rattle, stumble, rattle, trigger off shouting anger. His eye narrows. A shot. Hands grip schnaps. Defiance loads. Determination aims and a steely look quickly bags [another's] fate.

55. 'Shrapnel': The sky throws up clouds and bursts into smoke. Barrels flash. Flying feet flay stones. Eyes giggle at the chaos and lust in death.

56-57. 'Attack of Fear': Dread. Me and me and me and me. Dreading roaring crashing dreading. Dreaming splintering burning dazzling. Dazzling star-shells roaring dreading. Crashing. Dread. Me.

57. Wretched, cowardly, insidious horror.

58. 'War-Grave': Stakes implore crossed arms. Writing fears the pale unknown. Flowers impertinence. Dusts intimidate. Faint light runs with tears, glazes forgetfulness.

59. Obituary: On 1 September 1915 there fell, leading his Company in an assault across a canal: Reserve Captain August Stramm, holder of the Iron Cross 2nd Class, the Austrian Cross of Merit (War), recommended for the Iron Cross 1st Class. A member of the Regiment since January, he made a major contribution to the Regiment's successes, partly as Battalion Commander. His name is closely bound up with the history of the Regiment, which has lost one of its out-

Translations of German Quotations 173

standing officers in him. As a loyal comrade-in-arms and regimental officer tirelessly concerned for the welfare of his men he will live in our memories. For the officers of the Regiment, Ahlers, Major, commanding Reserve Infantry Regiment 272.

60. The poems printed here give me the impression of a *very* limited talent; but within these limitations a passionate response to life; language for him, was a material from which he struck fire ... *He was on the right track.*

62. So long as people remain patriotic, so long as they retain their sentimental devotion to the country in which they happen to be born, so long will they also believe that their country is worth more than the neighbouring one, and that it is honourable to die for it – so long as this attitude persists, it will be impossible to end international war ... If we are serious in working for a 'united states of Europe', that is, if we want lasting peace between the nations, then we must feel ourselves to be Europeans, or, better, compatriots and co-inheritors of the whole world.

62. Chauvinism is a perpetual menace to mankind. It, and it alone, can turn millions of rational beings into madmen overnight.

62-63. This book – poems from the field of slaughter – refuge of a currently homeless idea, I throw in the face of the age ... F.P.

64. 'Suppose War is Comming': Suppose war is coming. There's been peace for too long. Then things will get serious. Trumpet calls will galvanise you. And nights will be ablaze. You will freeze in your tent. You'll feel hot all over. You'll go hungry. Drown. Be blown up. Bleed to death. Fields will rattle to death. Church-towers will topple. Horizons will be in flames. Winds will gust. Cities will come crashing down. The thunder of heavy guns will fill up the horizon. From the hills all around smoke will rise and shells will explode overhead.

65. 'Leaving for the Front': Before dying I must just make my

poem. Quiet, comrades, don't disturb me.
   We are going off to war. Death is our bond.
Oh, if only my girl-friend would stop howling.
   What do I matter? I'm happy to go.
My mother's crying. You need to be made of iron.
   The sun is falling down on to the horizon. Soon they'll be throwing me into a nice mass grave.
   In the sky the good old sunset is glowing red.
In thirteen days maybe I'll be dead.

66.   'Romantic Journey': On top of the wobbliest ammunition cart, like a little toad finely carved in black wood, hands gently clenched, rifle on his back (strapped on loosely), lighted cigar in wry mouth, idle as a monk, keen as a dog - he's holding valerian drops pressed to his heart - looking comically serious, looking crazy in the yellow moonlight, there sits: Kuno.

66-67.   'Prayer Before Battle': The men are singing fervently, every man thinking of himself: God, protect me from accidents, Father, Son and Holy Ghost, don't let shells hit me, don't let those bastards, our enemies, catch me or shoot me, don't let me snuff it like a dog for my dear Fatherland.

67.   Look, I'd like to go on living, milking cows, stuffing girls and beating up that blighter Joe, getting tight many more times before I die like a Christian. Look, I'll pray well and willingly. I'll say seven rosaries a day, if you, God, in your mercy will kill my friend Huber, or Meier, and spare me.

68.   But if I get my lot, don't let me be too badly wounded. Send me a slight leg wound, a small arm injury, so that I may return home as a hero who has a tale to tell.

68-69.   'The Battle of Saarburg': The earth is growing mouldy with mist. The evening is heavy as lead. Electrical crackling bursts out all round, and with a whimper everything breaks asunder.
   Like old rags the villages are smouldering on the horizon. I am lying God-forsaken in the rattling frontline.
   Many copper enemy birds whirl around my heart and head. I brace myself in the greyness and face death.

	Translations of German Quotations

71.   'Glory Surrounds the Flag': Glory surrounds the flag! Arise! Arise! Drummers call and hoofbeat rings out. Leave behind song and the Mecca of night. Everything is glowing and bright.

   Come forward out of your bitter agonies! Shake your golden mane. Be dismembered hyenas, a scream in your heart and bronze uproar. Glow through the land! Bleed and pray!

71.   In Dieuze I saw my first soldiers' graves. In Fort Manonvillers, which had just been shot up, I found a tattered Rabelais among the débris . . . If only one could understand it, make sense of it. What has broken out now is the Devil and all his works. The ideals are so many little labels stuck on as an afterthought. Everything, but everything, is on the point of collapse . . . The whole world has gone mad.

72.   'This Is When': This is when the behemoth raises its snout out of the salt waters. Men jump from burning barges into green slime lit up by flames.

   Their souls are needlessly sold at white elephant stalls for a pittance, their hearts drained of blood, their spirits dead. Avenging angels are going around with rods.

   They burst violently into houses, no bolt withstanding their fury; they flit around vestry cornices.

   Tearing away laths and tiles, their breath steaming. Black sunshine hangs like a sulphurous pall over this hellish crucible.

72-73.   'I Did Not Like': I did not like the death's head hussars and the mortars with girls' names, and when at last the great days came, I quietly slipped away.

   I must confess to God and to you, mesdames: while they were sobbing over biers, I, like Absalom, was caught by my long hair in the tree of woe of all their dramas.

   You will find in these lines too many a martyr play and dashing adventure. One does not only die from mines and rifles.

   One is not only torn to pieces by shells. My nights were invaded by monsters which made me experience Hell.

Translations of German Quotations

73.   'Big Bertha': Big Bertha is my name, twenty-four [centimetres] my girth; I know what I can do; my range is seven miles.

73–74.   'Dance of Death, 1916': And so we die, and so we die, we're dying every day because it's so easy to die. In the morning still asleep and dreaming, gone by midday. By evening well and truly buried.
    Battle is our brothel. Our sun is made of blood. Death is our sign and password. Wife and child we abandon – what concern are they of ours? So long as we can be relied on.
    And so we murder, and so we murder. Every day we murder our partners in this dance of death. Brother, straighten up in front of me, brother, your breast! Brother, you who must fall and die.
    We don't grumble, we don't grouse. We keep our mouths shut all the time until our hip-bones are wrenched out [*scil.*: with dancing so much]. Our bed is hard, our bread is dry. God is bloody and defiled.
    We thank you, we thank you, *Herr Kaiser*, for your kindness in choosing us to die. Sleep on, sleep peacefully, until you are raised from the dead by our poor bodies pushing up the daisies.

75.   I know of no other poet in German today who in this deepest of bloodbaths shows such a pure humanity as does Wilhelm Klemm in his war poems.

76.   His poems have even been noticed abroad, as editors of journals have told me in their letters. In the midst of so much bloodthirsty bellowing – a human being.

76.   humane poems from the field of slaughter

76.   I have striven for the greatest possible simplicity. German war poems are positively awful. It's shocking what is being printed in the newspapers. And always the same sort of stuff.

76.   I am sure that our beloved country will fare well and that nothing will happen to me ... we must and shall prevail.
The war has really begun for us now.

One is unable to stop and think.

This war is something splendid. Like a hand of cards when everybody passes, which changes everything. I am a firm believer in mass hypnosis.

We are living in a great age.

The enthusiasm remains remarkable.

Those were terribly edgy and exhausting days, this retreat-like withdrawal by day and night. Our unit [field hospital] has already had all sorts of experiences ... it's ridiculous how quickly one gets used to everything ... The wounded are in a sorry plight ... We are all hoping that the war with France will be over soon; the French are suffering even more than our people are.

77. —This hanging around is terrible.
 —So we exist from day to day ... peace has become an unlikely story.
 —Every morning it crosses our minds that something may happen to us. It seems almost natural for men to be wounded and to die every day.
 —War can be so dreadful that one longs for the bullet which will free one from all the tension and misery - to some extent this is the secret which makes the men able to endure such indescribable suffering.
 —At the front everything is really all one. Every day one can be killed in one way or another.
 —My surroundings always get me down so much ... The wounded follow me into my dreams.
 —You have no idea how depressing it is to be wading through this misery all the time. I'm not getting used to it, on the contrary, I'm getting more and more edgy.

77. these war-poems are anti-war poems; and while others were wallowing in bellicosity and jingoism, he had the courage to depict the horrors of war in uncanny poetic hyperbole, and in autumn 1914, during the Battle of the Marne, to declare: 'My heart is as big as France and Germany together, pierced by all the shells in the world.'

79. 'Lights': Lights are going out. Night and desolation are bursting in. Our hearts shudder more deeply - Blind angels rise up

178   *Translations of German Quotations*

             distraught – Flutter of wings and a moaning without respite.

79.   'Invocation': O great event, unthinkable war! I see you, in your spectral beauty, crossing countless streets and countless faces – I hear you rumbling and roaring, dying and screaming.

79.   'Moving Forward': The sky glows fantastically. Golden feathers scattered across an inspired azure. The crimson remains of the shot-up village gleam between the malachite of the trees.

81.   'Afternoon Battle': Until the rain came on, towards evening. Falling on friend and foe alike, on the field of honour and dishonour. On man and horse, on advance and withdrawal. On the dead and the living.

81-82. 'Leaving for the Front': The shadows made a black thicket, a sleepy sound is coming from the river down below, and the moon-bowl is pouring out its light – trees and stones are made of voices singing.

            A little castle is standing there, white, covered with a web of dark fairy-tales. A tower has an oddly innocent look. In the churchyard a little dance of death is going on.

            The whole scene is going to heaven. The mile began. Far off, with a deep note, can be heard the unassuming whistle of a train – Farewell, Agatha. We shall never meet again!

82.   'Dying': The blood oozes shyly through the tunic. The grimy grey limbs quietly wither. Lips are paler and thinner, noses more pointed. Perspiration glistens on smoothed brows.

            Eyes open, all with the same look. They all look blue, all peaceful and staring, full of infinite remoteness and benignity; and forgive the world and us these hellish goings-on.

83.   'Field Hospital': Straw rustles everywhere. The candle-stumps stare solemnly. Across the nocturnal vault of the church moans and choked words drift aimlessly.

            There's a stench of blood, rubbish, shit and sweat. Bandages ooze beneath torn uniforms. Clammy, trembling limbs, wasted faces. Dying heads slump down, half sitting up.

In the distance the storm of the battle thunders on, day and night, groaning and grumbling furiously and solemnly – and to the dying men waiting patiently for their graves it sounds like God's words.

84. 'Deserted House': The double doors of the ribs are opening. Already the blue divans of the lungs are swelling, and the crimson cushion of the liver, streaked with green, and between them, resplendent in red lace, a silent baldachin with four chapels, the heart, from whose dark tabernacle, instead of the hoped-for divine miracle, flow only the black roses of the blood. And in the brain's deathly pale labyrinths, and in the full vault of the stomach, and in the master sculpture of solemn bones you will not find the much-vaunted one. Already the soul, that eternal nomad, has struck its invisible tent.

85. 'Battle of the Marne': Slowly the stones begin to stir and to speak. The blades of grass freeze into green metal. The woods, low, dense hideouts, swallow distant columns. Heaven, that chalk-white mystery, threatens to burst.

Two colossal hours contract into minutes. The empty horizon distends itself above us, my heart is as big as France and Germany together, pierced by all the shells in the world.

The battery raises its lion's voice, six times out into the countryside. Shells howl. Silence. In the distance the infantry-fire rattles on for days on end, for weeks on end.

85-86. 'Evening at the Front': Every evening an officer comes into the damp tent and tells us who has fallen. Every hungry evening when we long lie shivering there are dead men among us who will die tomorrow.

One had his head blown off, there a hand is dangling, here someone without a foot is wailing, a captain got it straight in the chest, and the rain, the rain goes on dripping incessantly.

Throughout the night the cannons go on echoing away. In the distance villages burn with little red tongues. O God, how is this destined to end? Oh questing bullet, when will you come to me?

86. 'Rethel': The huge nocturnal chimneys rise up solemnly

from the pyramids of rubble from burned-out factories. The crazily beautiful moonlight swaggers pinkly over mountains of bricks.

A pitch-black street swallows up the column. High up in the ruined façade the moon is playing. Flitting through night-blue window-hollows and hiding behind reckless gables.

And now the ruined town is gleaming deathly white. White with horror. White with silence. And the dark army with grey ghostly helmets moves through it, muffled wave after muffled wave, at midnight.

87. We got there towards one o'clock in the morning; the moon was shining with the pallor of death. First a bunch of gallows, the chimneys of the ruined factories. Through a field of rubble we came to a dark old street, here and there tall, burned-out buildings, a half-collapsed house, a cellar yawning blackly. Not a sound – just the usual smell of decomposition and the muffled sound of the somnolent columns. Then suddenly a marble white area of ruins opened up, perhaps the size of Leipzig city centre, the mountains of bricks pale pink in the moonlight, the streets dug up, snow-white, the remains of walls eaten away . . .

87-88. 'At the Front': The countryside is desolate. The fields look tear-stained. A grey cart is going along an evil road. The roof has slipped off a house. Dead horses lie rotting in pools.

The brown lines back there are trenches. On the horizon a farm is taking its time to burn. Shells explode, echo away – pop, pop pauuu. Cavalrymen disappear slowly in a bare copse.

Clouds of shrapnel burst open and fade away. A defile takes us in. Infantrymen are halted there, wet and muddy. Death is as much a matter of indifference as the rain which is coming on. Who cares about yesterday, today, or tomorrow?

And the barbed wire runs across the whole of Europe. The forts sleep gently. Villages and towns stink out of their terrible ruins. Like broken dolls the dead lie between the lines.

80-90. 'Villages': The houses look as though they are made of gingerbread and have been half eaten up. The blue sky has so much space in them, smiles through so many round holes in piles of rubble and through empty shell cases. Everything, absolutely everything has been destroyed.

You can safely walk through the daylight street, pink and white with the debris of walls. The other side does not shoot all the time and an individual is never hit.

The church is an empty shell. And the tower - good Lord - has only one side left. Round the church is a cemetery full of soldiers' graves. The white crosses stand there as smartly as if they were still on parade.

There is a sweet scent of thistles from their mile-wide fields. The paths are overgrown. Poppies bloom amazingly, an intoxicating red with a touch of purple. Camomile grows in enormous clumps.

91.   I go in, like a member of the audience going into the theatre.

91-92.   'Trench Warfare': The machine-guns are saying their nightly offices. Some swallow their lines hurriedly. Trill their lines or die away darkly across huge railway lines. Rattle out a quick tercet.

One taps five times in a very deliberate way. Five times the bullets chirrup overhead. Spooky. One thanks one's lucky stars. But how far away the stars are over the trenches.

Happily the incendiary flares rise up in front of trees shot to pieces and silent ruins. How sweet the woods smell in November. Of night and ripe nuts. How long shall we go on being enchanted?

92.   'Snow': Now snow has fallen again. The land is white as a novel. Strange, unreal. A life without protection, our thoughts wander. Wake up, my friend!

Do you not hear the shooting? It is war, world war. Just think, world war! What haunted our forebodings, yellow, has come true. Do not look at the snowflakes, they are falling the same as ever. Take stilts of the imagination.

Stampede on spirit legs over all the events along God's ways and byways, which you will never understand. Until your breathless heart suddenly stops. And you find yourself again, under a steel helmet.

96.   The book contains no jingoistic poems, but is rather a book of sorrow and mourning.

Translations of German Quotations

97-98. 'Sister Mary': The slender grace of her hands made the magic of a shy boyhood come alive again and he saw primroses, yellow against the moss of the woods; saw his mother walking, smiling, in the summer sunlight with bunches of blue flowers; saw his little sisters pass by with flushed faces . . . images . . . images . . . her words, hovering and raining down on him, sweetly sang away his fever, cooling the sting of his burns . . . nightingales sang outside his sweetheart's window in May whenever her lovely voice passed by; did violets burst into flower one evening in March when she was in the room? There was gold somewhere about whenever she inclined her shining hair to one side; stars gleamed when her eyes opened over him in the dusk of the room . . . magic came alive again, children's parties in the garden. Boat trips on the Wasserrosensee, cuckoos calling wildly in the woods and timid games of hide-and-seek with the children next door; myriad stars and a moonlit July night . . . Her tender care made the fire of his fever abate . . . He saw girls dancing in the clover, his mother walking in the garden; he began to look happy again. Far, far away in the west the nightmare of the battle continued.

100-101. 'The Dead Soldier': Lay there like a solitude, like a pile of stones, whitish, spread out, in much rain. Why did Death scream at him in the night, that night full of moonlight, warm with the wind? – Head still full of memories of the other side of the Rhine: dancing wildly all night long and walking home along Castle Gate; in his blood the fresh wine or the garden with the red lanterns, and the pigeons flying off to their death at nightfall . . . Children will be solemnly dancing ring-a-ring-o'-roses by the roadside, in April it will rain, one evening the air will be full of beetles, but he is just a dark shape; mouth full of gentle words, which once hummed a wistful song on the way home one July night. Who killed him? A man who ran through the sweltering port, who saw nights glittering with stars, through the white archway of the balcony, southern with a new moon, red; or a man who accompanied circuses to the pandemonium of annual fairs, shabbily dressed, in a green jerkin, a bizarre, motley figure? . . . That mouth had many things left to say: maybe about gardens strolled through in autumn, maybe about ochre-coloured cattle, maybe about the poverty of his grey old mother; or that ear, pale, small, still full of thunderstorms, of deep waves of sound, enjoying hearing again the blackbirds in the pear-tree in spring, the shouting of the city children out in the country; in his eye this: a net full of white fish, bluish-looking stars; was not a Gothic doorway overgrown with ivy, gleaming in the dark, once reflected in it? ... Now he is just a dark shape, a death, a thing, a stone, destroyed beyond measure, filling the night with its outrage at man's cruelty.

102. 'Nocturnal Landscape': A constellation like a day; and behind it a horizon fingered and shrouded by light and flare, which went or came, fell or stood, restless, spectral; and, if it went, there was deep night; and, if it came, somewhere a village lay white and furtive, and a forest was made, and a valley full of sleep, with torrents, tangled things, with graves and towers of churches, in ruins, with rising mists, big-clouded and moist, with huts where sleeping men lay, where a dream walked, full of fever, full of strangeness, full of animal splendour, where a curtain of clouds suddenly split open; behind it grew a sea of stars or a realm of rockets, a light sprang up out of the ravine, terrible, roaring, wheel clatter rattled on roads, a man stepped darkly into the dark, his face dazed with a dreadful dream, saw questing the flight of fires, heard butchery down below, saw the city blazing ceaselessly behind the darkness. Heard a rumbling in the belly of the earth, ponderous, powerful, primal, heard traffic on roads, heading into the void, into the extended night, into a storm, dreadful in the west. - Unquiet the ear with the thousand hammers of the front, with the cavalry who came, stamping, headlong, with the horsemen who rode away to turn into shadows, engulfed by night, to rot, death slaughters them, to lie among weeds, weighty, fossilised, hands full of spiders, mouths red with scabs, eyes full of bottomless sleep, on their brows the bloom of obfuscation, blue, waxen, decaying in the smoke of night, which sank down, which shed its shadows far, which stretched, vaulting, from hill to hill, over woods and decay, over brains full of dream, over the hundred dead, ungathered, over the countless fires, over laughter and madness, over crosses in fields, over pain and despair, over

184 *Translations of German Quotations*

rubble and ash, over river and ruined village ...

104-105. 'Verdun': Uncanny, never seen before, fully of cruelty; in its skies strings of fire, streamers of smoke, white arrow lines, a greenish glow; its name: agony, bleeding-to-death, a thousand forms of death, a running sore, place of murder, grave, butchery, evil labyrinth; sent up from way behind their targets, on winter nights, monstrous, crazy, infamous, rumbling, full of ice and wind and with no moon, suddenly fired upon by the candles sticking up out of the woods, big, ponderous, brutal; drowned by big guns, old-fashioned, powerful, never-ending; smothered with a pall of fire, sulphur, gas and chlorine, by the stench of the dead, by portents and thunderbolts, gold and night, by fragments of clouds, great fountains of explosions, by curses and flashes of light, dazzling, glaringly bright, by swarms of daring fliers tremendously high up in the sky; crazily churned up by the fighting; crushed, smashed, livid with fabulous fires from a blown-up fort ... consigned to sleep by us, hostile, malevolent enough to destroy the most wonderful dreams of herons, violet evenings in late March, of silver mornings in the Main valley, of nightingales, blackbirds, moonlit nights on balconies, of a dress worn by pretty Margareta, of southern lovers, brown-skinned and dark-haired, of a boisterous party ... way behind smoke, fumes, gloom, stupendous, strong and vicious, full of death and murder, numberless, piled up; and upwards, on the horizon all the time full of gold and red, full of white fires and green flashes. - Who could think of ponds with sacred swans, of words of love, beautiful, rippling, when out there the doors of the fiery furnace were standing, open, and grim death's countless butchers! ...

106-107. 'A Day at Verdun': A pale grey day, the sound of an aeroplane ... Mines exploding house high; smoke; gas in the air; lull before the storm; silence for minutes on end ... Oh, that it might become sweeter, whiter, bluer; oh, that stars might appear, twinkling, as at home! ... It is so far, so far to home, so far to children, to the loved one's gentle grace, to sparkling springs, shady gardens, parties ... What? someone would shout, violently, vehemently, and who, burrowing away in tunnels, would hear this with dismay on his face? -

Gunfire pounds away at the sky for hours on end; then an incongruous silence. - There was much death. But who still cares about death? Death is common, common as water and leftover bread. It took men digging, men fighting, men asleep, men lying in wait, tense, everything unreal. - Oh, if only night's mists were about, sweet with dreams, how fervently I would pray the prayer of my earliest childhood, how silent I would be when rockets brush the stars, how I would plunge my brow in forgetfulness, in sea-spray, in inertia, homesickness, wonder, how calm I would be when outside everything is in such a turmoil, rocked by many winds; with what puzzlement I would fear this death and never comprehend it! ... Day dawning; the sound of an aeroplane ... Already dim squadrons are moving into the eternity of night just over.

108. 'A Night at Verdun': Then was it dark around a face, sometimes lit up by fire, tearful, staring ahead, listening to noises in the smoke ... A silver bird cried three times, a spent rocket fell in woods, scattering fire where it landed on the waterlogged path ... A look-out crawled through the wire, dazed, lay there, went on lying there, withdrawn, silent. Six times the sky was emblazoned with the path of a glowing shell and its streaming tail. - So long as death does not come, slyly, from in front or from behind! Wind whistles across the darkened scene; squadrons leave on their night flight, removing themselves to an infinite height. - White areas of light wash the span of night from side to side, from edge to edge, appearing at random. - Those heartless ones, whom does their vile anger kill in the depths of sleep, in the gentle embrace of dreams? But they are far away, things are hatching nearer at hand: A mortar bomb lands, terrible, splintering; nearer dangers are lurking silently in the belly of the earth ... further ... deeper ... men tunnelling away ... men hammering ... rust and lights underground ... There is a dull tremor as though a great mouth were calling out in its sleep at midnight ... Around men's brows everything subsides wearily: searchlights, aeroplanes and shellfire have become less frequent, all that remains are men tunnelling and hammering, blue in the slate ... Quietness, blessed peace; one is almost inclined to pray. - But then a shell fell

186 Translations of German Quotations

in the trench, killing sleeping men.

109-110. 'In the Trenches': Everything passes; only death remains, lurking. Everything passed into oblivion: home town, the yellow moonlit night, the village dance, everything vanished. We are lost men, we are men marked by the red mouth of death, we are so dark and so old, small as dwarfs. We are astonished that across the expanse of night stars should still sometimes sink below the woods, blue and deformed, that a flower should still blossom, innocent, among the gleaming bones by the wire. We are growing brutish, we are losing our souls, our sweet, dovelike souls; we are becoming godless and malevolently full of blasphemy. In many a deep darkness someone began to weep, convulsed, agonised. On many a summer morning when at home blue smoke was rising up over the range, someone or other lay stiff in the sap trench, with dried blood on his mouth, the shot below his heart. One climbed out of the tunnel, badly burned, aged, wretched, with one hand missing, many were no longer there because a mine had blown them to pieces in the night ... Prayers? ... Oh, often they began to flow from our lips, involuntary, confused, stammering, weary, when things became too much for us when everything came to a head: homesickness and the bombardment, when gas came billowing over, choking us, with yellow poison, when someone suddenly collapsed in a weird silence, quietly, soundlessly, wearily, when smoke, grey, burst from tunnels, smelling of flesh and old cloth... But when a flare burst into the night sky, green, beautiful, and suspended there, I (who?) would think: of curious wells, red marble amid coltsfoot and milkwort, in distant *palazzos* in the south; until in the light of flames, gleaming white, I fall into sleep, into the straw, overcast by sadness and dejection. -

111. 'In a Shellhole': What was it Ninette used to sing? ... Something gay, something southern. - I could cry that I am lying here amid murder and assaults, in a blue sea of rockets, in the wind's sighing, beneath turbulent night skies, in green waters full of snails and red worms, awaiting death, putrid and swollen, amid the dying screams of horses, amid the dying screams of men, I heard them, dark, calling out of the dark,

hanging in the wire: thus do birds sing who are ready to die, lonely, pining away, in the spring of their lives. And beyond the Rhine, far away, somebody opened a creaking door, and from the opening came prayer, the overwhelming prayer of a fatherless child ...

111-112. 'Screams': There were nights quite shattered with screams, with great screams of death, coming brokenly from the bottom of men's hearts, demented and full of lament, dark human sounds in which affliction sang, red and northern, screams in which oceans raged and furious storms. Were they calling out for their gay childhood? For secret paths in the woods? Screams which came night after night, eerie, growing ever fainter, ever quieter, coming deeply from behind a fence in front of which death grew, slowly, overwhelmingly and pitilessly, death by bleeding, death by starvation, death by loneliness, mighty and towering terribly - Who crawled out towards the mouth that screamed? No one, because the rifles rattled incessantly, on this side and the other, because death rode incessantly through night and flare-lit hours. Who broke out in tears at that terrible 'Help', 'Have pity', 'Save me', 'Mercy'? Struck into the heart like the song of dying birds, southern, lost, and alien - Death covered them with corrosion, green mud-death; in their screams pennons fluttered, sandhills lay, children's balls bounced, the beloved's shift gleamed ... Every evening still this is in my ears; why did I not die of it? of this: exhausted nights, harrowing cries, smoke over the helmet, stars, acrid, over neck wound, air full of moaning as they hung torn to shreds in the wire, flapping in the wind, with thighs laid open ... Who thought up all this? These nights full of adventure, these nights full of cruelty, shameful madness? - Rotted like weeds beneath night's gaily coloured vaults, yellow and red. To whom was their curse addressed? To whom was their prayer addressed? To a god who did not hear, who was asleep on cloudhills. Towards whom did their screams leap? Towards heartless men who went on shooting incessantly into the mighty darkness ... Oh, that heaven did not explode, that the earth did not open up, on to which their screaming flowed, distant and getting more and more timid, oh, that their mothers did not come, their faces lined with grief, that their children did not sob bitterly from the bottom of their hearts! Nothing happened to avert the death which bade them scream, long drawn out, dreadful, ending in a choking rattle. Stars hung silver among them, a white play of light. If a brow stood out, it was soon shrouded in smoke and noise . . .

112-113. 'The Deserter': Night; and into it the stars set with trembling light; a word, a shout, a clanking, stealthy and short-lived, beneath the cloud-bank a sea of searchlights, pale and spectral; a fire burning in the low-lying land behind copses, smoke from aeroplane exhausts dispersing with a pungent smell. A distant howitzer beginning to howl in the dark, powerful, loud-mouthed; then a flare curving up into the blackened sky. Beneath it they lay: dead, torn to pieces, withdrawn and with a cunning look, a rifle snapped at a picket, while beneath that same sky someone crawled away, went into the gallery full of thuds and rumbling noises, cut the wire entanglements, intent on his work . . . And as this was going on and the night was mild, he was thinking of the fountains and the belfry where the bells rang out in the morning; he thought of his wife and saw his arm covered in mud and hair, and as he thought this one man and another died, a corpse was lying in the darkness, rotting, the rats were eating intestines . . . He peered ahead, then the other side in trench, sap and barricade awoke and sent rockets up to join the uproar of the night. Did he see some delicacy, his home town, a ploughshare, his sisters? Did he hear a girl singing, the cry of an owl? Still he lay in the mist, hugging the ground, still among the dead, still rooted in agony; was he due to be lying there tomorrow, silent, cold, his body torn to shreds? Mist rose up from the woods, spreading whitely, the rumbling of wheels could be heard in the distance, in stone-lined saps lay a sleepy picket . . . Crawling on his stomach and moving one knee at a time; for half an hour a crater concealed him, it stank of rotting flesh, past puddles, squeezed through wire and undergrowth. Was captured wearing a queer smile, the wonder of it dawning in his mind − white, glorious, shapely: he was restored to his wife.

114-115. 'I Carried Secrets into Battle': I carried secrets with me into the Battle of Arras: gulls flying in September against a silver-grey sky, the red moon of Franconia, a beautiful face once glimpsed behind windows, midnight boat trips, an Andalusian nun in the early morning light, and Héloise's slender silk-clad form. I carried too: love songs, sung by servant girls in courtyards at dusk, Bamberg Cathedral, gravestones in Picardy, Spessartheide, trumpets in Beethoven concertos, a brow smooth as velvet, flaming meteors over North Germany, strong sweet Dutch gin, which we drank with street girls. These things I carried with me into the smoke rising in clouds, in a mind that was confused and very young. These things I carried in the face of death, towards flames, many-tongued, and this I knew: that for ten weeks I lay in a monastery in Bavaria behind hundred-year-old folios, knew that I cried out crazy things to God, cursing Him and praising Satan, that I lay for whole wonderfully warm, deep blue nights across Annunziata's silvery body, that I crossed Bohemia, that I wore my hair long in the summer breezes, that I cried out in delirium one day in July... Oh, what a great time that was, how rich, with dances, outings, light from windows, red skies at night, chasing butterflies, grasshoppers, grey birds, how it rose up, blue as a fairy-tale, from sea and horizon, open skies, lakes, lying in freshly mown meadows, gazing into the infinity of nightfall, hearing red-uniformed pipers in an ancient town and seeing the touchingly gawky nakedness of sixteen-year-olds bathing in the 'gelber Rosenteich', in my ears laughter from cafés, happy violin melodies from Italian operas, the flutes light and graceful, oh, if only I were walking again, with a girl, in early morning across the shingle, with children out into the starlit night of Apulia, with friends across the Saxon countryside, I once had the waters of the white Main flowing round me. Spent flares are falling in the wind now, green and ghostly, transforming midnight. Out of the darkness corpses gleam white and pale.

116-117. 'Standing To': I shall go into death as into a doorway filled with summer coolness, the scent of hay, and cobwebs: I shall never return to colourful butterflies, flowers and girls, to dancing and violin music. Somewhere or other I shall fall on stones, shot in the heart, to join someone else who fell wearily earlier; I shall have to wander through much smoke and fire and have beautiful eyes like the godly, inward-looking, dark as velvet, incredibly ardent ... What is death? A long sleep? Sleeping eternally deep down beneath grass and plants, among old gravel? Trumpery. Maybe I shall go to Heaven and enter the snow-white night of God's stars, His silken gardens, His golden evenings, His lakes ... I shall lie beneath the open sky, looking strange, ancient, portentous, my mind once again filled with days out in the Tyrol, fishing in the Isar, snowfields, the noise and excitement of the annual fair in prosperous villages in Franconia, prayers, songs, cuckoos calling, woods, and a train journey along the Rhine by night. Then I shall become like evening, secret, dark, puzzling, mysterious, benighted; then I shall be like earth, lifeless and void, and totally removed from the things around me: days, animals, tears, deep blue dreams, hunting, merrymaking, I shall go into death as into the doorway of my house, with a shot in the heart, painless, strangely small.

118.' 'At Death's Door': Only death is eternal, only the earth and, above it, the bell of Heaven.

121. I believe that my work has ceased to develop; I see this in my poems, of which I am in my heart of hearts almost ashamed, although people take pleasure in them. I don't want to see them again.

121. I wouldn't have been capable of visualising it like that, – no one can, for the experience is so new that it has never been a part of war before.

121. Alas, our poor fellow-countrymen expect to have the horrors of war served up on a plate all nicely embellished and adorned, to help them get into the mood. Expect to have colossal events brought down to their own petty level. As though art were anything but life given form!

121-122. For me, as man and poet, the time before 1917 is no longer relevant ... My poetry was old-fashioned, merely traditional ... In reality, for instance, no 'Prussian musketeer' exists. In reality the feeling of fighting for one's country was current only in the first year of the war. I have ceased to believe that human aims are more significant than human existence. There was a time when I actually believed that the state was more important than the individual ... and so I was inevitably a good, loyal servant of the state. But now that I realise that the state is abusing the power given to it by its members, I can no longer accept such a view of things.

122. God died with and in man.

123. 'Soldier's Farewell': Let me go, mother, let me go! All that crying will not do any good, for we are going to defend the Fatherland.

124. Farewell all, farewell! When we fall for you and for our future, let these words re-echo as our last salute: farewell all, farewell! A free German knows no cold compulsion: Germany must live even if we must die!

124. 'Ballad': The night is so dark and the battle so loud, that all the stars are dead and dispersed. In Germany a soldier's sweetheart is standing at the window voicing a silent prayer.

125. 'In the Trenches': Frenchman, comrade, that one got you fair and square! Do not be angry with me for shooting you!

125. We shall not hear it. We shall be lying dead and cold. No singing or fanfares for peace will waken us; mankind will be standing on our bodies looking into the new dawn.

126. 'Brothers': For a long time a dead man had been lying in front of our wire, the sun shone hot upon him, wind cooled him and dew.
    Every day I looked into his face, and each time I felt more and more certain; that must be my brother.
    I saw him all the time as he lay there before me, and heard his voice calling from some happy peaceful day.
    Often at night a sobbing which woke me with a start: Brother, dead brother, do you no longer love me?
    Until, despite all the bullets, I went across to him at night and brought him in. - Buried him: - An unknown comrade.
    My eyes deceived me. - My heart, you are not mistaken:

every dead man has my brother's face.

127. 'Where the Danger of Death is Greatest': Where the danger of death is greatest, there is no taunting and no hatred, just constant wariness and silence in the face of death.

It is fate that kills, not the enemy, and one day the killing must stop. And then those who are now innocently doing violence to one another will be united.

127. 'Under Artillery Fire, II': We have burrowed our way into the depths of the earth, in the darkness of our dug-outs we fancy there's safety, like children burying their faces in their mothers' laps. O, mother earth, your depths are not deep enough to shelter us. We wish a chasm would open up, dreadfully deep, we long for primeval forests to fall over our heads. In the depths of all our hearts there rages an ardent desire: that rivers and oceans might tear open the holy body of the earth between ourselves and the other side. Our poor tormented hearts beg and pray for earthquakes and deep night, for such a great calamity as will make an end to all strife and hatred among men.

128-129. 'Mass Graves' lie in the solitude of the heath in the lowland. Dark pine forests stand at a distance, the heath is brown and the sand is white. The pale blue sky stands high above shattered, deserted villages.

But clouds pass by lower down, white and grey clouds, sailing past. Their shadows steal down as though they were greeting the dead down below from comrades drifting on waves in the sea or lying washed up by the tide on a lonely shore.

Mass graves lie scattered over the countryside. Birds of a strange kind with long, hovering wings circle overhead, birds with black feathers and red breasts, sorrowful, loving, searching hours of longing of lonely lovers at home.

They sing the song of lament of mothers and brides-that-never-were, of men and children lamenting the proud heroes, the heroes of love and duty. Sing it, searching from mass grave to mass grave, incessantly, day and night.

Their powerless feet – longing's slender inadequate feet – scarcely touch the earth; they are not made for resting.

Black are their eyes, shining like pearls made of tears. Out of their gaping breasts, out of the feathers' metal, the red, throbbing heart gleams.

Thus do they fly and circle over the lands of the earth, over the oceans. Rarely, only rarely does a silvery cry ring out, full of sorrowful joy: a bird finding its love's goal; when the blood flows from the heart, it knows that where it flowed its love lies buried.

Once again it sings the song to its end, the song of the unknown men, the many unknown; redder and redder the stream of blood gushes from the heart and enters the dry, cracked earth. A black cross, the dying bird lies with spread wings, head raised, on the grave.

Softer the song becomes, now it is a song of wounds and dying, of meeting again and rising from the dead, until song and bird die away. And at home a grief-strengthened mother dries her last tears.

130. 'When Night Falls': When the last shadows of the setting sun slip across the battlefield, the dead soldiers rise from their graves, from graves in woodlands and glens, from graves in heath and dune, stand beside their grave-mounds praying, facing their home countries, on foreign soil.

A bird sings in the night.

Then they fall out, rise up, glide homewards, over ruined towns, over fields laid waste, over armies still fighting, past shimmering rivers, away, away to their homelands.

There, when night begins to fall, shadows draw near from the frontiers of the Fatherland, from mountain and ocean, like cloud-shadows, clouds, red at sunset, landing like larks on their nest.

Everywhere.

Over there, at the end of the wood, where between ripening cornfields a footpath, bordered with poppies and cornflowers, climbs upward, there are figures: happy gesture of outstretched arms; blessing hands touch nodding ears of corn, bowed necks lower eyes full of painful joy into the sea of stems, raise to their pale lips the bright red and blue of wild flowers. Kneel, arms stretched out towards the golden riches of life, in the flowering clover.

131.	'Soldiers': Shells have silenced the poems, it is no longer words which extol heroism. The poet's heart is bursting with anthems; his silent amazement is worth more than his song.
131.	Every man who returns from the war is a shining island of joy in the sea of sorrowing mankind.
131-132.	'The War-Invalid': You cannot understand my smile, comrades? I smile wherever I go and wherever I am. I am returning to life. For me everything has a different meaning. Even if my left arm longs for the right one (which is rotting somewhere), the feeling of loss burning like poison; yet the left one, which has quite a stretch, grabs life wherever it meets it. I know a land full of dead men. I once lay among them, wounded. Whenever my mind's eye recalls the scene, I taste blood in my mouth. A thousand dead are still being buried daily, I saw them fall, one by one. But I am alive and the world is mine. There is no greater happiness on earth than that of not being a soldier, not being in the war!
132.	I've written a very general poem about the war, called 'Der Invalide': it's very long and is full of the hatred of genocide which sometimes makes me feel like weeping with anger at mankind.
134-135.	'Profession': All along we were aware of our love for you, only we never put a name to it. When we were called, we set off in silence, not on our lips, but in our hearts the word Germany. Our love was shy; it lay hidden deep within us. Now that its time has come, it has risen up. For many nights now it has been guarding your house in east and west and has been serenly stepping through storm and violence, Germany. That no foreign foot may tread our native land one brother dies in Poland, another lies wounded in Flanders. We are all guarding the holy border of your frontier. Our most youthful life for your most withered tree, Germany. All along we were aware of our love for you, only we

never put a name to it. But the hour of your greatest danger gave glorious proof that your poorest son was also your loyalest son. Remember this, Germany.

135. In its hour of peril we shall not leave the Fatherland in the lurch.

135. a nation, of which the moving words of a front-line poet were to say that its poorest son was also its loyalest son.

136. I believe in Germany as in God.

136-137. 'Night March': Kitbags weighing heavily on our backs, spades rattling occasionally, rifles - tired shoulders hunched forwards, we move rank by rank into grey uncertainty.

Strangely unreal things glide past our long column. An alien country's alien patches of darkness pervade tense minds.

From spectrally shrouded ground phantoms rise up, wraithed in mist, and when they drift by close to us, everyone gets the faintly sweetish smell of death.

In the dark blue sky a flickering glow is reflected. Far off villages are blazing. Turned inward like tears long held back; the countryside sown with steel extends as far as far as the eye can see.

Only rarely does a flood of blue-white light fall on this extended scene of horror, as if the moon was trying to build a path of peace into the bloody world.

137. 'Morituri': Troops marching by night. All faces are the same: mud-stained and pale, helmeted.

Many a man suddenly raises his head out of his coat collar: did he not just hear his name called out?

Sweat pours into eyes, sweat bites into necks. Happy the man who knows nothing of other men's fates.

138. 'Song of the Shells': Iron birds of war, we plunge down from the air. Our ascent spells danger, our descent spells the grave.

Invisible wings clapped to our body, steel claws pointed to give them a deadly hold, we come crashing down on people and things and spread our hundred-toothed steel feathers.

If we then fly up again from the shaking earth, our flapping wings sweep away trees and houses. All tranquillity, every gentle sound fades away before our earth-shaking thunder-song. Always, whether we come whining from east or west, from south or north, the hideous song of murder howls before us.

Predator-birds of death, we swoop from the sky. Our ascent spells danger, our descent spells the grave.

139-140. 'The *Moulin Rouge*': Over there, where the narrow white ribbons of the road are joined in a knot, stands – it was once called *'moulin rouge'* – a pile of rubble . . . it's been blown to pieces . . .

Rafters and gables gutted, reddish walls blackened and burst apart, its dead eyes stare out into the countryside, fanned by the autumn wind and showers of drizzle.

Inside a haggard figure sits in solitude and silence at a round table. He's been carousing here for months, gorging here for months. Germans and French are all the same to him.

Now and then the solitary reveller rises and stretches his bony arms up into the light, so that a beam of light strikes his bone goblet, strikes the blood-bright wine.

When evening's shadows fall on meadows and streams, and night passes by in its silver boat, then across the fitful scene staggers drunken Death.

140-141. 'The Gardens of Death': From millions of sundered hearts the cold, unscented flowers shine forth. Never have the gardens of death flowered so profusely, never have earth and sea shone forth in its colours as they do this evening.

The flowers stand, bed by bed, in serried ranks.

The garden-master walks along the long rows, arms folded meditatively. When he waters the beds, he draws water from the stream of tears which flows through the gardens; silently he prepares fresh soil for fresh seeds. Then he leans on his rake, his unseeing eyes following the unbroken rows stretching away to heaven. Do the stars still follow the same course? The gardens of death are ablaze with a profusion of colour.

143. That is my view too: that any worthwhile depiction of war must transcend the merely physical, and must treat events in space and time (= battles) freely. For me, personally, there is one aspect of it that should be stressed above all others: the death: the mass death, the horror.

144. It is my belief that war as such cannot be described in literary terms. Not this war, anyway. Firstly, because it is so very complicated ... and secondly because it has no soul ... The ultimate inevitability which was the soul of so many of the earlier, smaller-scale wars is lacking in this war of ours.

  This war, when treated artistically, is more or less bound to appear just as the immensely and crazily bloody product of the age. War involves the negation or at least the diminution of the spiritual and the aggrandizement of the material.

  All forms of culture, and that includes 'literature' (currently so ill-reputed), is the product of peace, which it helps to uphold and which it serves. War is *always* destructive, however holy it may appear to be. War does not advance the cause of civilisation; on the contrary, it stunts or destroys it. For us, this particular war is war as such! My view of the war will therefore be a general one rather than a Pan-German one ... My work so far ... serves the cause of peace and human brotherhood.

  Our war is deadly serious and essentially tragic, not as theatrical and optimistically patriotic as it looks or can be made to seem from the writing desk.

145. my dear father Walt Whitman.
  He is always in the breast pocket of my tunic.
  As man and poet he is inexhaustible ... You really should get to know him. Knowing him and loving him is the only thing to do.

145. 'To Death': But spare me, Death; I am still in the first flush of youth, my life-work is still unaccomplished, the future is still wrapped in a haze – therefore spare me, Death.

  Sometime later, Death, when my life has been lived, when it has burned away into my work – when the tired heart is waning, when the world has nothing more to say to me, then carry me off, Death.

146. 'Sowing Seeds': Death is life, living - drifting, dreadfully beautiful - clouds, on high, always, everywhere.

146-147. 'Marching': They are all marching along smartly, their packs are not heavy, they shoulder arms vigorously and sing raggedly and boisterously. Left, left, left right left . . .

I don't sing because I don't want to; my blunderbuss is hurting me, I slouch along, my head is reeling - they're singing about Miller's dovecot [a reference to a popular song of the time]. Left, left, left right left . . .

They've all got a loving heart at home, a wife, a girlfriend or two - they get sausage sent and Lord knows what else, tobacco and warm underclothes - left, left, left right left . . .

I'm thinking of someone (heartless creature) who doesn't write, who doesn't even think of me - I'm all alone and nobody sends me anything, and on top of that I've got to go to battle soon! Left, left, left right left . . .

148-149. 'Book of War': Dear friend, now dead, your glazed eye no different from that of a hare that has been shot or a coldhearted contemptible traitor - For twelve years the winds of time buffeted us together, we automatically shared books and sandwiches, shared the same school-bench, the same needs, the same knowledge and lessons; my friend, your eye is dead.

That is why your mother is so sorrowful, grieving and sighing, but as unassuming as ever; that is why your kid sister and kid brothers so early in life are already experiencing the stormclouds of fate and the mighty reaping of death. Empty are the bed in your humble room and your place at the table at lunchtime. And it is because nobody waits for you any longer, that your mother is grey with grief.

You would have become a root, a seed-corn, a defiant shoot in the soil of life, a bearded father of friendly children. A field ploughed with pain swallowed you up, a field fertilised with blood was your undoing, the all-knowing and everlasting reaper trod you underfoot. What is the point of complaining and speaking of guilt? But you would have been a seed-corn and a father!

You could have been a seed-corn, and became a victim; a

bleeding scrap of flesh, you fell on the endless mountain of bloodless corpses. Even your death is no more than another's death. For thousands and thousands marched off in step into the black agony of oblivion. Regiment and brigade, army and further armies marched off to the bloodstained field of honour of the dead soldier. You were one victim.

Brimont is bare now and its woods have been pounded to the ground, not a pine-tree is left for me to make a cross for your grave. So you lie mutely in a field littered with wreckage, in heavy dreamless sleep. Neither hero nor commander – just an unknown soldier. Bones in the wind of decay. But one day you will be thrilled to hear the countless blessed legions of Peace go marching across the field where you are buried, so listen and wait for them.

149. here is the beginning of my war book. I think it is good, and this is the style in which it must be continued.

149-151. 'To the Soldiers of the Great War': Rise up! Out of trenches, muddy holes, concrete bunkers, quarries. Up out of mud and fire, chalk dust and stench of corpses! Come along! Comrades! For from front to front, from battlefield to battlefield, may the world's new red-letter day come to you all! Off with your steel helmets, caps, képis! And away with your rifles! Enough of this bloody enmity and murderous sense of honour.

You all I implore by your country's villages and towns to stamp out, to weed out the monstrous seeds of hatred, implore you by your love of your sisters, mothers, children, which alone still disposes your scarred heart to sing. By your love of your wife – I too love a woman! By your love of your mother – a mother's body bore me too! By your love of your child – for I love little ones! And the houses are full of cursing, praying, weeping!

Were you at Ypres, ruined Ypres? I too was there. At Mihiel, stricken Mihiel? I was there. At Dixmuide, surrounded by floods? I was out in front of you, in Verdun's hellish defiles, in the smoke and din like you, with you in the snow outside Dünaberg, freezing and getting more and more depressed, at the necrophagous Somme I was opposite you. I was opposite you everywhere, but you did not know it!

Enemy beside enemy, man beside man and body beside body, warm and close together.

I was a soldier and a man and did my duty, just like you, thirsty, sleepless, sick – always on the march or on guard. Hourly surrounded by falling, screaming, smoking death, hourly aching for home, loved ones, one's own town, like you and you and all of you. – Tear open your tunic! Bare your barrel of a chest! I see the grazing shot dating from 1915, the scab, and there on your forehead the sewn-up gash from the attack at Tahüre – But so that you will not think I'm putting it on, I'll repay you in the same coin: I open my shirt: here is the multi-coloured scar on my arm! Battle's brand! Long after the war a fond souvenir of scramble and alarm. How proud we are of our wounds. You proud of yours, but no prouder than I am of mine.

You did not give better blood nor greater vitality, and the same churned-up sand drank our vital juices! Did the dreadful crump of that shell blow your brother to blazes? Did not your uncle fall, your cousin, your godfather? Does not your bearded father lie buried in his grave? And your friend, your jolly friend from school? Hermann and Fritz, my cousins, bled to death, and my helpful friend, the young one, the one who was fair-haired and kind. And at home his bed is waiting for him, and in her shabby room his mother, grey with grief, has been waiting ever since 1916, 1917; where is his cross and his grave?

Frenchman, from Brest, Bordeaux, Garonne; Ukrainian, Cossack from the Urals, from Dnjestr and Don; Austrians, Bulgarians, Turks and Serbs, all of you in the raging whirlpool of action and dying – Britisher from London, York, Manchester, soldier, comrade-in-arms, truly fellow human being and best of men – American, from the populous states of freedom: throw away partisanship, national pride and antagonism! If you were an honourable enemy, become an honourable friend. Here is my hand, so that hand in hand may now be linked together and our new day find us sincere and humane.

For all of you the world is great and beautiful! Look! Marvel! After battle and blood's groaning: how freely green seas flow into their horizons; how mornings and evenings glow in pure brightness, how mountains rise up out of the valleys, how billions of living beings tremble all around us! Oh, our greatest blessing of all is: life!

Oh, that brother may again really be called brother! That east and west may recognise the same values! That joy may again flash into all nations, and man be roused to goodness by man!

From front to front and battlefield to battlefield, let us sing the birthday of the new world! Out of every chest let a single tune ring forth! The psalm of peace, of reconciliation, of revolt! And may the surging, radiant song, the thrilling, brother-embracing, the wild and divinely compassionate song of thousandfold love ring out around the earth!

154. 'Legend of the Dead Soldier': And when the war, in its fourth spring, showed no sign of ending, our soldier did the logical thing and died a hero's death.

154. But the soldier does as he's been told and dies a hero's death.

155. 'The Dying Soldier': Captain, send for the court-martial! I'm not dying for no Emperor! Captain, you are the Emperor's man! When I'm dead, I'll not salute!

When I am with my Maker, the Emperor's throne will be below me, and I shall have nothing but scorn for his command! Where do I live? Where my son is playing.

When I have awoken to life immortal, my last letter from the front will arrive. Death called, death called, death called, death called! Oh, how deep my love is!

Captain, you are crazy to have me sent here. My heart got burned in the firing-line: I'm not dying for any Fatherland!

You'll not force me, you'll not force me! Look how death is breaking my bonds! Go on, court-martial death! I'm dying, but not for the Emperor!

156-157. At the beginning of the war there was a rainbow. Birds, black, wheeled against grey clouds. Pigeons shone silver as on their circular journey they turned through a narrow strip of sunlight.

Battle takes place hard by battle. They lied like troopers. Row upon row of stoved-in heads fill one with horror. Shells often explode as they tumble on beginning to lose velocity.

The shells' pain-bow grows all the time.

Caught between death and the bow of peace, they clutch their rifle barrels more firmly, to defend their homeland, spitting at the enemy, leaning on one another as they totter, tumbling over hills, like waves of the seas, staggering on, attracted magnetically by Death.

158.   you go around threatening people with your damn great sword

158.   Tigers' eyes glowing with hate all around you

158.   Flares climb high up into the sky, fireworks extending the night and the sputtering light of a decaying moon. With your gun you stand there rigid as the houses that are lit up.

Flares of bristling tiger's fur. A trigger is lying in wait for any movement revealed by the light to watchful eye, as though the day were not yet dead in which one man was another's prey, one man's mouth at another's throat, until the organ-cry of death is heard.

With eyes wide open you stare at the brilliance of the colourful predator, burning brightly in the night. Until night and snow conceal me again, grey-green eyes keep these wild melodies awake.

158-159. Where wolves ran through the bright night snow, the night was full of sudden hunger: wild cries filled the air. Long-necked shells and shrapnel call out. Iron teeth without lips. Hotly hungering for my ribs.

In the tension of the snowy light of dawn we are once again beset by the baying voices of death raging towards us with deafening explosions.

159.   Many forms of predator threaten, multicellular, shells; unicellular forms only make a little hole. I am invited to a mythical celebration. Harpies search high and low. On the whole they are lenient. They could do terrible damage. Many an arm is missing its body, the head which used to direct it. O Glory, o Honour, o Heroism! On a white field the sweet red flower stands out beautifully.

160-161. Once you would come sneaking along softly, insidiously innocuous, wholly nondescript: then we hated your bland, civilian nature from whose capriciousness no one was safe.

In an undertone men spoke of the strokes of your scythe. You were what men feared in every danger. You wanted more! - Now your reputation has faded. It is withering and shrinking with the number of your victims.

Now you crouch behind gun barrels, big-mouthed, insensate, roar your frightfulness a thousand times more loudly into our deaf ears. Cowardly and contemptible is such superiority. He who blusters too much, my friend, arouses suspicion! Cousin Death, you have lost this game!

BIBLIOGRAPHY

Primary Material

Anthologies

Anz, T. and Vogl, J. (eds.), *Die Dichter und der Krieg. Deutsche Lyrik 1914-1918*, Munich, 1982.
Bab, J. (ed.), *1914. Der deutsche Krieg im deutschen Gedicht*, 12 numbers, Berlin, n.d.
Biese, A. (ed.), *Poesie des Krieges*, 2 vols, Berlin, 1915.
Bridgwater, P. (tr. and ed.), 'German Poems of the 1914-18 War', *The Journals of Pierre Menard*, No. 3, July 1969.
Deppe, W.G., Middleton, C. and Schönherr, H. (tr. and eds.), *Ohne Hass und Fahne. Kriegsgedichte des 20. Jahrhunderts*, Hamburg, 1959.
Heynen, W. (ed.), *Deutsche Kriegsgedichte. Eine Auswahl aus den Jahren 1914-1918*, Offenbach, 1918.
Pfemfert, F. (ed.), *1914-1916. Eine Anthologie*, Berlin - Wilmersdorf, 1916.
Rubiner, L. (ed.), *Kameraden der Menschheit. Dichtungen zur Weltrevolution*, Potsdam, 1919.
Schickele, R. (ed.), *Menschliche Gedichte im Krieg*, Zürich, 1918.
Silkin, J. (ed.), *The Penguin Book of First World War Poetry*, Harmondsworth, 1979.
Tat-Bücher für Feldpost, 4 numbers, Jena, 1914-15.
Volkmann, E. (ed.), *Deutsche Dichtung im Weltkrieg 1914-18*, Leipzig, 1934.

Collections by Authors of Poems Discussed in the Text

Ball, H., *Gesammelte Gedichte*, Zürich, 1963.
Baum, P., *Schützengrabenverse*, Berlin, 1916.
Brecht, B., *Gedichte*, Frankfurt/M. : I, 1960; VIII, 1965.
Bröger, K., *Aus meiner Kriegszeit. Gedichte*, Nuremberg, 1915.
Bröger, K., *Kamerad, als wir marschiert. Kriegsgedichte*, Jena, 1916.
Bröger, K., *Soldaten der Erde. Neue Kriegsgedichte*, Jena, 1918.
Bröger, K., *Sturz und Erhebung. Gesamtausgabe der Gedichte*, Jena, 1943 [=1944].
Eisenstein, K., von, *Lieder im Kampf*, Berlin and Munich, 1916.
Engelke, G., *Schulter an Schulter. Gedichte von drei Arbeitern: Gerrit*

Engelke, Heinrich Lersch und Karl Zielke, Jena, 1916.
Engelke, G., *Rhythmus des neuen Europa*, Jena, 1921.
Engelke, G., *Das Gesamtwerk*, Munich, 1960.
George, S., *Der Krieg*, Berlin, 1917.
George, S., *Drei Gesänge*, Berlin, 1921.
Heym, G., *Umbra vitai. Nachgelassene Gedichte.* Munich, 1924 (repr. 1962; many other editions).
Klemm, W., *Gloria. Kriegsgedichte aus dem Feld*, Munich [1915].
Klemm, W., *Aufforderung. Gesammelte Verse*, Berlin - Wilmersdorf, 1917 (repr. Wiesbaden, 1961).
Kraus, K., *Worte in Versen* 9 vols, Vienna and Leipzig, 1916-22.
Lersch, H., *Kriegsgedichte*, 10 numbers, München-Gladbach, 1915-18.
Lersch, H., *Herz! Aufglühe dein Blut. Gedichte im Krieg*, Jena, 1916.
Lersch, H., *Deutschland! Lieder und Gesänge von Volk und Vaterland*, Jena, 1918.
Lersch, H., *Deutschland muss leben*, Jena, 1935 (several reprints).
Lersch, H., *Ausgewählte Werke*, 2 vols, Düsseldorf-Köln, 1965-6.
Lichtenstein, A., *Gesammelte Gedichte*, Zürich, 1962.
Rilke, R.M., 'Fünf Gesänge, August 1914', first publ. in *Kriegs-Almanach 1915* of the Insel-Verlag; repr. in later editions of his *Neue Gedichte*.
Schnack, A., *Tier rang gewaltig mit Tier*, Berlin, 1920.
Stramm, A., *Tropfblut*, Berlin, 1919 (and subsequent editions of poems).
Trakl, G., *Sebastian im Traum*, Leipzig, 1915.
Trakl, G., *Die Dichtungen*, Leipzig, 1919.
Trakl, G., *Dichtungen und Briefe*, 2 vols, Salzburg, 1969.
Zuckmayer, C., *Der Baum*, Berlin, 1926.

Secondary Material

Bab, J., *Die deutsche Kriegslyrik 1914-1918*, Stettin, 1920.
Bowra, C.M., *Poetry and the First World War*, Oxford, 1961.
Bowra, C.M., *Poetry and Politics 1900-1960*, Cambridge, 1966.
Bridgwater, P., 'German Poetry and the First World War', *European Studies Review*, I, No. 2, 1971, 147-86.
Bridgwater, P., 'The War-Poetry of August Stramm', *New German Studies*, VIII, 1980, 29-53.
Bridgwater, P., 'Georg Trakl and the Poetry of the First World War', in: *Londoner Trakl-Symposion*, ed. W.E. Yuill and W. Methlagl,

Salzburg, 1981, 96-113.
Bridgwater, P., *The Poetry of Heym and Lichtenstein* (forthcoming).
Johnston, J.H., *English Poetry of the First World War*, Princeton, 1964.
Korte, H., *Der Krieg in der Lyrik des Expressionismus*, Bonn, 1981.
Peacock, R., 'The Great War in German Lyrical Poetry, 1914-18', *Proceedings of the Leeds Philosophical Society*, Literary and Historical Section, Vol. III, 1934, 189-243.
Philippi, K.P., *Volk des Zorns. Studien zur 'poetischen Mobilmachung' in der deutschen Literatur am Beginn des Ersten Weltkriegs*, Munich, 1979.
Volkmann, E., 'Einführung' to his anthology *Deutsche Dichtung im Weltkrieg 1914-1918*, Leipzig, 1934.

INDEX OF POEMS

Hugo Ball
Das ist die Zeit 71-2
Glanz um die Fahne 71
Ich liebte nicht . . . 72-3
Totentanz 1916 73-5

Peter Baum
Am Beginn des Krieges stand . . . 156-7
Leuchtkugeln steigen hoch hinauf 158
Viele Tiere dräuen . . . 159-60
Wo Wölfe durch die blanke Schneenacht liefen 158-9

Bertolt Brecht
Bekenntnis 134-6

Karl Bröger
Das rote Wirtshaus 139-40
Die Gärten des Todes 140-1
Nachtmarsch 136-7
Sang der Granaten 138

Karl von Eisenstein
Sonett an den Tod von Anno 14 160-1

Gerrit Engelke
An den Tod 145-6
An die Soldaten des Grossen Krieges 149-52
Buch des Krieges 148-9, 151
Im Marschieren 146-7

Gorch Fock
De dicke Berta 73

Bruno Frank
Dort, wo der Tod am nächsten droht 126-7

Index of Poems

Stefan George
Der Krieg 21-5

Georg Heym
Der Krieg 6-9

Wilhelm Klemm
Abend im Feld 85-6
Abschied 81-2
An der Front 87-9
Anrufung 79
Dörfer 89-90
Feuerüberfall 90-1
Lazarett 83
Lichter 79
Rethel 86-7
Schlacht an der Marne 84-5
Schnee 92-3
Stellung 91-2
Sterben 82-3
Verlassnes Haus 83-4

Edlef Koeppen
Loretto 11

Karl Kraus
Der neue Krieg 1
Der sterbende Soldat 155

Heinrich Lersch
Ballade 124-5
Brüder 126
Der Kriegsinvalide 131-2
Im Artilleriefeuer II 127-8
Im Schützengraben 125-6
Massengräber 128-30, 133
Soldaten 131
Soldatenabschied 123-4
Wenn es Abend wird 130-1

Alfred Lichtenstein
Abschied 65
Die Schlacht bei Saarburg 68-70

Doch kommt ein Krieg 64
Gebet vor der Schlacht 66-8
Romantische Fahrt 65-6

Rainer Maria Rilke
Fünf Gesänge, August 1914 3-6, 8-9

Anton Schnack
Der Tote 100-1
Der Überläufer 112-14
Eine Nacht 108-9
Ein Tag 106-8
Ich trug Geheimnisse in die Schlacht 114-16
Im Graben 109-10
Im Granatloch 110-11
In Bereitschaft 116-18
Nächtliche Landschaft 101-4
Schreie 111-12
Schwester Maria 97-9
Verdun 104-6

August Stramm
Angststurm 56-8
Feuertaufe 52-5
Krieg 49-51
Krieggrab 58-9
Patrouille 51-2
Schlachtfeld 43-6
Schrapnell 55-6
Sturmangriff 47-9
Wunde 46-7

Georg Trakl
Grodek 33-6
Im Osten 30-2
Klage 32-3
Menschheit 25-9
Trompeten 29-30

Carl Zuckmayer
Morituri 137-8

For Product Safety Concerns and Information please contact our EU
representative GPSR@taylorandfrancis.com
Taylor & Francis Verlag GmbH, Kaufingerstraße 24, 80331 München, Germany

www.ingramcontent.com/pod-product-compliance
Lightning Source LLC
Chambersburg PA
CBHW052112300426
44116CB00010B/1638